Dust or Magic

Secrets of successful
multimedia design

❝An idea can turn to dust or magic,
depending on the talent that rubs
against it**❞**

Matsuo Basho
(1644–1694)

Dust or Magic

> Secrets of successful
> multimedia design

Bob Hughes

 Addison-Wesley

An imprint of **PEARSON EDUCATION**

Harlow, England · London · New York · Reading, Massachusetts · San Francisco · Toronto · Don Mills, Ontario · Sydney
Tokyo · Singapore · Hong Kong · Seoul · Taipei · Cape Town · Madrid · Mexico City · Amsterdam · Munich · Paris · Milan

PEARSON EDUCATION LIMITED

Head Office:
Edinburgh Gate
Harlow CM20 2JE
Tel: +44 (0)1279 623623
Fax: +44 (0)1279 431059

London Office:
128 Long Acre
London WC2E 9AN
Tel +44 (0)207 447 2000
Fax: +44 (0)207 240 5771

Website: www.awl.com/cseng

First published in 2000

ISBN 0-201-36071-3

British Library Cataloguing in Publication Data
A catalogue record for this book can be obtained from the British Library.

10 9 8 7 6 5 4 3 2 1

Typeset by Pantek Arts
Printed and bound in the United States of America

The publisher's policy is to use paper manufactured from sustainable forests.

Contents

Companion Web site

Visit http://www.dustormagic.net

Cover image acknowledgement

Cover graphic by Alex Mayhew, Creative Director of Real World's "Ceremony of Innocence" CD-ROM.

Trademark notice

Section **1**

Cyberia

"My romantic vision is that in the information revolution we're reliving evolution**"**

Jerome Wiesner,
President of MIT 1971–80,
quoted by Stewart Brand in
The Media Lab (1987)

Introduction:
The emancipation of the serfs

THIS IS A BOOK FOR SERFS of all ages and income levels. It is *mainly* for the "infoserfs" who work in "Cyberia" – but every serf is warmly welcome, especially if they're interested in computers and take serfdom seriously.

It talks about a revolution – but not an obvious one. This one is so big you can easily not notice it – yet it is right under your nose and you (as practicing serf) are one of its co-architects. It is the "creative revolution" caused by people who make things; the revolution that made computers (and civilization and Cyberia) possible in the first place.

What is "Cyberia"? The word started off as a rather inspired, ironic term for the multimedia workplaces of the early 1990s. These often felt like a strange, featherbedded Gulag Archipelago where the KGB uniforms had been swapped for corporate suits.

I try to be a bit more rigorous: my Cyberia is the "landscape of possibilities" you enter when you tackle a job on a computer. These possibilities are no different from the ones in other kinds of work – there are just more of them, and they are very much more sharply defined.

Crafty peasants, great captains, and the world of work

My Cyberia is part of the bigger world of work, and has the same relationship to it that a mountain massif has to the country it emerges from. It is a unique, new, vantage point. This "world of work" has two major traditions which coexist uneasily.

First, there's the "serf" or "peasant tradition," where things are made by small groups and by individuals. There's a lot of variety here: the people are all "one-offs" and so are the things they make. Some things they make are exquisite, others are rough and ready but they all do the job. You can often tell exactly where a thing was made to within a few miles just by looking at it, and even who made it. The makers think with their hands as much as with their brains. There's a large emphasis on what the anthropologist Claude Lévi-Strauss calls "*bricolage*": fiddling with whatever comes to hand in an intuitive way to reach your goal. Trust is endemic. Work projects aren't strictly segregated from the rest of life; they blend in with housework, childcare and leisure; and they tend to be of fairly short duration: a few months at most.

Then there's the industrial tradition, where things are made by big, well-organized teams modeled (according to some historians) on the crews of eighteenth-century battleships, and led by "captains of industry." Everything is carefully segregated here to avoid explosions. Thinking is done in a separate place from the doing, and by separate people. Work is separate from life. People even dress differently when they come here, and to some extent become different people: they are more uniform – although within the uniformity there's a well-organized system of distinctions that run vertically (between levels of authority) and horizontally (between specialisms). The products of this system are uniform too – which is often very welcome. The absolute minimum is left to trust. There is great emphasis on discipline. Production is meticulously planned in advance. Where messing about is unavoidable, licensed practitioners do it (designers, etc.) working in quarantine from the "troops." Very big things are done – over quite long timescales: years and decades. Everything is so specialized that hardly anyone can see the "big picture," which is in any case well protected from the vulgar view by tier upon tier of policemen. This produces the illusion that the "important person" at the top is a great visionary who has some wonderful ability to "make things happen" – and its corollary, that "ordinary people" don't do anything very much.

Who really won the Battle of Trafalgar?   The British Royal Navy destroyed a French/Spanish fleet off Cape Trafalgar in 1805. The victory is ascribed to Admiral Lord Horatio Nelson, his tactic of "crossing the enemy's T," and his gunners' ability to fire three rounds for every one fired by the French (this too is ascribed to Nelson's enlightened management).

What history does not say (although it stares every visitor to HMS *Victory* in the face) is that the Royal Navy had a wickedly simple advantage. Every single gun had a little flintlock trigger; the giant 32-pounders are like ridiculously oversized pistols, fired at the twitch of a string. French guns were fired by a slow fuse. Neither navy's guns were easily trainable. It was a matter of catching your target as it hove briefly into the limited field of view. A French gun-captain had to estimate where his target would be when the gun fired. His British counterpart simply watched for an enemy gun-port and pulled the string. It made overwhelming accuracy almost unavoidable – evidenced by the devastation wrought in seconds on French ships like the *Bucentaure* that were raked *en passant* from the stern.

Whose idea were the triggers? Not Nelson's. He believed in courage, not technology (he had firmly rejected an offer of improved gunsights). I have discovered that triggers were made standard in the Royal Navy in 1755, but whether it was an admiral, a Sea Lord, a gun-founder or an inventive gun-captain who had the non-obvious idea, then went through all the palaver of trying it, testing it, and finally getting it adopted, I cannot say. Whoever it was, it was they who made history – and in a way that's much closer to humdrum, everyday work experience than the do-or-die heroics of the great Nelson (which cost him his life). Whether by coincidence or not, it's only now, in the Cyberian age, that History has begun to take an interest in this kind of history.[1]

The great unraveling begins

The military/industrial tradition can be a fine thing to be a part of: to march in step can be intensely exhilarating; the order and logicality can be a great relief from the chaos of family life; but it can also be hell, and outrageously destructive. The peasant life is no picnic yet we tend to feel nostalgic nowadays for the peasant way of doing things – and (it transpires) there are good solid reasons for feeling this way.

The industrial tradition seems absolutely dominant. But as soon as it enters Cyberia the situation is reversed. The peasant tradition (or something very like it) comes into its own. Major pieces of software are produced on a "cottage industry" basis. Instead of minding their machines, people play with them, using them as a "medium of creative expression." These apparently trivial activities increasingly dominate the scene: computer games alone are a $17-billion-a-year business (1998), and nearly all done "peasant-style."

Meanwhile the industrial tradition becomes spectacularly unraveled. Instead of coming in late, computer projects that are run industrial-style often don't come in at all. Instead of ending up a bit over budget and a bit behind schedule, they regularly end up costing many times their original budget, taking twice or three times as long as planned – and then don't work.

Is this because computer work raises completely new kinds of problem? Apparently not.

In 1975 a senior IBM engineer called Fred Brooks analyzed the problem in an important book called *The Mythical Man-Month*, and explained that the industrial approach was at the heart of it. He then discovered that he'd touched a deeper nerve than he'd thought. People from quite unrelated disciplines like the law, medicine, and social science told him that he'd pinpointed long-running problems in their own fields, and his book had given them badly needed arguments with which to tackle them.

During the 1980s a treasure trove of evidence began pouring in from the new field of Human Factors (and the related field of "Human–Computer Interaction," or HCI). As computers became more complex, usability problems emerged, which forced computer companies to take a serious interest in human psychology. The psychologists found that the problems people were having with computers were also present in everything else – from ovens and video recorders, to cars, buildings, road systems, and the organizations where they worked. A well-known name in this field is Donald A. Norman whose 1988 classic *The Psychology of Everyday Things* is now read as avidly by town planners, architects, and product designers as by software developers.

If work is a landscape, it's one whose basic features are everywhere – but only become blindingly obvious when you reach the central massif where little ridges finally rear up into mountains, and little depressions in the ground widen into great valleys and canyons. Here you can see the country's true anatomy. Having been here, you can see the lowlands with new eyes, and how whole classes of long-running problems arise. For me, these new perceptions are some of the chief benefits of the computer age.

The landscape of human needs

Work practices are like a country's agriculture, which you can easily mistake for the landscape itself. The more powerful the civilization, the less concern it has for underlying landscape features. A peasant economy will use a limestone ridge's thin turf for grazing and the adjacent plain for crops. An advanced economy can treat it all the same: limestone land can be made to support the same crops as the loam, by aggressive use of nitrate fertilizer – or you can use other nitrates to blow the whole thing up, and then pulverize it to make concrete. Eventually one may find that the peasants' approach was the better one.

So, what are these "geological features" of the world of work? They are simple human needs – mediated by basic but far from simple human factors that you'd blush to mention in a corporate boardroom: emotion, intuition, trust, personal idiosyncrasy, curiosity, playfulness – and the basic urge to make delightful, useful things for other people whether you're paid to do it or not; features industrial culture tends to consider minor, redundant, woolly, and "soft." The unprecedentedly complex, stubborn constraints of the computer-medium have finally made them as non-ignorable as the British craftsman and visionary, William Morris, asserted 150 years ago.

William Morris and the power of everyday things[2]   William Morris (1834–96) anticipated present-day understanding of intuition, emotion, unconscious awareness, and tactile intelligence by well over a century – and a good job too. He recognized their role in traditional crafts – which he forced onto the cultural agenda just when industrialism seemed most hell-bent on eliminating them entirely.

He didn't preserve them as zoo specimens. He mastered many of them himself, showed how they could evolve in an industrial world, draw ideas from it, become an inspiration and even a challenge to it, through a work regime that prefigures Cyberia's best in all key respects: the insistence on hands-on knowledge, on experimentation, on compact teams of multi-skilled workers with broad personal horizons, and that work should be interesting and enjoyable.

He is the great, original champion of "everyday things" which, he insisted, affect and inform us constantly, unconsciously, and far more powerfully than the reasoning mind easily comprehends. In this he prefigures Donald Norman – but he went much further, connecting it to the intuitive, unconscious aspects of work itself, of fulfilling work to fulfilled lives, and of these to a truly and sustainably rich society – which he fought politically to create. He then proved these connections not just with words (of which he wrote millions) but with a non-stop flood of beautiful, useful things produced in happy, solidly viable workshops. No Cyberian yet has launched a program as complete and public as his although some seem to be headed in that direction. New knowledge about "soft" human factors should give them confidence: it is ammunition Morris could never have dreamed of having. A latter-day Morris will be pushing on an open door.

Morris implanted the idea of "well-made things" and all the values that go with them so deeply into the Western mind that we can easily fail to notice we have them: just like his "everyday things" in fact.

Recent research shows that "soft," human factors are anything but soft. If anything, emotion and intuition are tougher, quicker, cleverer, and vastly more efficient than even Morris dared to claim.

The quest for "electronic brains" in the 1960s and 70s provoked a spate of discoveries about how the mind works at the level of neurones and synapses. The upshot, in the early 1990s, was not an electronic brain, but new respect for the human one, for the body that goes with it, and for all the soft, "fluffy" things Morris talked about. Emotion and intuition are now major subjects for science. We find that it is impossible to think rationally if emotion is impaired. Stress and anxiety *do* impair thought: you can see it on a PET-scan. Hands *are* just as important for thinking as brains.

The unconscious mind *does* take in far more information, and processes it *measurably* more quickly and accurately, than the conscious part of the mind does, or even notices. Most of what we know, we know unconsciously – and we really *do* do our best thinking "without thinking." These are no longer matters for impassioned argument, but of plain scientific fact. Names to conjure with here include Michael Gazzaniga, Richard Gregory, Joseph LeDoux, Antonio Damasio, and Pawel Lewicki.[3]

The work finally begins to establish a "causal link" between hierarchical work regimes (which strive to eliminate intuition, emotion, and individuality from the workplace and cause stress within it) and their high human, social, and financial cost. And it shows just why really great work is not and never can be done that way.

The most successful work of every kind, wherever you look, is typically done quasi peasant-style by small teams of idiosyncratic individuals, using their hands and their "feelings" every bit as much as their brains. This has become commonplace in computer work.

Jeff Hawkin's hand-made PalmPilot   I'll mention just one computer-media example here: 3Com's phenomenally successful PalmPilot handheld organizer. This was designed by Jeff Hawkins.[4] His prototype was a block of wood that he cut in his garage workshop, shaped and refined, and carried around for months in his shirt-pocket, pretending that it was a computer. So when you use a PalmPilot, you encounter no other hand but his; you even use his own actual handwriting: his "Graffiti" handwriting-recognition system. There are now dozens of much bigger companies in the "handheld" business but none has achieved anything like the success his tiny company achieved. Many of them boast features that, on paper, should leave the PalmPilot standing – but in practice the Pilot's "feel" is what wins the day, and this is mainly appreciated unconsciously.

In the "industrial lowlands" around Cyberia, the best work is also done this way – although you may not know it.

One man's best-selling car: the Mini   Consider two cars: the classic British Mini launched in 1959, and its (intended) successor, the Metro (1982). The Mini was designed almost entirely by Alec Issigonis. The Metro benefited from far more market research, analysis, and "design input" than its predecessor, but it is generally regarded as a classic victim of "design by committee." It never made the same impact as the Mini – and the Mini has in fact outlived it: it is a "design classic," immune to fashion. One could write a book to analyze the reasons for the Mini's success and the Metro's relative failure, but the general verdict is: the Mini was one man's labor of love – and people love it because it carries Alec Issigonis's handwriting all the way through.

This Mini belongs to Rolf Göpffarth, a computer scientist from Bonn, Germany (picture shown with his kind permission). There are lots of Minis near where I live but I thought I'd show you Rolf's because he's so fond of it that he put it on the Web at www.unibonn.de/~uzs2e6/minid.html (Rolf's Mini page). His site also has information about Issigonis, and links to other Mini pages.

"Mini stories" are commonplace in the computer world, significant rarities in the rest of the world – but throughout the world the overwhelming tendency is for authorship to remain concealed. For every Alec Issigonis who achieves a certain recognition in his lifetime there are thousands who don't – and that's perpetuated in computerdom. Most PalmPilot users have never heard of Jeff Hawkins. They assume it was made by something called 3Com: an office building. It took me quite a while to discover that one of CD-ROM's landmarks (the "Living Books" series) was made by a man called Mark Schlichting. His name appears nowhere on the software box – only those of his publishers: Random House and Brøderbund. Here, things seem to have gone backwards: books at least carry their author's names but computer titles very often don't.

It is important to know "who did that" – and it's a much bigger issue than simply "denial of the author's rights." It is extremely important for makers to know about other makers – and for users to know who made the things they use.

The computer, the community, and the end of the "authorless artifact"

What first made me want to write this book was the realization, around ten years ago, that the computer-media world was just chock-full of the most extraordinarily diverse, interesting, and helpful people, but hardly anyone seemed to know about them. Often they didn't even know about each other. This meant that people were working much harder than they needed to, with much less success than they deserved, reinventing perfectly good wheels and falling into the same old pitfalls over and over again.

It was like being in an extremely rugged terrain of steep ridges and deep, narrow ravines. There were plenty of other people nearby, but they were totally hidden from view. It is of course not a uniquely Cyberian phenomenon.

The "unseen local community" problem   In 1845 an expedition led by Sir John Franklin, in the ships *Erebus* and *Terror*, set out to find a north-west passage from Baffin's Bay to the Barents Sea, and disappeared. Nearly a century later, some of the expedition's remains were discovered. It seems the lime-juice had frozen, destroying its vitamin-C content, and everyone died of scurvy. The team that discovered the remains interviewed local Inuit people whose ancestors had been in the area at the time of the tragedy. Franklin's people had had no idea there were any Inuit nearby. The "locals" had watched the whole thing, rather afraid of these odd-looking beings, and very puzzled that they seemed so intent on doing things the hard way. This seems a very suitable metaphor for many work projects – which fail in needless isolation.

Ignorance is bad for users.

A Harvard educationist called Brenda Matthis[5] points out that "authorless software" presents you with somebody's world-view – which you just don't question. You don't even realize that it is someone's world-view. It's just "the way it is." What seem to be "natural laws" are in fact someone's assumptions – and they are bound to be half-baked ones to some extent. Thus, interactive games and multimedia encyclopedias (like Microsoft's Encarta) can stupefy people instead of enlightening or empowering them.

Taking this insight down into the "industrial lowlands," one sees that "authorlessness" is the established norm. Books may carry their authors' names, as do fine-art items and certain underpants but they are the exceptions that prove the rule. We seldom know who made the houses we live in, the offices where we work, the chairs, desks, and phones we use, the clothes we wear, or even the food we eat or the crockery we eat it from – and we know even less about how they came to make them. Most of the fabric of everyday life is not, apparently, made by anybody at all – which is even more stupefying than (according to some people) Encarta is.

Things are always made the way they are for particular, human reasons – ranging from self-centered laziness, to dire necessity and panic, to sudden insight and care; but when the "authorship" is hidden the history is hidden too. We just assume things are supposed to be that way (the way rocks and trees are).[6] If we can't cope with them we must be stupid. If they please us we thank the superhuman genius of Sony, Coca-Cola, or God. Either way, we slide into a true "cargo-cult" mentality, which blinds us to the real natures of things – *and* to our own abilities: it seems that "good stuff" cannot be done by mere mortals like ourselves; conversely, people like us don't do the "bad stuff" either. People who feel this way are not much use to anyone.

But when you peel back the surfaces of things the exact opposite happens. A "mere mortal" is what you find – and one who's surprisingly like yourself. It cuts the "bad stuff" down to size – yet it doesn't reduce your appreciation of "the good stuff"; it increases it enormously – *and* it enhances your self-respect: a fragile item in most people, and essential for anyone who strives to do "good stuff." Things that seem awesome, impossible for a "mere mortal" to achieve, turn out to be what they are *precisely because* of some aspect of their creator's own, unique, and idiosyncratic kind of "mere mortality." This makes you realize that your own "mere mortality" may be some use after all!

For example:

Geniuses aren't what you expect   I had been aware of "Conway's 'Game of Life'" for years – it is a fundamental example of "artificial life," "emergence," "complex systems," etc.[7] All I knew about Conway was that he was a legendary Cambridge and Princeton mathematician who invented "Life" back in the 1960s. The mathematics writer Martin Gardner has called him "one of the world's undisputed geniuses."[8] I assumed he was long dead. Then I saw an announcement that he was not only alive, but giving a talk just down the road from where I live. I went, expecting some ancient, posh, distant Cambridge-don stereotype. When I got there I thought I'd got the wrong room: here was a wiry middle-aged rascal with a shock of brown hair and a slight Scouse (Liverpool) accent, getting members of the audience to do mathematical tricks with skipping ropes. He told us afterwards that he'd discovered his passion for tricks and games in the playground of his Liverpool primary school in the 1940s and 50s, and everything grew from there. In the course of that short meeting the remote, towering edifice of math collapsed into something infinitely friendlier and closer to hand than I had ever imagined it could be.

Discovering "who did that?" is some of the best therapy there is – whether the thing in question is a mathematical theory, a song, a chair, a website, or a massacre.

This is precisely where the computer begins actively to make a real difference. It can present you with an event or an artifact, without stripping away its origins as other media do. A Mini on the street gives no hint of the story behind it – but the one on Rolf's Mini page comes with a trail of links that bring more and more of the story to light as time goes by. This reverses the historic trend to "authorlessness." Self-serving governments can gag the local press, but not the Internet – at least, not yet.

The Voyager Company's work (Chapter 2.2) showed that "revealing authorship" has immense emotional impact – and marked this out as ripe and profitable territory for new-media developers to explore.

The new mind-science begins to explain how this works. Knowing the maker (or culprit) explains things that you'd been affected by, *but not been aware of consciously.*

Afterwards, things that were unconsciously enjoyed (or suffered) become consciously appreciated – and this gives a very special and important kind of pleasure. It confirms to us that our subjective feelings about things had a real basis. We learn to trust and respect ourselves: the *sine qua non* for doing "good stuff."

Notes

1 I refer to the "history from below" movement – whose leaders (in Britain) include the late Raphael Samuel, and Christopher Hill: mentioned in the introduction to Section 2.

2 The best account of Morris is Fiona McCarthy's *William Morris – a Life for our Time.*

3 It was Gazzaniga who discovered that the two halves of the brain are specialized – leading to a spate of popular books about "right-brain thinking." His latest work is *The Mind's Past.* Gregory is the long-time champion of "hands-on science," and has shown how physical inter-action is essential for thought. LeDoux and Damasio have both written recent important books that demonstrate the key role played by emotion and intuition – and the "neural circuits" that are involved. See the bibliography for details. Lewicki heads the Nonconscious Information Processing Laboratory at Tulsa Oklahoma: http://centum.utulsa.edu/~PSY_PL/www/. For a very good overview and analysis of this entire field see Guy Claxton's *Hare Brain, Tortoise Mind.*

4 Hawkins had previously designed one of the very first "handhelds": the GRiDPad – which failed to catch on (as Apple's wonderful Newton probably failed) because it was too big and costly. For more of the story, read David Jackson's March 1998 *Time* article "Palm-To-Palm Combat" (see bibliography).

5 See her paper "Authorship in Software" – presented at the International Workshop on Hypermedia and Narrative – at the Open University's Meno project website: http://meno.open.ac.uk/meno/ht97.html. My own "Narrative as Landscape" is also there.

6 Clifford Reeves and Byron Nass have written a whole book about this phenomenon: *The Media Equation*, Cambridge University Press, 1996.

7 Briefly: you have an arbitrarily large checkers or "Go" board on which counters are placed at random. Then, they "breed" or "die" according to a few very simple rules. It turns out that "organisms" emerge: patterns of counters called "blinkers," then bigger ones called "gliders" that travel across the board, then "glider guns" that emit gliders – and so on. For a really good explanation of the Game of Life, try Phil Johnson-Laird's *The Computer and the Mind.* I recom-mend an interview with Conway by Charles Seife, which you can find on the World Wide Web at http://www.users.cloud9.net/~cgseife/conway.html.

8 "A quarter-century of recreational mathematics," *Scientific American*, August, 1998.

The computer as a "medium"

WHY SHOULD SOMETHING designed to calculate tide tables, population statistics, and shell trajectories become a creative medium (and a strikingly successful one – at least some of the time) before its wrapping-paper, so to speak, has even been tidied away? The computer has only been around for 50 years[1] – the blink of an eye in historical terms.

The answer may be pretty simple: people use everything they get their hands on as media – but what are "media"?

The history and mystery of media: a quick but plausible explanation

This is my theory. I find it helpful and maybe you will too.

The habit of "using things as media" runs so deep we barely realize that we have it – but it could well be what makes people "people."

The broad-brush definition of "a medium" is: *anything that you can use to give somebody else an experience of some kind, in your absence.* (There's more to it than this – see below – but it will do for now.)

A "medium" starts off as an innocent "material," which humans exploit for some sensible, businesslike purpose. That's all people did for most of our history (about 100,000 years;[2] 2,000,000 years if you include our tool-using hominid ancestors). But then, about 40–50,000 years ago, people started using materials as "media" as well: to impress, delight, and sometimes to terrify other people. Arrowheads and knives became smooth and beautiful. Jewellery and pottery appeared – and the makers weren't content with pots that just "did the job": they decorated them and gave them attractive shapes, almost from the very first.

Since those days, people have always used their materials as media when time permitted (and often when it didn't), even when the "official purpose" of the task was severely functional. The urge to make things beautiful, impressive, or just pretty is so ingrained that the 1930s Modernist idea of making things "purely functional" came as a shock. This tendency seems just as strong in modern humans as in ancient ones, and therefore a fundamental human attribute.

As I said, it's not *quite* that simple:

1   Sometimes it turns out that beauty goes hand-in-hand with functionality (not always, and when it does, it comes as a surprise. The impulse to "beautify" comes first). However, the "functionality of beauty" is real, and is a central mystery – not just of art and design, but also of science.

2   Also, "media" serve as "private playspaces." They are "extensions of the mind" – and this is one of their most important roles. It could predate the "communicative" use of media. As we'll see, it is a huge factor in the computer's history.

All media have "constraints": the "stick-whittling" analogy

Whether used for public or private purposes, *the medium itself defines what you can do*. It has "constraints" – and these have to be discovered, then exploited. Until you discover the constraints, they run the show. This is what happens when you first whittle a stick with a penknife: the grain guides the knife, the feeling is pleasant, you carry on until suddenly there's no stick left. Exactly the same thing seems to happen when we use computers – as we'll see.

The computer is used as a "medium" much more than people like to think

Nobody, as far as I know, has yet tackled the question of just when people started using computers as media, or thinking about them in that way. Did Alan Turing or John von Neumann play with their machines with the idea of setting up experiences for other people? Turing and von Neumann certainly used them as "personal playspaces." They were both famously playful characters. That playfulness, more than any "official" purpose, is perhaps the real foundation-stone of this entire, very serious-looking edifice we call "the computer industry." Maybe computing machinery is fundamentally funny stuff.

Whether it is or isn't, innocent fun of the stick-whittling variety is endemic – and explains a very big problem: this technology, which is supposedly all about logical control, is to a large extent out of control.

Computers and the stick-whittling problem

Since the 1970s, people like Fred Brooks have been pointing to the ways software projects overrun their budgets and deadlines – and then don't work.

In 1995, in a landmark book called *The Trouble with Computers*, Thomas Landauer showed that computerization has actually reduced productivity throughout entire industries and national economies.

In Britain in 1997, Mark Carrington and Philip Languuth found that …

Banks now spend 10 times more per employee on IT than they did in 1980 – yet operating costs have escalated massively to £23.6 billion per annum [$37 billion at 1997 exchange rates] largely because of the technology investment.

Meanwhile, the ratio between operating costs and income has remained static.

Overall costs have only been reduced by staff cuts.[3]

There's definitely something funny going on! Multimedia and the Web are not immune: profitable productions have been very much more the exception than the rule. For example, the world's major publishers entered the CD-ROM arena *en masse* in the early 90s, and most of them failed. In October 1997, the research company Dataquest found that a mere 4 percent of CD-ROM titles had been profitable.[4]

So what *is* the problem? Landauer thinks the very promise of computers is at the root of it. And it's not that the computers fail to deliver on their promises: they often do that very well, and we feel very satisfied with the results. The problem is often that what they're promising is not *quite* what's really needed – but the promise is so nice we go along with it anyway.

For example: one of Landauer's sources (Paul Attewell) reports that middle managers *feel* their laptops make them very much more productive. Indeed, in the firms he studied, "internal productivity" went up 78 percent. More work was definitely being done. Yet the firms' *actual output* stayed absolutely flat. The 78 percent increase was an increase in report-writing.[5]

Web-design workers may put this down to "typical middle-management foolishness" – while doing exactly the same thing themselves. Many happy, productive hours, days, and weeks are often spent honing graphics, animations, and Java applets that, quite possibly …

(a) impair the job's effectiveness (e.g., they take so long to download onto the user's computer that the user gives up) and

(b) become the "tail that wags the dog": assets in which so much love and money have been invested that they can't be dumped when needs change. They have to be used in future, even if they're no longer relevant, and even when they get in the way of better solutions.

▨ Considered *as a tool*, the computer's empowerment is *surreptitiously selective*. It doesn't, actually, make *everything* easy; it makes *some* things *enormously* easy, and can easily carry you in directions that lead you miles away from your original goal.

▨ Considered *as a medium*, the computer evidently has properties and constraints that guide *us* rather better than we guide *it*. Being unaware of them we tend to "go with the grain" – and produce reports nobody will read and graphics nobody wants. There is, of course, no possibility of ignoring the grain, and certainly no possibility of abolishing it. What we have to do is get a feel for the medium. Maybe the current "crisis of computing" is exactly what we should expect, when people get their hands on an exciting new medium.

Notes

1   Precisely 50 years as it happens. I write this in 1998 – the anniversary of Manchester University's "Baby": the first "stored-program" computer.

2   The dates come from Steven Mithen's *The Prehistory of Mind* (Thames & Hudson 1996). *Homo Sapiens Sapiens* (our own sub-species) first appears around 100,000 years ago but didn't become dominant until the "neolithic revolution" that started around 40,000 years ago. The neolithic's "hallmark" was once considered to be the appearance of pottery; then farming. However, use of media could be a better benchmark: this is the subject of an ongoing discussion.

3   Carrington and Languuth, *The Banking Revolution: Salvation or Slaughter?*

4   From article by Emma Keelan, in *The Guardian Online*, 20 November 1997.

5   Landauer, *The Trouble With Computers*, p. 332.

1.2

The computer as a landscape

"STICKWHITTLING" DESCRIBES quite well the experience of using a computer to "fine-tune" graphics, PowerPoint presentations, and memos beyond the call of duty – but when you make an interactive program, especially when you build things in code, your time- and effort-wasting options grow exponentially, along hair-raisingly many axes. The seductions and obstacles multiply. You can start off along an easy-looking route then find (after days of happy effort) that you "can't get there from here," or spend days on a problem that, it then turns out, would have taken five minutes if you'd tackled it from a slightly different angle.

It seems very like exploring a highly convoluted, exhilarating, but totally unforgiving landscape, in the dark. The language we use suggests it, and it can feel like it physically.[1] I call this landscape "Cyberia."

Cyberia is not the same as Cyberspace   "Cyberia" and "Cyberspace" are often used interchangeably, but "Cyberspace" is rather different: it is the strictly notional space where we interact online, which is everywhere and nowhere. The word was coined by William Gibson in his 1984 novel *Neuromancer*. His hero, Case, finds the word defined thus (by his intelligent information-machine, or "deck"):

Cyberspace. A consensual hallucination experienced daily by billions of legitimate operators, in every nation, by children being taught mathematical concepts … A graphic representation of data abstracted from the banks of every computer in the human system. Unthinkable complexity. Lines of light ranged in the nonspace of the mind, clusters and constellations of data. Like city lights, receding … .

"What's that?" Molly asked, as he flipped the channel selector.

"Kid's show." A discontinuous flood of images as the selector cycled. "Off," he said to the Hosaka.[2]

Just for your interest, Gibson says, in the "Author's Afterword" to Voyager's 1991 electronic edition, that he invented the word (and wrote the novel) not on a computer, but on a 1930s Hermes portable typewriter.

> "Cyberia" is the computer's "possibility landscape": the "realm of things that are do-able through computer control." Every project explores some part of it.

> "Possibility spaces" are in fact more real than most things in the "real world" – although sometimes the real world does a passable imitation:

Getting there via Tibet   Sometime in the 1970s a French climbing team had reached Everest's main peak from the southern, Nepalese, side, and was descending in a hurry to avoid oncoming night. One climber slipped and took the rest with him; they slid hundreds of feet; the rope snagged on a rock and snapped, and the man on the right-hand end vanished over the edge (his name was Bourgeois – a Belgian).

The survivors searched for him in vain, then made their way back to base camp, and finally flew home from Kathmandu to Paris, where an emotional memorial service was held.

A year later Bourgeois's wife got a phone call from him. The fall had carried him just 50 feet below and a little to the right of his companions (i.e., to the north) but he couldn't climb back up. With night falling there was only one thing for it: descend as fast as possible. What he didn't know was that he was descending into Tibet – not Nepal. He eventually bivouacked in the ruins of the Great Rongbuk Monastery, was arrested by Chinese troops, taken first to Lhasa then Beijing and finally released.[3]

This kind of impromptu but life-changing Grand Tour is a recurring feature of computer work.

> It is a truism of life generally that tiny steps can have huge, unexpected consequences. In computer work, the effect seems to be hugely amplified and one can actually feel it at work.

> The "mountain landscape" metaphor corresponds very well with current scientific thinking about Life, the Universe, and Everything.

You, me, and the typewriter   For example, many of the things that make up our environment and dominate our lives are accidents, forced on us by minor decisions made "further up the mountain." The classic example is the "QWERTY" keyboard with which I struggled daily to write these words (as did William Gibson, when he first typed the word "cyberspace"). It was designed originally for typewriters – each key mechanically linked to a little hammer that put the letter on the page; the arrangement of keys was made deliberately difficult because the hammers would get entangled if the typist worked too fast. By the time better input-methods were possible, a whole new industry had grown up around QWERTY and the alternatives didn't get a look-in. This is just one of many examples studied by the Santa Fé Institute economist Brian Arthur.[4]

Other examples are you, me, and the dog: we are all "descended" (as we so aptly say) from a life-form that, like the modern plaice or the flounder, had its head (or what passed for a head in those days) turned around the wrong way. To this day, the right-hand sides of our bodies are controlled by the left-hand sides of our brains, and vice versa.

Scientists call these landscapes, in which keyboards, humans, dogs, and everything else exist, "phase space," "possibility space," or "evolutionary space."[5]

The massif of contradictions: a quick tour of Cyberia

The "mountain landscape" idea can free us from some delusive and dangerous myths – the first of which is that "somebody, somewhere knows precisely where we're going." In a real landscape, nobody *ever* knows precisely where they're going – and the ones who think they do are ones to avoid. But omniscience is a very popular notion in large organizations, which probably helps explain why they do so badly in Cyberia.

Industries and organizations have a terrible tendency to pretend that they're little islands of pre-Darwinian order in our chaotic universe. They progress inexorably along their appointed path, under the inspired leadership of a few rare geniuses chosen by God. Modest things are supplanted by better things, which give way to truly superb things: as shown below:

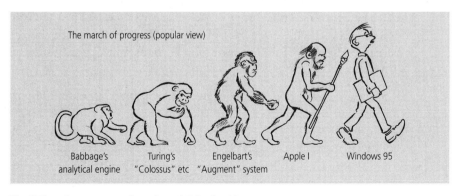

The march of progress (popular view)

| Babbage's analytical engine | Turing's "Colossus" etc | Engelbart's "Augment" system | Apple I | Windows 95 |

The "Triumphant progress" version of Cyberian history

... a sort of "ascent of man." We get the impression of a process that was destined to happen just this way. It is perhaps advantageous to give that kind of impression to shareholders and important customers – but it does not really square with the rather more shambolic situation on the ground.

Taking our mountain metaphor (and a leaf from the chaos theorists' book), let's take a vantage point approximately 30,000 feet above the action:

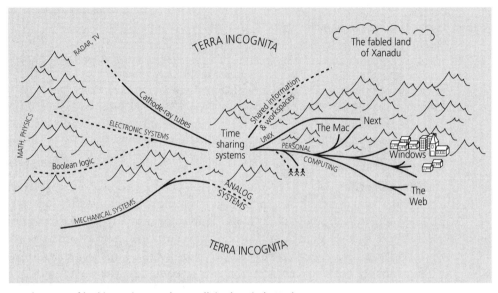

Another way of looking at it: a random walk in the Hindu Kush

Here we have a rather more exciting picture: a vast, and still *largely unexplored* "land of possibility." The march of progress shown in the first figure is just one of many possible routes into its interior, and not necessarily the best one either. Any sense of security we feel at the "trail-head" could well be the false security of the crowd. What warmth there is could just the body-heat of fellow-travelers. Perhaps Bill Gates has led us all up Shit Creek!

If he has, let's not get too outraged. Shit Creek is an essential part of the journey – mountaineers say: no Shit Creek, no Mount Everest. What *is* silly is to pretend Shit Creek doesn't exist. The *really* silly thing is to put your faith unquestioningly in the "guy in front." He may look as if he knows where he's going, he may be highly experienced – but he can be wrong. He is merely doing his best.

Some lessons of the "Cyberia" metaphor

So far, we've only tickled the fringes of Cyberia – but enough people have ventured into it to get some idea of its nature:

- The "routes" people have found into it so far are almost certainly not the ideal routes. (No exploration ever hits on the best routes first time.)

- We've probably bypassed some good alternative routes already. Maybe we should backtrack and revisit them.

- Maps (like project master plans) need to be as good as possible – but they can never tell the whole story. To get that, you need to explore and try various routes, "hands-on."

- It's an unforgiving terrain: more like the Himalayas than Holland. Every step takes effort, and wasted effort can be fatal. We often find ourselves in "you can't get there from here" situations.

- Lightweight reconnoitering is essential; huge all-or-nothing expeditions usually come to grief.

Beware the kingdoms of Cyberia

When humans invade any new territory, especially a fertile one, they tend to gravitate into little tribal groups – each developing its own culture, heroes, hierarchy, language, distinctive mode of dress, legal code, defense department, and warlords (elected or self-appointed) to head up the whole operation and maintain national purity.

The computer is no different – only it happens much faster here. Maybe the added anxiety of being in an invisible world accentuates the huddling instinct. Here, we already have quite large "kingdoms" of corporate computing, applications programming, games development, "cyberarts," "multimedia," the Web, etc. – each with its own "national literature" (its journals, etc.), "national holidays" (its conferences) and other badges of difference. Most of these new kingdoms have frontier controls, and even internal caste systems. For example, "Multimedia" has its CD-ROM workers and Web workers – and members of the CD-ROM caste are not necessarily accepted by the Web caste, and both seem to despise the ancient Interactive Video caste.

What would Norbert Wiener have said about this?   Norbert Wiener was the man who coined the original word, cybernetics, in 1947, which he defined as "the science of communication and control." He was one of the very first and greatest advocates of the digital way of doing things. He was alarmed at the way the world was heading and found this type of empire-building, and "the accepted techniques of mass attack and the division of labor"[6] at the root of the problem. He totally believed that "multidisciplinary" ways of working were mankind's only hope.

It's a bit sad, really: this is all one landscape – and unlike the Earth's landscape, there seems to be plenty of it to go around. However, these "national boundaries" are very premature, and also doomed because:

We change this landscape by exploring it

Creativity makes waves – and this is not mixing metaphors: real rock behaves like a fluid in geological time, and in Cyberia time goes faster. The Cyberian landscape is always changing – and it does this as a result of our own explorations. The effect can be catalytic: as when an enzyme causes a whole mass of protein to fold itself into a completely new shape, with new properties.

Alan Kay (the great evangelist of personal computing) said, "The best way to predict the future is to invent it" – but although we *do* invent the future, the effects of our inventions are unpredictable.

Sometimes, quite little changes that somebody makes can "ripple through" the whole landscape and lock it into a completely new configuration. Sometimes the new configuration is more stable than the old one, and people can move in and start exploiting it in earnest. Bill Atkinson's HyperCard (Chapter 1.7) did this, and Tim Berners-Lee's invention, the World Wide Web. At the same time other areas that people were exploiting vanish, or become inaccessible. But the new landscape is never permanent – and the rewards tend to go to people who are aware of the landscape's tendency to change, the *ways* in which it can change, and therefore have the kinds of ideas that can cope with change.

Now, I'll quickly describe the ways Cyberia has been shaped by its explorers. It has already gone through a lot of changes – and is certain to go through many more. What follows is highly selective, and I know I have omitted some very important people. But this isn't a history of new media – other books do that job very well already and I'll provide references to them as we go. The aim is simply to help you develop a feel for the way people affect things here.

Notes

1   This isn't scientific, but of 36 programmers and multimedia workers I asked at a meeting recently, about half said they frequently felt they were working in an invisible landscape when writing code. There is a possible neural reason for this – but unfortunately it won't fit into this book.

2   *Neuromancer* (Voyager Expanded Book edition) p. 103.

3   Bourgeois told this story to the English writer Peter Gillman, who published it in the *Sunday Times* Colour Supplement some time in the 1970s.

4   Belfast-born economist Brian W. Arthur is one of the founders of the Santa Fé Institute – the "home of chaos theory." For a good introduction to his and the other Institute members' work, see Mitchell Waldrop's *Complexity* (Penguin, 1989). Or visit the Santa Fé website at http://www.santafe.org.

5   Ian Stewart and Jack Cohen give a very good explanation of "phase space" in *Figments of Reality – The Evolution of the Curious Mind*. Another excellent person to read, to get a handle on this way of thinking, is Richard Dawkins – e.g., his *The Blind Watchmaker* and the more recent *Climbing Mount Improbable*: these are superb conducted tours of "evolutionary space."

6   From the introduction to Norbert Wiener's *Cybernetics, or control and communication in the animal and the machine*, MIT Press, 1948.

1.3

Cyberia's geological past

CYBERIA IS AS ALLURING as a beautiful, fertile volcanic island. It is hard to imagine that it has ever been, or could ever be, any different.

Cyber-talk *sounds* well aware of the situation, but the awareness is really quite shallow. We talk constantly about new things because there are so many of them in this wonderful new environment – but most of this talk is of the "exciting new kinds of yam" variety, or "great new ways to extract timber." This takes our eye off the ball: we talk agriculture and forget that the landscape sets the real agenda, and it will change, as it has already changed, dramatically and abruptly. Yam-growing and timber extraction may cease to be options. But whatever the new landscape is like, it will still be a landscape. The valuable, durable skill will always be exploration skill rather than exploitation skill.

The still-relevant beauty of the analog era

Cyberia underwent one major seismic upheaval very recently: the shift from "analog" to "digital" computing. Geology being what it is, there's no reason to assume analog won't resurface again in the future – so it's worth being aware of it.

Analog machines – usually made from mechanically engineered parts but also from electronic and even chemical components, and from hybrid collections of components – allowed *continuously varying* input and output (as opposed to the "discrete", or "quantized" input and output you get from digital machines). They are so called because the machine itself physically resembles the system you are modeling (it is its "analog"). Thus, astrolabes are "analog computers" for predicting eclipses. In the case of the astrolabe, *the machine was its own interface*. A real work of art. Analog machines were often purpose-built to do one particular job, and many designs gave instantaneous, error-free results.

Whether analog ever resurfaces or not, it should be a rich source of inspiration and ideas: we are often trying to present abstract processes in the most physical way possible, and that is just what analog technology did. Unfortunately analog machines are hardly written about these days so the best sources tend to be quite old.[1]

Gordon Pask (of whom more in Chapter 1.5) seems to have been a major poet of the analog era.

Turing's world

The "analog landscape" was changed utterly by a tiny but fiendishly efficient idea released into the environment in 1936, by the British mathematician Alan Turing: the "finite state machine" using "binary logic." Turing is best known for his part in the codebreaking effort that led to allied victory in World War II. His life-work was very strongly grounded in the idea of "phase space" (particularly, the n-dimensional version known as "Hilbert space"[2]). He is regarded by many as computing's true father and his story is one of the great Cyberian classics (Andrew Hodge wrote it: *Alan Turing, the Enigma*[3]).

In 1936 Turing proposed an imaginary, completely dumb machine, that could carry out all kinds of procedures: the "finite-state machine" or "Turing Machine." At around the same time, he provided the "atomic structure" of the new environment by marrying binary arithmetic with Boolean Logic (the now-familiar but then old and quaint algebra of "if - then-else" type statements devised in 1854 by George Boole at the University of Cork, to represent the "Laws of Thought"). In 1937 he even built part of an experimental "binary multiplier" in the workshop at Princeton, and it worked. We were "in" (as hackers say).

This "seed idea" spread through possibility space the way most changes do: very slowly at first, then rapidly, and by the 1960s had taken it over completely. In 1950 he posed the question, "is there a limit to the kinds of things that can be done by a moronic device, mindlessly following procedures?" (my paraphrase). The answer to this question is still "we don't know" and seems likely to stay that way.

Turing's machines are "universal machines." They can be any machine you like.

The poetry of the machine

Turing doesn't seem to have been into "media" as such – but he (and fellow pioneers like John von Neumann) had a very strong, even a guiding sense that "the machine" had a certain "truth and beauty" of its own. Engineers have always recognized the inherent beauty of machines – even if it remained a closed book to the official guardians of truth and beauty: the artists.

If we really want to get to grips with machine aesthetics,[4] analog machines obviously need to be considered – but even more, we should probably study the thoughts of men (mostly – and why mostly men?) like Newcomen, Brunel, Edison, and Joseph Marie Jacquard whose punch-card-driven mechanical loom (patented in 1804) provided a model for early computers.

Artists in Cyberia (and then Siberia): the other Russian revolution

Throughout the industrial revolution artists shrank instinctively from "the machine": it represented all that was bad and degrading. But in the early years of the century a few embraced it: for example, El Lissitsky, Kasimir Malevich, Vladimir Tatlin, the sculptor Jacob Epstein, and the English "vorticists." The Russians seem to have been the prime movers.

Malevich, especially, was after a kind of art that went below the surfaces of things. He pushed beyond the limits of representational art, then of cubism, thence to "constructivism." The Russians seem to have recognized with special clarity something genuinely different in the "poetry of the machine," and they explored it vigorously. Steam locomotives, production processes, aero-engines are utterly rule-driven, notorious for their intolerance of "fuzziness." This made them seem merely "inhuman" to most artists, but El Lissitsky and Malevich recognized something at work there like a huge, alien life-form, and celebrated it in a journal called *Veshch* ("Thing," or "Object") – still available in good art libraries.

The Russians had a special vantage point from which to observe the "shape of events." It had become almost a visible thing in Russia thanks to a delayed, then explosive industrial revolution that caused seismic social change, immediately interrupted by savage industrialized war, revolution, and an even crueler civil war whose icons included the armored train and the popular cinema – all in barely more than 30 years. Minds that survived that were almost bound to come away with unique insights.

It is worth considering what would have happened, had Russia not suffered its three wars and its Stalinist purges, and the computer revolution had started in Moscow or Leningrad instead of MIT, Stanford, and Manchester. Russian computing seems, even so, to have added a lot to the common wealth.

Mechanized multimedia

"Multimedia" is not necessarily a cybernetic art – you can blend sound, music, images, etc. and create "immersive" experiences very well indeed without a computer (and people have done that for millennia – see below). The computer certainly gives multimedia huge new powers – and makes the experience *replicable*.

But people seem to have known for a very long time that multimedia+machinery is a winning combination – and explored whatever "possibility space" was available very energetically and inventively indeed.

Various artists of the 1920s built contrivances to give an immersive, multimedia experience. Two are: Laszlo Maholy-Nagy, who built something called "The Light-Space Modulator"; and Kurt Schwitters, who built rooms called "Mertzbau" – one of which is preserved at Newcastle University, England.

The new mass-media certainly had the idea, exploiting the "possibility space" provided by current technology to the absolute limit. The early French film director Abel Gance used machinery and media in astonishing ways: live orchestras, massed choirs, whole sections of the film gorgeously colored frame by frame by hand, multiple projection screens.

Current mainstream cinema seems tame by comparison – although Disney and Universal Studio "experiences" carry on the tradition.

Theater and multimedia

Some, like Randall Packer,[5] think the operatic composer Richard Wagner was "the first artist in cyberspace." In 1876 he built a state-of-the-art opera house at Bayreuth, in which he deliberately set out to integrate all existing art forms: music, dance, poetry, painting, and architecture. He even had a word for it: *Gesamtkunstwerk* ("Total Art"). But if Wagner qualifies, then we ought to include the dramatists of ancient Greece: Aeschylus, Sophocles, Euripides et al., whose theatre seems to have been intensely "multimedia".[6] Brenda Laurel – one of the most insightful writers on our medium – draws heavily on the ancient Greek drama in her *Computers as Theater*.

Sixteenth-century Europe produced some astonishing adventures in multimedia – mechanized and manual. Court culture of England and France was one of highly artificial environments: palaces, mazes, and "masque" plays – involving spectacular stage machinery. "The masque" was one of those art forms that is "written on the wind": unlike Shakespeare's theater, it left little in the way of written records from which later generations might reconstitute it – yet it seems to have been one of the major art forms of the day. Perhaps related to the masque is Giulio Camillo's almost legendary "Memory Theater." You'll find a wonderful account of this in Frances Yates's influential book *The Art of Memory*.

Camillo (born c. 1480) created quite a stir in early sixteenth-century Europe with a wooden "memory theater" that was quite the research project of its day. Partly funded by King François I of France, the idea was that "*whoever is admitted as spectator will be able to discourse on any subject no less fluently than Cicero*" [Vigilius Zuichemus, writing to Erasmus from Padua in 1532. Yates, p. 135]. Does that sound like a typically over-ambitious product-brief for a multimedia encyclopedia? Many new-media workers have been inspired by Yates's account of Camillo's work. Indeed, the computer you're using now probably owes a lot to it: according to Stewart Brand, it was the "art of memory" that gave Nicholas Negroponte the initial idea for "Put That There" – an early expression of what became today's desktop interface (see Stewart Brand's *The Media Lab*).

Camillo (who abandoned a professorial chair at Bologna to develop his theater and ended up broke) lived, like us, at a time of great intellectual ferment, wholesale reorganization of beliefs, not to mention expansion of scholarly enquiry, of empires, of commerce, and the explosion of knowledge and rival systems of belief that went with this. As it happened, another technology took the strain, and the limelight, in a quite different way: print.

Yet Camillo's tradition flourished and developed for a further century and, Yates argues, never really died.

Notes

1   ... although there's a good, short chapter in A.K. Dewdney's *The New Turing Omnibus*. See also Gordon Pask's *Microman*, and good computer histories like H.H. Goldstine's 1972 classic *The Computer: From Pascal to von Neumann*.

2   If you are a Lingo programmer, Peter Small (Chapter 2.1) will take you though Hilbert space in his "Magical A-Life Avatars." See also, his website at www.avatarnets.com.

3   See also Andrew Hodge's website at Wadham College Oxford, which has more information on Turing, and a Turing Machine that you can try – also numerous links to computer history sites: http://www.wadham.ac.uk/~ahodges/main.html.

4   David Gelernter pleads for recognition of machine aesthetics in *Machine Beauty: Elegance and the Heart of Technology* (1998). He uses a fairly limited range of examples, drawn from his own experience as a computer scientist, but at least he has made a start.

5   Randall has a nice little website about all this entitled "From Wagner to Virtual Reality," at http://www.cel.sfsu.edu/MSP/timeline/Home.html.

6   There is, I believe, quite an extensive literature on the stage machinery used in the "classic period" of Greek theater. Recently, researchers at Athens University have discovered that the masks used by actors were themselves much more "technological" than had been thought.

1.4

Bush, Engelbart, Nelson, and the quest for Xanadu

LIKE BLIND MEN WITH AN ELEPHANT, people start exploring a new "possibility space" with no idea of its overall shape – or even that it might have one. Sometimes it never occurs to them that they're dealing with the same large thing until it rolls over on them in its sleep.

From 1945 a very definite sense of "what's out there" starts to develop. Many people are involved but three names stand out: Vannevar Bush, Douglas C. Engelbart, and Theodor Holm (Ted) Nelson. By rights I should add a fourth, Tim Berners-Lee,[1] but I have not had the time to do him anything like justice. They've given workers in the new territory their first major bearing-point. Nelson's name for it is "Xanadu": a world where nothing is ever lost, so the value of everything is enhanced – and anyone can get to it and contribute to it. Xanadu is hard to reach – but unlike Coleridge's Xanadu[2] it is more than a dream. Industry has lurched off in directions that make it much harder to reach than it need have been but even so we may get there yet.

Who else have I missed out?   Loads of people – certainly including brilliant ones I've never heard of (but would have if we'd reached Xanadu). Were I writing a full-blown history here, I would also mention H.G. Wells: the British writer whose ideas influenced the work far more than has been generally realized.[3] I would also tell you about Alan Kay, who pioneered the idea of "personal computing" in the 1970s. I would write at great and exciting length about Gordon Pask, the "mad genius" English apostle of Wiener's cybernetic vision, who (I'm told) built remarkable machines for "driving through knowledge" in the 1960s. However, you can get these excellent stories elsewhere.

Bush, Engelbart, and Nelson can be portrayed as an evolutionary series, or as Olympic runners, carrying the "sacred flame" in relay. I think the reality is a little bit different from that, and more interesting.

Vannevar Bush[4] proposes "a new profession of trailblazers"

Bush (with pipe as always) in **1949**, trying a device that used similar technology to his imagined "memex": a photo-typesetting machine developed in France and refined at MIT by Samuel Caldwell (seen here) and others. It used electrical relays and motors, and photographic film. **Photo by courtesy of MIT Museum**

The classic route into Cyberia starts, traditionally, with an article published in 1945, entitled "As We May Think," by Vannevar Bush ("Vannevar" takes emphasis on the second syllable: like "retriever"). Bush had spent World War II at the head of Roosevelt's Office of Scientific Research and Development (OSRD) – supervising work on radar, code-breaking, munitions, and the atomic bomb, among other things.

In this article, Bush describes an imaginary knowledge-machine, the "memex" (all lowercase for some reason), a desk-sized workstation "...*in which an individual stores all his books, records, and communications, and which is mechanized so that it may be consulted with exceeding speed and flexibility.*"

It is one of the most influential texts in computing history[5] – and that's rather pleasantly surprising: it is short, not terribly technical, and it was published, not in a heavyweight scientific journal, but in a popular magazine: *Atlantic Monthly*.

The vision he presents is a wonderful one – and written in words anyone can grasp: in refreshing contrast to the fearsome "headline science" of 1947 (atomic power, "electronic brains," radar). Its lucidity must have helped – also, the media had rather latched onto Bush as the "acceptable face of science": he looked avuncular and smoked a pipe. Bush himself was surprised that the article attracted so much attention. This is not to deny that the memex was a brilliant idea – just to show that brilliant ideas may rely, for their acceptance, on all kinds of quirky factors.

Nearly all accounts of cybermedia talk about the memex – not about Bush himself, his thinking, and his motives. Very little was available about him until Pascal Zachary's biography *Endless Frontier* appeared in 1997. Bush has been adopted as an icon of the digital age – but the man Zachary describes is not a "computer visionary" in the current sense. On the contrary, he is like a last survivor of the race of hands-on engineers, inventors, and "tinkerers" typified by Franklin, Bell, and Edison – a race that had pretty well vanished by 1947 – and he never got to grips with digital technology. He opposed an initiative of Norbert Wiener's for developing a digital device in 1944 – although that may simply have been because Wiener's project was too long-term to help with the war effort.

One can see how much the memex owed to Bush's "outmoded" heritage. He had "*a deep feeling for the soul of wheels and motors*,"[6] says Paul Bridgeman, reviewing Zachary's book. His great love was analog machines, where abstract processes are made concrete – and you can observe, hear, and feel them as the machine works its way through the problem.

This desire for physicality, the conviction that we understand things as much with our hands and physical senses as with our minds, continues to be a powerful inspiration, although the "possibility space" of analog computing, in which he envisaged the memex taking shape, has been bypassed.

When the USA entered World War II Bush was already in his 50s, and working as Director of the Carnegie Institution after a long and immensely successful career at MIT. He had earlier built an important analog computer: the "Differential Analyzer," which became a vital military asset – used for generating the ballistic tables on which artillery relied.

From the Carnegie, he became head of OSRD where his role became overwhelmingly a bureaucratic one as the wartime scientific effort grew. By the end, he seems to have been an almost tragic figure – a great public figure, but one whose own lifelong passions had been irrevocably sidelined by the very events he'd supervised. On the other hand his vision was sharpened. He'd probably been more exposed than any man in the world to the curse of "info-glut": the enormous problem of finding the information one needs – or even knowing that it is there. For example:

Mendel's concept of the laws of genetics was lost to the world for a generation because his publication did not reach the hands of the few who were capable of grasping it and extending it; and this sort of catastrophe is undoubtedly being repeated all about us, as truly significant attainments become lost in the mass of the inconsequential. ("As We May Think")

His proposed solution, the "memex," was to be *"an enlarged intimate supplement to [the user's] memory."* It would store text and pictures on microfilm. The user would have several screens so as to view several documents side by side. Photocell technology would allow the user to link sections of any document with any other – and add his or her own notes.

It was, as Zachary points out, a personal device – long before anybody had thought of computers as tools of "personal empowerment" – and he spelled out detailed "scenarios for use."

The owner of the memex, let us say, is interested in the origin and properties of the bow and arrow. Specifically he is studying why the short Turkish bow was apparently superior to the English long bow in the skirmishes of the Crusades. He has dozens of possibly pertinent books and articles in his memex. First he runs through an encyclopedia, finds an interesting but sketchy article, leaves it projected. Next, in a history, he finds another pertinent item, and ties the two together. Thus he goes, building a trail of many items. Occasionally he inserts a comment of his own, either linking it into the main trail or joining it by a side trail to a particular item. When it becomes evident that the elastic properties of available materials had a great deal to do with the bow, he branches off on a side trail which takes him through textbooks on elasticity and tables of physical constants. He inserts a page of longhand analysis of his own. Thus he builds a trail of his interest through the maze of materials available to him. And his trails do not fade. Several years later, his talk with a friend turns to the queer ways in which a people resist innovations, even of vital interest. He has an example, in the fact that the outranged Europeans still failed to adopt the Turkish bow. In fact he has a trail on it. A touch brings up the code book. Tapping a few keys projects the head of the trail. ("As We May Think")

Bush envisaged that these "trails" would become *documents in their own right,* and he anticipates *"a new profession of trail blazers, those who find delight in the task of establishing useful trails through the enormous mass of the common record."*

Bush's vision continues to delight and inspire. Its technologies seem old-fashioned and Heath-Robinsonesque – but perhaps that's what gives the idea its vitality. They help us to imagine how the business of "navigating through knowledge" could take on a physical quality. Certain features of his vision have been realized in far superior ways, but his central idea stands unconquered and seems to loom ever larger. For all the power of modern computers, it is still not possible for someone to "fly" as effortlessly through an "information space" as Bush's imaginary memex-user. Tim Berners-Lee's invention, the World Wide Web, gives us a very good taste of what he had in mind – but the nearest most of us get is perhaps when we use computer games like "Tomb Raider" and "Wipeout."

Modern computers mostly compound the "info-glut" problem by "atomizing" information into billions of documents – most of which are copies or modified versions of existing ones (the "multiple copies" problem). As I write this, some of the world's biggest, fastest computers are losing the battle just to index the fraction of the world's knowledge that is available on the Web.

Bush knew that *the routes by which we find knowledge are at least as important as the knowledge itself.*

Bush never attempted to build a memex – probably not because he didn't know how, but for the very simple reason that he knew he was getting old, and knew too well how intensely hard it is to turn a good idea into reality: he had traveled that route enough times for one lifetime.

Douglas Engelbart and "Augment"

After World War II, many people felt, like Bush, that the human mind needed urgent help. Doug Engelbart's work seems a good demonstration of the way a pressing common need produces similar-looking insights, almost spontaneously, in different places, with little apparent connection.[7]

He can be mistaken for Vannevar Bush's heir, picking up the big idea where its creator left off. But that is not exactly the case. Engelbart saw the same "possibility landscape" Bush did, but from a different angle. Unlike Bush, Engelbart was young, healthy, and optimistic enough when the vision hit him to attempt the backbreaking slog of making it a physical reality.

Engelbart does not sound like a natural-born mover-and-shaker: a quietly spoken, hands-on engineer ("a saintly man," Ted Nelson calls him). Big organizations at first backed him with state-of-the-art equipment and generous funding – then abandoned him completely when, in the 1970s, fashion shifted away from the idea of helping human beings, to the idea of replacing them with Artificial Intelligence. Happily he has survived the rout of "hard AI" and "Engelbart's Unfinished Revolution"[8] is right back on the agenda. Now in his 70s (he was born in 1925) he runs, with his daughter Christina, a flourishing consultancy called Bootstrap Institute,

Douglas Engelbart – photo by courtesy of his Bootstrap Institute (www.bootstrap.org)

which has just launched a chapter in Japan. They have a valuable website at www.bootstrap.org.

Like Bush's, Engelbart's work comes from deep concern for the human condition – but it grew from very different life-experiences and apparently, for some reason, an acute feeling of personal responsibility.

Engelbart grew up in a poor, rural part of Oregon during the Great Depression of the 1930s; his father died when he was ten, and he knew real if not lethal hardship. He pulled himself up by his own bootstraps, and eventually turned "bootstrapping" into a well-worked-out philosophy. He started an engineering degree at Corvallis Oregon, was drafted into the US Navy, sailed for the Philippines just as Japan surrendered, and witnessed appalling suffering there.

He worked as a radar technician. The experience of work with the mysterious cathode-ray tube (CRT) would eventually help him to the idea of the "shared information-space." Later (1951) he realized that *"any signals that came out of a machine could drive any kind of hardware – they could drive whatever you wanted on a display. ... I thought, 'Boy! That's just great!'"* (*Workstation History*)

He found Bush's memex article in the Red Cross library; it impressed him, but didn't seem to have any immediate personal relevance at that point.[9] He went back to college, finished his degree, got a job operating the wind tunnel at what later became NASA's Ames Research Center, at Mountain View, Northern California. Then, in 1951, when he was about to get married, the sense of responsibility and mission struck him, in a series of "flashes":

FLASH-1: The difficulty of mankind's problems was increasing at a greater rate than our ability to cope. (We are in trouble.)

FLASH-2: Boosting mankind's ability to deal with complex, urgent problems would be an attractive candidate as an arena in which a young person might try to "make the most difference."

Yes, but there's that question of what does the young electrical engineer do about it? Retread for role as educator, research psychologist, legislator, ... ? Is there any handle there that an electrical engineer could ... 2C6

FLASH-3: Ahah – graphic vision surges forth of me sitting at a large CRT console, working in ways that are rapidly evolving in front of my eyes (beginning from memories of the radar-screen consoles I used to service). 2C6

Well, the imagery of FLASH-3 evolved within a few days to include mixed text and graphic portrayals on the CRT, and on to extensions of the symbology and methodology that we humans could employ to do our heavy thinking; and also, images of other people at consoles attached to the same computer complex, simultaneously working in a collaboration mode that would be much closer and more effective than we had ever been able to accomplish. 2D

Within weeks I had committed my career to "augmenting the human intellect."[10]

He decided that electronics was the route to take – even though there were hardly any computers anywhere at that time and they appeared a very marginal technology. He enrolled at Berkeley for a PhD in Electronic Engineering – one of the few places where this was possible, and even here there were no actual computers. He went thence to a job at Stanford University's commercial spin-off, Stanford Research Institute (SRI), and for three solid years worked on his vision, studied and costed ways of accomplishing it. Finally in 1963 (12 years after the original "flashes") he presented his findings in a paper called "*A Conceptual Framework for the Augmentation of Man's Intellect*" – which is downloadable from the Bootstrap site.

Engelbart knew that his idea would never fly unless he could find a market that needed and could afford to pay for it. Its first users would be big business and government organizations.

He set up a lab at SRI that, by 1968, had produced a digital upgrade to the memex idea that not only went beyond Bush's vision, but worked, which thousands of people subsequently used to do real work, and which directly begat the modern, graphical style of personal computing – although its most revolutionary features were lost in transmission, and the whole idea very nearly came to grief. The system was at first called NLS (oN Line System), then "Augment."

Augment workstation of c. 1964–6. The small box on the right is the mouse. To the left, a special keyset for quickly inputting commands. Its cost was roughly $80,000. Picture by courtesy of Bootstrap Institute

The key idea was what he called a "workstation." It had a CRT display (an outrageously expensive novelty in computing in those days: one that he used in 1962 cost $80,000, but he had worked out that would change). The CRT served as a "portal" onto an "information space" that you shared with other workstation users. You could keep your bit of it private if you wanted to, or make it available to other users so that they could see and comment on your work (in real time) and even make changes. We would now call this "cyberspace" – but Engelbart's was a rather fuller-blooded implementation in many ways.

The workspace contained all the documents you needed (reference materials and jobs in progress) and an ever-expanding range of tools for working on them – including things called "wordprocessors" and "outliners." You could create and work on documents, link them, discuss them with distant colleagues , and "publish" them when they were finished. If it sounds like the World Wide Web that's not surprising: it inspired it.

The CRT display used "screen windows" to display different documents and menus side by side; you manipulated them with a keyboard, a special keyset and, Engelbart's most famous invention, a "mouse."

Workstations were linked to each other by Tymnet (the proprietary computer network of the mainframe-sharing company Tymshare, which soon bought and supported the project) and via the ARPAnet (the Internet's precursor).

Engelbart demonstrated the system at a conference in San Francisco in December 1968, and had it filmed. It was hugely influential: many of the people who subsequently paved the way for "multimedia" were working in the San Francisco area at the time, and saw either the demo itself, or the film. It was a completely new vision of computer use. Appropriately the 30th anniversary was celebrated on the Web in December 1998 with a live "webcast" by Engelbart himself (see the "Unrev" site at http://unrev. stanford.edu).

Augment developed apace into the 1970s; costs fell, its features got better and better – and then funding stopped. Over on the east coast an enticing new vista had been opened up – Artificial Intelligence – and smart money migrated there *en masse*.

As it happened, the "hard AI" route led into a dead-end – but by the time that became clear, Augment had long been unplugged, its people and technologies dispersed, and personal computing had started off along an easy but narrow track that would prove very difficult to get out of. However, Engelbart's vision inspired people to make the effort, and they have regained an impressive amount of it.

Much of Augment's technology was taken up by Xerox (in its "Alto" system), and from there, various bits and pieces of the vision made their way into Apple's Lisa, then the MacIntosh, and finally Microsoft Windows.

Important bits are still missing.

- **Augment's "Portal" has become the PC's "shrine."** We have adopted Engelbart's peripherals, but not the central idea: the big, shared workspace. His Augment workstations were windows on a shared world; by contrast, today's PCs are like handsome private shrines, with small, relatively rough windows to cyberspace tacked on as an afterthought.

- **Instead of gaining interaction-channels, we've lost one.** Like today's PCs, Augment had a keyboard and a "mouse." But it also had a keyset, used with the mouse, so that you could manipulate stuff on the screen with both hands. Given the importance of tactile involvement for perception, it would have made sense to build on this, maybe adding "treadle" controls and then, perhaps, ways of sensing the user's position, posture, and gestures. Instead we have gone backwards: all we have is the keyboard and the mouse. But some people do things differently: arcade-games players, physically handicapped people, and the VR community.

- **"Device Independence" has *nearly* been left behind.** Engelbart's system could drive any kind of display. In the 1960s displays came in many varieties, some of which now seem exotic and even futuristic –

what does this mean?

[handwritten: , yeah. Who decided this as the standard]

the world had not standardized on raster-scanning displays as the "desktop standard." Today we again have a plethora of display devices: Personal Digital Assistants like the 3Com PalmPilot and its various competitors, and multi-functional cellular phones – and a shortage of ways of making them share and display the same data. But here the outlook is better: Tim Berners-Lee had exactly this goal in mind when he built the World Wide Web. His work has given us a second opportunity to achieve device-independence. But as the Web becomes a "big-money" game, commercial interests are pushing it away from device-independence.

Engelbart's story contains important lessons for creative workers, of which I want to single out three for special mention:

■ **Mere ease of use is a "false god."** Engelbart believes *it is essential that users make some commitment to the system, in terms of learning new ways of working*, i.e., if we simply accept that systems have to be "totally intuitive" and "easy to use" then much of the computer's power will be soaked up achieving that end, and we'll drastically reduce the benefits people get from it. The idea that became NLS, and then Augment, was called H-LAM/T, which stands for "*Human using Language, Artifacts and Methodology in which he is Trained*" (my emphasis).

[handwritten: where do the 2&6 computers exist in all of this? But m...]

■ **Having the idea is just the beginning**. It is intrinsically hard to get people to understand new ideas: they interpret them in terms of what they already know, and miss the point. So *communicating an idea is a job in itself*. Engelbart spent three years on his "framework document"; then he led the computer community by the hand every step of the way, by building systems that actually worked, and which they could use. The idea, ultimately, was *passed on from hand to hand* in an absolutely literal, physical sense.

■ **What you do comes out of who you are and what you know**. Engelbart's work seems to be as much the expression of his particular temperament and experience (during the Depression and in the Philippines) as the "necessary outcome" of particular technologies. Every one of us has different experience and temperament – and can make equally different contributions based on them.

Ted Nelson and the Road to Xanadu

Theodor Holm Nelson is sometimes called the personal computing revolution's Tom Paine (Paine was the English revolutionary who wrote "Common Sense" – one of the founding texts of the American Revolution of 1776). He is certainly fiercely articulate, a great sloganizer, with a daunting command of all manner of detail, and someone who would rather spend most of his life on the margins than do anything half-baked. He is absolutely on the side of the people who do the work.

In terms of "products," you could say he hasn't achieved much. His life-work, Project Xanadu, has been in progress since 1960, and there has never been a public released version. But in another way he's accomplished more than anyone: he has turned the ideas of Bush, Engelbart (and numerous otherwise unsung heroes) into something like a crusade – complete with an agenda, slogans, martyrs, heroes, and a sophisticated ideology that goes way beyond the computer *per se*. He is the nearest thing to a Cyberian William Morris.

Transcopyright picture of Ted Nelson from his home page at http://www.xanadu.net. Note the "Transcopyright" Emblem: Transcopyright allows anyone to use an image on a web-page – but without physically copying it (eliminating the "multiple copies" nightmare referred to above).

Nelson invented the words "hypertext" and "hypermedia". He defined things called "thinkertoys" that "help you envision complex alternatives." He described what we now call "cyberspace" (his term was "docuverse") and its geography, its characteristics, and its possibilities. He provides a treasure-chest of ideas, references to worthwhile people and things, and agendas for action in three now-legendary self-published books: *Computer Lib, Dream Machines* (1974) and the later *Literary Machines*, which describes Project Xanadu: "*the most audacious and specific plan for knowledge, freedom and a better world yet to come out of computerdom*".[11]

Xanadu (which he's now working on in Japan) aims to provide a solid, commercial implementation of Bush's "big idea": a global system, accessible by all kinds of computers, where any kind of document can be "transcluded" in any other – without making separate copies. It is a

The cover of the first, self-published edition of Nelson's manifesto *Computer Lib* **(1974)**

"write-once" medium. This makes it radically different from existing systems. What is more, it provides for automatic payment of royalties on a pro-rata basis, whenever your own words are "transcluded" among someone else's.

The real issue here is not just "better software." It is human freedom, and the way any system of any kind can be made, by hard careful work, to help freedom, or allowed by laziness to destroy it.

This is the theme one finds wherever one turns in his work. Here's a typical snippet from *Dream Machines* (page 152[12]). It's from a book about Jack Tramiel, the man who founded Commodore (the company that produced one of the first "personal computers," the Commodore PET, and the Amiga):

"People who knew he was in Auschwitz were frequently shocked by the way that Jack talked about being in the camps. Sometimes he would get that faraway look in his eye and shake his head in disbelief.

"'You know,' he once told me, 'it's hard to believe it really happened. But it can happen again. In America. Americans like to make rules, and that scares me. If you have too many rules you get locked in a system. It's the system that says this one dies and that one doesn't, not the people. [. . .] that's why we need more Commodores. We need more mavericks, just so the rules don't take over.'"[13]

This does not sound like computer science to most people! Are personal computers really such a big deal? Do they really have any part in mankind's great debates? Is the freedom they offer (or the slavery they threaten) really on a par with Auschwitz? Is this at all relevant to someone who simply (wants) to make a living as, perhaps, a website designer?

Ted Nelson believes it is. Little things lead to greater ones. If the computer really is the "universal machine" of Turing and von Neumann, then its effects will be universal – and whether we end up as the controllers or the totally controlled depends on the little steps and decisions taken now. Today's tyranny in the "Save" dialog-box helps smooth the path to tomorrow's political tyranny, perhaps.

Nelson came to computers in 1960 as a sociology postgraduate at Swarthmore College in Pennsylvania. Writing, however, was his first love. He discovered, in the computer, a means of escaping from the tyranny of "hierarchies": first the hierarchies implicit in text itself (the frustration of having to keep ideas and notes in particular places or categories, when they really "want" to be anywhere and everywhere: *everything is deeply intertwingled*," as he puts it). So he built a system for handling his own notes: a bizarre thing to do in 1960.

Then, it seems, he realized that this "intertwingularity" was totally at odds with the education system he'd spent so long in and been so uncomfortable with. It dawned on him that education is organized on a literally feudal and territorial basis, with arbitrary barriers dividing the sea of knowledge into little fiefdoms where "*the pupil must pay homage to the Duchess of History, the Count of Mathematics.*" As for "the curriculum," he notes that the very word means "little race track" in Latin. Again, it is a system of control. "*A curriculum promotes a false simplification of any subject, cutting the subject's many interconnections and leaving a skeleton of sequence which is only a caricature of its richness and intrinsic fascination.*" (*Literary Machines* 1/20).

From there (this was the 1960s, the era of the Vietnam war) it was a short step to realizing that all of society is managed this way. He recognized that the "feudalism" isn't always deliberate policy. It's simply the outcome of allowing things to take their own course; of "good men keeping silent," to use one of his favourite quotations, from Edmund Burke. And of course, the whole ethos of computing was overtly one of control. That is literally what "cybernetics" means. The question was "who is to control what?"

"*If the computer is a universal control system, let's give kids universes to control.*"

Nelson, DM 131

As Nelson's "quest for Xanadu" took him from Swarthmore, to the Philadelphia suburb King of Prussia, to Chicago, to Austin, to Sausalito, to Sapporo, to Tokyo, his theme expanded beyond software into human freedom, enabled by computers, and his writings made him a rallying-point for people who shared that concern.

"Ted succeeded with Computer Lib to rally a rabble of latent crackpots into an anarchistic army which breached the sanctum of Official Computerdom and brought computers to everyone." Lee Felsenstein (designer of the Osborn personal computer), in an endorsement for Dream Machines

This "anarchistic vision" is a big part of the spiritual birthright of anyone who chooses to work in multimedia. Nelson can take a lot of credit for it – but he's not at all woolly-minded about it, and not everyone qualifies for membership of his "elect." Not all people who think they're on the side of the angels are actually "good guys" in Nelson's terms.

Libertarian, reformist, or revolutionary – which are you? Nelson's "angelic host" seems to contain three distinct political factions. I'm not sure my names for them are the ones he would use, but whatever they're called, you meet them at every level in your work – not just in books:

- First (proceeding from Right to Left) are the "Libertarians," who believe the benefits of the computer will arrive automatically as long as we don't inhibit the "natural process." The MIT Media Lab's famous director, Nicholas Negroponte, is probably a libertarian; also perhaps John Perry Barlow (Electronic Frontier Foundation). Most followers of Margaret Thatcher and the economist Milton Friedman definitely are. (Opponents of this position sometimes call them "panglossians," after Dr. Pangloss, in Voltaire's "Candide" – 1759 – who believed that "all"s for the best in this best of all possible worlds".)

- Then there are "Reformists," who recognize that events don't automatically shape themselves the way we'd like, but they believe it's always possible to work with the situation as we find it, and coax it along more positive channels by timely, sensitive, and thoughtful intervention. Most of us fall into this category – possibly because we have livelihoods to earn and can't afford to rock the boat.

- Thirdly, there is Nelson's camp. These are the "true Revolutionaries," and they don't trust "the natural course of events" one inch. If you want good things to happen, they say, you must decide what you want, and make a stand. This, they admit, is much harder than "going with the flow" but they insist it is safer in the long run.

Where you take your stand is up to you: on particular issues as they come up (be "bolshie," "make waves"); or you can plant yourself outside the madness and start building the future you actually want – and that is what Nelson has done.

He doesn't recommend "going with the flow."

Pragmatism and the <u>desire to get along in the world lead people to put up with what</u> <u>should not be put up with.</u> But nothing really stops anyone from creating the good and the elegant except habit, inertia and desuetude – and the fact that doing right is much harder than not doing right.

(Literary Machines 87.1, 1/3)

Notes

1 Tim Berners-Lee invented the World Wide Web almost singlehandedly on a NeXT computer, while working at the European high-energy physics research center CERN, in Geneva. You can pick his story up at his World Wide Web Consortium's website: http://www.w3.org/.

2 Samuel Taylor Coleridge read about Xanadu in 1816 in Samuel Purchas's *Purchas his Pilgrim* (an early work of travel literature – 1625), and put it into his famous poem-fragment *Kubla Khan*. Coleridge said he dreamed the whole thing (while under the influence of opium – taken to combat rheumatic fever), started to write it out from memory when he awoke, then was interrupted and forgot the rest. Nelson's "Xanadu" probably wouldn't have helped in that particular case – but every technology has its limits.

3 Wells was the focus in the 1920s and 30s of an extensive network of scientists and thinkers that stood against totalitarianism and nationalism, and crusaded for access to information, internationalism, and scientific freedom. Wells in fact proposed something rather like Vannevar Bush's "Memex" in 1936: a "World Encyclopedia" which would:

… spread like a nervous network … knitting all the intellectual workers of the world through a common interest and a common medium of expression into a more and more conscious co-operating unity.

The article is in *World Brain*, Doubleday Doran NY. Originally presented at the Royal Institution in London on Friday 20 Nov 1936. I found the reference in *Hypertext in Context* – McKnight, Dillon & Richardson, Cambridge University Press, 1991, p.8.

4 MIT held a symposium in honor of Vannevar Bush in October 1995, attended by Engelbart, Nelson, Tim Berners-Lee, and many other key players in this story. The proceedings are on the Web at http://www-eecs.mit.edu/AY95-96/events/bush.

5 … and naturally you can find it on the World Wide Web. Go to http://www.cs .brown.edu/memex/ and follow the links. This site is at Brown University – a major center for "hypermedia" research, and I mention it again later.

6 Paul Bridgman's words – in a review, for *New Scientist*, of Pascal Zachary's biography of Bush. Bridgman is the curator of Communications at London's Science Museum – and a lifelong admirer of Vannevar Bush.

7 The classic example is Newton's and Leibniz's almost simultaneous invention of a mathematics to cope with several variables at once: the Calculus. The common need there was to account accurately for planetary motion – against a background of rapidly expanding maritime power and commerce, which had pressing need of better navigational science.

8 See the "Unfinished Revolution" website at Stanford – created to celebrate the 30th anniversary of Engelbart's famous Augment demo – http://unrev.stanford.edu.

9 Bush's biographer Pascal Zachary describes him as "infected with memex fever" but Christina Engelbart says that's definitely an overstatement. Later, as Zachary says, he would write to Bush that he was working "along a vector you had described," but Bush never replied.

10 "Workstation History and the Augmented Knowledge Workshop" – Douglas C. Engelbart 4 December 1985 The enigmatic numbers at the ends of the paragraphs are inherited from his "Augment" system – which gave each paragraph a unique identifier.

11 He self-published both books in 1974. In 1987 Microsoft Press published them in one volume *Computer Lib and Dream Machines*, ISBN 0-914845-49-7 and this should still be available. *Literary Machines* describes Project Xanadu. It exists in various editions. Mine is version 87.1 (1987) but references should tally with yours, thanks to its distinctive page-numbering system. The current edition is from Mindful Press (Nelson's own imprint) and can be ordered from Eastgate Systems (Mark Bernstein's hypertext software and publishing company) at http://www.eastgate.com/products/Cat_Books.html#Nelson. For more on Nelson himself see Mind-Meld's "Digital Be-In" site (http://www.be-in.com/9/home/).

12 *Dream Machines* and *Computer Lib* have no index and finding a specific piece of information can be infuriatingly difficult, so I'm giving you the page numbers.

13 Quoted by Michael S. Tomczyk in *The Home Computer Wars: an insider's account of Commodore and Jack Tramiel* (Compute! Publications 1984).

1.5

Early explorations: From "time-sharing" to the personal computer

❝Computing has always been personal❞

Ted Nelson (*Computer Lib*)

THE COMPUTER FIRST BECAME a "medium" in surreptitious ways in the early 1960s, when Digital Equipment Corporation (DEC) brought out the first of its PDP series of "mini-computers." These were fairly big machines but much smaller than the mainframes. They sat in the department or office where the programmers sat – and the programmers could think of them as "their machines." The PDPs had three features that revolutionized computer use: real-time processing, time-sharing, and CRT displays.

Real-time processing meant you could now interact with a computer: you could type in a command or a program and get the result back immediately. *For the first time people were able to have dialogs with the machine.*

This sense of dialog seems to have been something people latched onto very swiftly. It was a real kick: "*for the hardcore programmers of the era, that was a taste of the forbidden fruit.*"[1]

Time-sharing allowed several people to use the computer (apparently) simultaneously; each user would have a terminal, and processor clock-cycles were apportioned to each in turn. Nobody would notice the delay as long as there weren't too many users connected, and none of them attempted anything too elaborate. Time-sharing also allowed users to interact with each other, via the computer.

CRT displays gave the computer a "face," in which you could read its "mind"; the fact that you, as programmer, could define the "mind behind the face" made this very interesting indeed!

And of course setups like these gave many more people access to computers, so they could have ideas about them, and play with those ideas. People are diverse, so the ideas were diverse too. In fact, there is so much diversity at this point that I'll have to be highly selective and very brief, and just give you a few snapshots of the kinds of things that were done. To explore this fascinating period further see Howard Rheingold's *"Tools for Thought"* and *"Virtual Reality"* (1989 and 1991), Ted Nelson's books (see previous chapter), and other works that I'll mention as we go along.

Playworlds

The first graphical computer game, "Spacewar," was written by "hackers" at MIT in 1962, not long after they got their first PDP-1 hooked up to a CRT monitor. "Spacewar" used primitive graphics, but you could play it over the Internet's precursor (the ARPAnet) against hackers at other sites.

Later on, in 1976, along came "Adventure" (by William Crowther and Don Woods): a text-only game inspired, apparently, by Tolkien's epic fantasy *"Lord of the Rings"* via Gary Gygax's original role-playing game "Dungeons and Dragons" (1974). It created a quite astonishing sense of place – just with unadorned text: no graphics at all. "Adventure" was a sort of "rite of passage" for a whole generation of computer workers through the late 1970s and 80s. There's a very nice description of the game in Tracy Kidder's *"Soul of a New Machine"*:

Later on, though, I wandered into a maze that really scared me.

YOU ARE IN A MAZE OF TWISTY LITTLE PASSAGES, ALL ALIKE.

You have to find your way around this maze if you hope to begin to master Adventure, because this one contains the vending machine with the batteries for your indispensable flashlight and, moreover, harbors the lair of the kleptomaniacal pirate who is forever sneaking up behind you and snatching away your treasures." (Kidder (1981), p. 84)

"Adventure" spawned a massive family of text adventures, of which "Zork" (three versions) was the most famous game, and Infocom the most famous publishing name. Not only are these still around, they're thriving. The population explosion in text-only PDAs like the 3Com PalmPilot seems to have given them a new lease of life – and you can find hundreds of them on the Internet.[2] Considered as life-forms, both "Spacewar" and "Adventure" have proved massively successful.

Why games? Brenda Laurel begins her seminal 1991 book *Computers as Theatre* by describing the almost spontaneous "blossoming" of "Spacewar," in 1962. She asked the guys involved. It seemed "the natural thing to do," they said. Laurel wrote:

Why was Spacewar *the 'natural' thing to do? Why not a pie chart or an automated kaleidoscope or a desktop? Its designers identified* action *as the key ingredient and conceived* Spacewar *as a game that could provide a good balance between thinking and doing for its players. They regarded the computer as a machine naturally suited for representing things that you could see, control, and play with. Its interesting potential lay not in its ability to perform calculations but in its capacity to* represent action in which humans could participate.

This desire for "participatory action" wasn't something computer scientists had foreseen. Here, it was "participatory action" of the eternal, playful, barroom variety, and it had never known the luxury of a "medium" of its own before. Now it invaded the computer as swiftly and irresistibly as seeds invade a patch of freshly turned earth.

Other human types found the new machines fertile ground for quite other primal urges.

Taming the world of text

People started using computers in what, to some people's minds, was a hugely trivial activity: writing. (Engelbart had of course been ploughing this particular furrow already for some years, but his work was not yet widely known.)

As we've seen, in 1960, at Swarthmore College in Pennsylvania, Ted Nelson seized on the new computer as a way of managing his own exasperatingly "intertwingled" ideas.

Writing is very much an exploration process – and a notoriously difficult one. Even when writing a letter, you try "different ways in" before you can "get going." A writer lives in a sea of ideas, each connected to innumerable others in all directions. To make matters worse they're invisible, so we have to remember them, and our short-term memory is notoriously limited (seven items – give or take two). A machine with vast short-term memory, a display, and the ability to manage all those links seems like the ultimate, heaven-sent "prosthesis" for the writer. (And what is more, the number of professional writers may be tiny but the amount of writing that's done in the world is vast: reports, memos, minutes, letters. So there was vast market potential for computer-based writing tools.)

The computer could actualize the spatial quality of writing – turn it into something like a landscape that you could define and explore. In the same way, it promised to revolutionize reading.

At Brown University on Long Island, Andries Van Dam[3] (perhaps better known as one of the pioneers of computer graphics) launched a writing program. The computer administrators were outraged to find people writing poetry on the new machines. He went on to build a hypertext system. Brown remains a major center of effort for hypertext to this day - and hypertext has become one of the most important vectors of cybermedia development. For more on this see David Bolter's book *Writing Space*, and George Landow's *Hypertext*.

Hypertext does not seem to have revolutionized either writing or reading in the way these people hoped it would – at least, not yet. The Web has brought some of its benefits – on a massive scale – but the greater dream still thrives, in a delightful "side-valley" of Cyberia that is visited mainly by discerning and literary folk. Eastgate Systems, of Watertown, Massachusetts, is one of the best points of entry. They publish a number of fascinating hypertext fictions, and a hypertext editor called "StorySpace" – and you can find them at www.eastgate.com.

Perhaps hypertext's promise was just too big for the mainstream – or the route to "wordprocessing" was too easy and obvious. The wordprocessor tackles the problems of *typing*, rather than writing: a much more modest promise, but one that had a ready-made market and was much easier to explain – and therefore to sell.

Artificial/Virtual Reality – physical involvement with the computer

At Madison Wisconsin in 1968 or thereabouts, Myron Krueger, an arts postgraduate, had the idea of using the computer to build what he called "responsive environments." His first experiments, on the university campus, involved "buildings that wave back": the computer controlled the room-lighting in one of the faculty buildings; sensors on the sidewalk below allowed passers-by to instigate and control a lightshow from the building. In 1969 he produced two computer-mediated "playspaces," "Glowflow" and "Metaplay," followed by a succession of other increasingly ambitious projects though the 1970s and 80s.

Why "artificial reality"? It seems Krueger's point of departure into cyberspace was "happenings" – the anarchic genre of performance art that flourished briefly in the 1960s – and the sensual, sybaritic ethos of that period, which suited him down to the ground. He believes passionately in the wisdom of the physical senses, and the need to bring physicality back into intellectual life. He proposed a "kung-fu typewriter" to "put the labor back into work"; the "hugaphone" to bring physical contact to phone conversations; also "teledildonics" – the first mention of cybersex.

Krueger's work led indirectly to what we now know as "Virtual Reality." For more on this see Krueger's own classic book *Artificial Reality*, and Howard Rheingold's *Virtual Reality*.

Visualizing abstract ideas

Drawing must have seemed an even more trivial use of expensive machines than writing to most computer managers. But graphics became a "hot" area of endeavor almost as soon as graphical displays became available – and the place to be was the University of Utah. Dave Evans set the department up and his students included Ed Catmull (who would later form Pixar with animater John Lassiter – creator of Disney's 1995 feature "*Toy Story*"), Frank Crow, Lance Williams, Alan Kay, and Jim Blinn.

Blinn became one of the great pioneers of the portrayal of abstract scientific and mathematical ideas through computer graphics, at CalTech (the home, till his death, of that great visualizer of ideas Richard Feynman). Later on at CalTech, an English physicist, Steven Wolfram, created "Mathematica": the remarkable personal computer application that turns mathematics into a visual artform.

Dave Evans's colleague was Ivan Sutherland. Between 1960 and 1964, as a postgraduate student at MIT, Sutherland had built a landmark system called "Sketchpad" that had features still almost unheard of in commercial PC graphics software. Using a light pen you could draw and connect, then rearrange, group, and make multiple "instances" of all kinds of shapes, and text.

Ted Nelson says: "*The mind-blowing thing about Sketchpad was the way you could move and manipulate the picture on the screen, with all its parts. One overall picture could be constructed out of a hundred copies of a basic picture; then a change in the basic picture would immediately be shown in all hundred places. … or you could draw meshing gears on screen and with the light pen make one gear turn by turning the other*" (*Dream Machines*, p. 96).

Dave and Ivan went on to form the Evans and Sutherland flight-simulator company, but only one PC drawing package that I know of has implemented Sketchpad's "instancing" feature: Aldus Corporation's "Intellidraw"

– which disappeared after Aldus merged with Adobe in 1995. Like so many really great computer applications, it committed the heinous sin of being "uncategorizable" – and paid the price.

Benoit Mandelbrot's work, which led to his discovery of "fractals," began at about this time. His starting point was the problem of visualizing the "chaotic" fluctuations of stock prices on Wall Street.

Exploring "musical space"

Electronic music is such a rich area that I must apologize for my brevity here – and urge you to look at Simon Crab's *120 Years of Electronic Music*[4] (yes, it really does go back that far!). But I think one observation needs to be made: the computer-music systems of the "time-sharing" and earlier periods were more revolutionary in many ways than the ones we have now.

Where, in the 1950s and 60s, people were experimenting with completely new ways of modeling music (graphically, spatially) today's SoundEdit, CuBase, etc. have brought us right back to musical staves, with key and time signatures, and keyboards – all of which were "necessary kludges" in the first place – imposed on us by the limitations of seventeenth-century technology. It is like what happened with computer-based writing – where adventurous early hypertext systems were driven into the background of computer folk memory by the modern wordprocessor: which is essentially an electronic typewriter.

There are plenty of famous examples of adventurous music (notably at MIT, mentioned by Stewart Brand in his classic *The Media Lab*) so I'll mention just one, relatively little-known example.

The British cyberneticist Gordon Pask developed a system called "Musicolour" in the mid-1950s[5] that allowed you to make music, generated a lightshow in response, amplified variations in your performance, and you could choose to go along with these "suggestions" or not. Finally, Musicolour could get "bored" if you carried on playing the same old thing. Its lights would cease to respond – encouraging the player to introduce a new variation. Thus, the performer was having a real dialog with the machine.

As Paul Pangaro[6] describes it:

The result (at least when the performer cooperated) was a continuous flow of improvisation; a "conversation" where the performer and apparatus flowed into the other with action and response.

Pangaro points out that this was far more interactive than most of the point-and-click interfaces that pass for "interactive" nowadays, which *"are more like command-line instructions dressed up in drag."*

Pask developed his ideas in a difficult but worth-trying book called *Conversation Theory.* Ted Nelson has called him a "fabulous man."

Building "minds" and exploring them

The challenge of imitating human intelligence was there right at the start of computer history: both John von Neumann and Alan Turing were thinking about it even before they had any computers with which to try it. The first computers were often referred to as "electronic brains." The story of Artificial Intelligence is a long and fascinating one that began with the hypothesis that the brain is a computer, and concludes (for the time being) with the general opinion that (a) it is not and (b) brains work so closely with their bodies that it's foolish to try to replicate them as independent entities anyway.

In the late 1980s there was quite a lot of excitement about "expert systems." Here, you took an expert in, say, bulldozer-maintenance, interviewed him, and loaded his expertise into an "expert system shell" (a glorified database). If the interviewer did the job well enough the resulting program would allow a novice to carry out certain servicing operations. At one time, it seemed as if we might be able to build complete, synthetic lawyers and brain surgeons this way, but no: again, "constraint" was the key to success: keep the area of expertise small.

This kind of thing is used, for example, by programs that monitor your Web activity to guess your interests – and feed suitable advertising into your browser.

Attempts to model "mind" in the computer have proved, not that the computer is necessarily stupid, but that it is different, and that the mind is *very* different from the way we thought it was.

By some accounts the quest for "artificial intelligence" was a failure. In fact, it advanced the cause of "mind science" to a quite enormous degree – and produced some very useful inventions.

These include "Eliza" and her daughters, the "chatterbots." Eliza (by Joseph Weizenbaum of MIT in 1963) is a surprisingly convincing psychoanalyst. I won't waste space by describing her here since you can try her yourself: versions exist for all computers,[7] even PDAs, and she is thoroughly "analyzed" by many writers. What she proved, which is so useful for us, is that *a system can be made to seem surprisingly intelligent and natural, using surprisingly few rules, provided the user's expectations are well-enough constrained* (i.e., Eliza remains convincing if you stick to the patient–analyst dialog). On the Web (and in some MUDs) you can find yourself in conversation with "chatterbots" that work on the same principle.[8]

Notes

1 Howard Rheingold, *Virtual Reality*, p. 78.

2 For example, Stephen van Egmond maintains a huge "Interactive Fiction" archive at http://www.truespectra.com/~svanegmo. I found a version of "Adventure" (for the Mac) at Jacob Munkhammar's site (in Trondheim, Norway): http://www.stud.ntnu.no/~jacob/JMUNK/s/ Software.html. See also Leisa ReFalo's site at http://www.geocities.com/Heartland/9590/ interactive.htm and http://www.tapped.com/fiction.htm (downloadable classics for PalmPilot users – all the Zorks, plus Hitchhiker's Guide to the Galaxy, Planetfall, and many new "han-drolled" games).

3 Andries Van Dam's website is at http://www.cs.brown.edu/people/avd/home.html.

4 Not yet published – but large parts are accessible on the Web at http://www.obsolete.com. Crab is one of Britain's leading Web designers.

5 See Pask's own account in "A comment, a case history and a plan." In *Cybernetics, Art and Ideas*, ed. J. Reichart, Studio Vista, London, 1971.

6 "Pask as Dramaturg" by Paul Pangaro (1993) *Systems Research*, **10**(3), edited by Ranulph Glanville. Also available on the Web. (Sorry – I've lost the URL but your search engine should find it. Mine did.)

7 Tom Bender of San Antonio Texas has a very nice $5 shareware version of Eliza for the Mac that you can download from http://members.aol.com/tombb. Tom also offers "Azile – Eliza's evil twin," and a truly excellent little Texan wordprocessor called TexEdit, which I use a lot.

8 Janet Murray describes "Elizas," "Chatterbots," and many other interesting things in her 1997 book *Hamlet on the Holodeck* – and has links to sites where you can try them at: http://web.mit.edu/jhmurray/www/HOH.html.

1.6

The beginnings of a mass medium: Interactive Video

Philips and Sony launched the laserdisk in 1978 – a 12-inch silver disk that could store an entire movie (but in analog form – not digitally). The quality was vastly superior to home videotape. They hoped to create a big, new domestic market in videodisks but the technology was expensive, video companies were reluctant to invest, and the Babel of video standards (PAL, NTSC, and SECAM) impeded international marketing.

To the rescue came the new, cheap(ish) personal computers: the Commodore PET, Radio Shack TRS-80, Superbrain, Apple II, and others. Inventive people harnessed these to videoplayers and "Interactive Video" (IV) was born.[1]

IV *could* be described as a retrograde development: it used the computer merely as "digital glue," to integrate materials produced in traditional, analog media. It was not really a "personal medium": you could not easily produce an IV title on your own on the kitchen table. It was also rather hamstrung by the need to have two monitors: an analog one for the video, and a digital one for the computer-based media (text, menu-choices, computer animations) – or an expensive "overlay card" to integrate the two. Nonetheless IV was a superb proving-ground for the new medium and it became a vibrant little industry in the 1980s. It delivered excellent full-screen video, and some of the work done for that medium provides lasting inspiration.

It spawned many ideas and conventions now taken for granted in "multimedia," opened up some exciting "possibility spaces" that were largely forgotten when CD-ROM became the mainstream "delivery medium," and provided some very valuable (not to mention expensive) lessons in "how not to do it."

How not to do it: IV as TV

Sadly, most of the IV projects that the public got to see were out-and-out disasters: notably, the early "kiosk" systems deployed by banks. Here, it seems, the developers mistook IV for TV – and subjected users to lengthy explanations and wordy introductions from "talking heads" (with no option of shutting them up) and long, beautifully photographed, scene-setting title sequences with soothing music and warm brown voice-overs that drove you wild with irritation: all you actually wanted was to get at the information.

For anyone with eyes this was an important lesson: when something is supposedly "interactive," making it non-interactive is a disaster – unless you play it very carefully.

These "corporate kiosk disasters" demonstrate a recurrent problem of new technology and big business. It is very difficult for a big business to use new technologies well because new technologies tend to come from little companies that have no "track record" – but "track record" is what insecure big-business managers look for. Hence, the work tends to go to big, reassuring-looking businesses that in fact know very little about the new technology. I believe many of those corporate kiosk disasters were made by TV and video companies.

IV scored its "greatest hits" outside the public eye, in education and training establishments.

"Ninety percent of the bangs for 10 percent of the bucks": IV on the cheap

Some of its most effective uses were almost embarassingly low-tech. In 1989 I met a lecturer from a very minor British university who had made a really crude IV system that used videotapes of his math lectures. Using a very simple computer interface, students could play and replay his black-board demonstrations of the mathematical proofs they found difficult, whenever they needed to. This simple facility had transformed his department. From being almost bottom of the league, its students were now achieving Oxford- or Cambridge-level results. The system had cost almost nothing, apart from the lecturer's evenings and weekends.

Simulations

The laserdisk's superb graphic quality and controllability made it superb for "simulations." Maybe DVI (Digital Video Interactive) will give us a chance to resurrect some of the techniques that were discovered by the IV pioneers:

Fast action from still images, on a Royal Navy frigate

I saw a remarkable disk, produced for the Royal Navy's recruitment office, sometime in 1989. It was a "virtual tour" of the frigate HMS *Manchester*; it allowed you to travel all over the ship as fast as you liked from the engine room to the bridge to the mess-deck to the main gun-turret – and even fire the guns, peppering the sky with real flak-bursts.

It was done, not with video or computer-generated graphics, but with thousands of still photographs. This made it possible to cover far more the ship than other techniques would have done, with better visual quality, and from different angles (so you could go down companionways, and go back up them again). Plus, you could travel at whatever speed you liked. You used a joystick. Push it hard forward and you travelled fast, ease back and you'd slow up. The pin-sharp clarity created a tremendous sense of "being there," which made it very exciting – much more like the mad, running-around sequences in the film *Titanic*, than the relatively low-resolution computer-generated scenes you explore in "Tomb Raider" or "Final Fantasy."

I thought it would be impossible to discover who had made this disk – but by chance I recently discovered that the author was a man called William Donelson, who had earlier worked on MIT Media Lab's famous "Aspen Disk" (described by Stewart Brand in his book *The Media Lab*). Donelson settled in Britain, where he went on to make IV "virtual tours" of North Sea oil-rigs – to familiarize oil-workers with these dangerous environments before setting foot there.

Donelson, Beckett, and their company's logo

Donelson continues to do "good stuff" with another very interesting individual: the Honorable William Beckett (who told me the story, on a bus in Edinburgh in summer 1998). Beckett is himself a hero of "armchair exploration" with a fascinating story of his own. They continue to work with the photographer who took the stills for "HMS *Manchester*": Ricky Gauld. You can follow their story further at http://www.armchair-travel.com/.

Witnessing realistic crimes

There was a plethora of IV training applications: one that I saw in 1989 was for London's Metropolitan Police and made you the witness to various incidents, including a street robbery. It had all the confusing abruptness of a real-life crime (very different from the gracefully choreographed TV and film crimes we normally see. These prepare you for the violence: real life doesn't). You were then asked to recall, for example, what clothes the assailant was wearing, his facial features, what he actually said, and various details of the scene. This was surprisingly difficult. It was an excellent use of the new medium: it exposed you to the problem of observation and recall under stress in a way that was not possible before. I don't know what became of the disk or even who made it, and very few members of the public ever saw it.

Life-and-death decisions on the battlefield – and the power of sound

At Dartmouth College Medical School, Joe Henderson employed similar dramatic techniques during the early 1990s in two big IV productions, "Regimental Surgeon" and "Traumabase," to familiarize doctors with battlefield conditions – specifically civilian doctors, drafted in times of emergency. Henderson says: "*Well-executed simulations should provide a sense of having had a life experience*" ["Designing Realities", in "*Virtual Reality theory practice and promise*," Meckler, 1991]. As the "rookie," you received a briefing, then found yourself in a helicopter, airlifted into a M.A.S.H.-style field dressing station with people yelling at you, asking your advice, required to make life-and-death decisions. It was not without a certain gallows humor.

Like most IV systems it required two screens: one for the PC display – presenting you with your choices and instructions – the other a video screen. At the "decision points," the action had to stop while you chose an option. These broke the flow of the interaction – you tended to relax into a more contemplative mood, which defeated the purpose: to get people to make good decisions under pressure. Henderson combated this cleverly – by keeping the sound running while the action was paused – and this reversed the "relax" effect. Users now felt under *increased* pressure.

Henderson proved this by monitoring his users' pulse rates as they used the system; sure enough, their pulses began to race as they faced the "choices" screen: a classic demonstration of the power of sound to create an illusion of reality. Henderson and his colleagues continue to develop fascinating virtual reality applications – see http://iml.dartmouth.edu/ (the Dartmouth Interactive Media Lab website).

Getting a grip on basic physics: Apple's "Visual Almanac"

IV was an excellent explanatory medium. Apple's "Visual Almanac" (produced by Bob Mohl)[2] featured beautifully filmed demonstrations of "playground physics" where the laws of Newtonian motion were demonstrated by (among other things) kids on merry-go-rounds. I remember a bird's-eye shot of the merry-go-round where you could change its velocity by changing the children's position on it: as they huddled together at its center, it span faster; as they leaned out from the edge it span slowly. Then you could superimpose a computer animation revealing that the children had traveled exactly the same distance in both cases.

A team at Newcastle University, England, produced an even more comprehensive physics disk-set called "Interactive Physics" – and brought it to market. However, the reliance on expensive videodisk hardware put it beyond most schools' budgets.

Apple anticipated the same marketing problem with "Visual Almanac" – so they released it (1989) on CD-ROM. However, the CD had nothing like as much impact. The slower system response and poorer video quality seemed to kill the experience stone dead.

Had DVD been available (or laserdisk players cheaper) this kind of interactivity might now be the norm, rather than the rare exception.

Users as authors: the BBC's "Domesday Disk"

One of the most interesting uses of the computer is to integrate many people's first-hand testimony, producing works that are true "community efforts." This was first done in Britain, by the BBC's Interactive Video Unit, in its famous "Domesday Disk" – launched in 1986, the 900th anniversary of William the Conqueror's Domesday Survey of England.

The BBC had earlier sponsored Acorn Computer of Cambridge, England (still flourishing: their ARM chip powered Apple's Newton, and is used in DTV set-top boxes, printers, and many other devices) to develop a microcomputer for followers of a national computer literacy project. The computer, affectionately known as the "Beeb," had a "massive 64k of RAM."

The Domesday System (whose chief architects were Peter Armstrong and Andy Finney) consisted of a Beeb, driving a videodisk player laden with video, maps, statistics, pictures – many of which were collected and created by schoolchildren and local-history groups. This was a landmark in new media – showing how the medium could become a communal thing. Sadly, only a few thousand Domesday Systems were sold. Now that we have the Web and DVD, which are ideal for that type of project, it would be well worth revisiting – if you can find a copy, and a "Beeb" to drive it!

Some laserdisk projects achieved much greater fame than the ones I've mentioned. The most famous ones were the "Elastic Charles": an interactive video magazine produced at MIT (which is on the Charles River), and the "Aspen Disk" (a "virtual tour" of Aspen, Colorado, produced by the Media Lab's Andrew Lipmann in 1978. Willian Donelson – mentioned above – was part of that team). You can read about these projects in Stewart Brand's *The Media Lab*.

Notes

1 They also harnessed them to racks of slide projectors, tape recorders, dry-ice machines and even firework displays, to create audio-visual spectaculars for product launches and corporate bonanzas. The art form never acquired a generally agreed name, but "multivision" and "multimedia" were used.

2 The last time I saw Bob Mohl he was working in Paris, on a barge, under the name of "Floating Point Media."

1.7

From the Mac to the Seedy ROM: Cyberia opened to the masses, then to the corporate bulldozers

❝As great visions move out, all the best parts get stripped away❞

Alan Kay (Quoted in Nelson's *Computer Lib*, p. 23)

"TIME-SHARING" HAD REVEALED a quite unexpected, enticing landscape in the 1960s, crying out for exploration. Hackers and academics, a few adventurous artists, and a handful of computer-games visionaries got on with it enthusiastically – but the attraction still wasn't at all clear to anybody who hadn't had direct, personal experience of using the computer. In the 1980s the Personal Computer opened this secret landscape up to thousands more – but it was still hidden from the eyes of non-initiates by the cold, command-line interfaces of the Unix, CP/M, and DOS-style operating systems of those early days.

Then, in 1984, came the Mac: the first would-be mass-market[1] graphical computer.

For a whole new group of users, the Mac was a revelation. You could actually draw and paint directly onto the screen! (albeit in black and white). What's more, it had a revolutionary new storage medium: a neat little plastic-covered $3\frac{1}{2}$" floppy disk (from Sony) on which you could store a whole 400k (a complete Dickens novel's worth) and then send it through the mail. In other words – a distribution medium!

People were exploiting these new "media" possibilities almost immediately.

Guide: almost "hypertext for the rest of us"

A team of computer-science researchers from Edinburgh University (one of them was called Ian Ritchie) built a delightful little hypertext application called "Guide" that allowed you to build, then "explore" hyperlinked texts and graphics – and create standalone hypertexts for distribution on floppy disk. They formed a company to sell it (Office Workstations Limited – OWL International in the USA).

Guide was supremely quick and easy to use and it seemed to many that "hypertext" had finally arrived. For a while, it was the computer software of choice on several US university humanities courses; it was adopted by a number of corporates for documentation – and looked set to become the workhorse of a new "hypermedium."

WorldBuilder: "roll-your-own games"

A programmer and Adventure/Zork enthusiast called Bill Appleton seized on the Mac, as a way of turning text adventure games into graphical ones. He built a tool with which to do it in 1985, and called it "WorldBuilder." It allowed you to build navigable graphic worlds that people could explore by clicking on screen "hotspots," by making menu choices, using keyboard shortcuts, or by typing in commands ("go north," "use shield," etc.), or answers to questions. It was pretty quick and easy to use; there was a scripting language of sorts but nothing too complicated; you could even do little animations.

As with Guide, you could make standalone versions, and distribute them on floppy disk or via Electronic Bulletin Boards. WorldBuilder had the *potential* to be a more general-purpose information-delivery and presentation tool – but I don't know whether anyone ever used it that way.

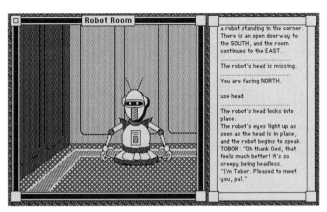

A typical screen from Bill Appleton's WorldBuilder (this is from the demo/tutorial included with the 32-bit version developed by Ray Dunakin – shown here with his permission. The robot comes to life after you've collected its various components, stashed away in various parts of the "world").

You can still get WorldBuilder at various places on the Web,[2] and I believe one of Appleton's own shareware games is still around: "Radical Castle."

At one point in this game (which I've never rediscovered or I'd include a screenshot here) you meet the programmer, chained to his Macintosh in a tiny, rat-infested room at the very top of one of the castle's towers. He "hurls a barbed insult at your head," and you have to duck quickly. Many people seem to have "cut their creative teeth" on WorldBuilder. One of them was the legendary Robert Carr (see Chapter 2.1).

Marc Canter and VideoWorks

Another pioneering little app was called VideoWorks – from a small Chicago company called MacroMind, a "software rock and roll band" led by a musician and computer-games developer called Marc Canter, who'd been working for the videogame company that created Pac-Man: Bally/Midway.

VideoWorks came out in May 1985 – only a year after the Mac's launch. It was a tiny (93k) sprite-animation package with no interactive features: a most unlikely candidate for leadership in the coming revolution. Yet it evolved into the industry-standard workhorse of interactive design: MacroMedia Director – in which the original VideoWorks scoresheet is still recognizable. If anyone wants an example of the way the computer seems to repeat the unlikely course of biological evolution, VideoWorks/Director is it.

Then, in 1987, HyperCard appeared. It was "freeware" – bundled with every new Mac. Guide became a "niche" product (it transferred to Microsoft Windows and is used nowadays mainly for corporate intranet work). WorldBuilder went into limbo – and Appleton decided to beat HyperCard at its own game, with a superb, full-color HyperCard worka-like called SuperCard. Videoworks survived by sheer adaptability and would later steal the whole show. I'll pick up its story in a moment.

HyperCard – the first developer community

HyperCard is really what got "multimedia" started on its present course. A huge "developer community" formed around it that was unlike anything that had happened before. It involved people from all walks of life. Many of them had never used computers before – let alone built anything with them. Diversity flourished. Many of the results were lovable only in the eyes of their creators – but that's democracy for you, and without it, some of the most original and inspiring works we have today would never have happened. As Brian Thomas (Chapter 2.1) has said, "HyperCard then was what the Web is today."

The first few months of HyperCard's existence produced at least three creations, two of them by complete computer novices, that would inspire future developments: Brian Thomas's "If Monks Had Macs …" (Chapter 2.1), Amanda Goodenough's "Inigo Gets Out," and the Miller brothers' first efforts, which would shortly become "The Manhole" – and eventually led to the blockbusters "Myst" and "Riven."

Inigo. **The final screen of Amanda Goodenough's "Inigo Gets Out" (1987) – an extremely simple but delightful piece of pure "point-and-clickery." Very influential in its day, it is still well worth experiencing. It showed that the computer *could* be a medium for quick, spontaneous creations. Voyager commissioned further "Amandastories," which are still available from Learn Technologies Inc. (www.learntech.com/voyager)**

The Manhole – **Cyan Inc© (1988). Same basic principle as Amanda's work (you click hidden "hotspots" to move through the story) but a quite colossal amount of work was poured into every single screen (this is one of hundreds) with every pixel carefully drawn by hand. The sheer depth of detail was unprecedented. After "The Manhole" Rand and Robyn Miller created "Cosmic Osmo" (1991), "Spelunx – the Caves of Mr Seudo," then "Myst" (1993) and "Riven" (1997) – which became PlayStation hits. Each title "upped the ante" by an order of magnitude, in terms of sheer quantity of work. As late as "Riven," the Millers were still using HyperCard as their main production tool. They have a fascinating and informative website at www.cyan.com. Image from The Manhole © 1987 Cyan, Inc. All rights reserved The Manhole ® Cyan, Inc.**

Meanwhile some wonderfully diverse things were happening on other PC platforms – especially the Commodore Amiga.

A digression

Commodore's amazing Amiga, and the magical Mandala

The original Mac was "graphical" – but only just. For its first three years it only offered 1-bit, black-and-white graphics. It made the transition to color with some difficulty – and against some resistance from "Mac purists." That resistance was not as silly as it may sound – but the fact is, the Mac was never conceived as a color machine.

Commodore's Amiga (launched in 1985 – a year after the Mac) was a color machine from the ground up, and in many ways a better multimedia option than the Mac (still is, in many opinions). It used a very clever set of dedicated chips for sound and graphics, designed by a guy called Jay Miner (an Atari veteran). Not only was it a color machine, it gave millions of colors – not just 256. Even better, it used multiple "bitplanes" (graphic layers) – just like arcade machines. What's more, it supported real-time rendering of 3-D objects, and video (which could have its own bitplane, behind or in front of the computer graphics). In other words, a radically different kind of machine from the Mac – and probably a much better choice as a "multimedia medium."

During the late 1980s and early 90s the Amiga was the games machine of choice. Games like Rollerball brought richly rendered, real-time 3-D graphics to home users for the first time. With NewTek's "VideoToaster" (add-on graphics-processing board), Amiga users could produce the kind of stunning graphics and animations hitherto only possible with vastly expensive Symbolics and Sun workstations. In the hands of people like Todd Rundgren, it was the workhorse of a whole new industry: the music video. Amigas are still used in games houses because there are still areas where they eclipse everything else – even though the architecture is 15 years old.

Mandala – from the Vivid Group's website (www.vividgroup.com)

A digression cont.

And there was a quite remarkable authoring tool called "Mandala." The famous Virtual Reality pioneer Jaron Lanier[3] developed a visual programming language of the same name somewhat earlier – but I'm afraid I don't know whether there was any connection. The Amiga's Mandala was created by a Toronto-based Virtual Reality artist called Vincent John Vincent, and programmer Francis MacDougall, in 1986. Vincent's Vivid Group still markets the Mandala system.

Taking full advantage of the Amiga's "multiple bitplane" architecture, Mandala allowed you to create a graphic world on the computer, and then, via a video camera, incorporate yourself into it! You stood in front of the monitor (or large projection screen) and could see yourself on the screen, interacting with whatever strange or magical things the author had placed there: you could bounce a virtual ball, dance with virtual dancers, hit virtual drums and play virtual guitars, talk to elves, move mountains!

Oakland, California-based artist Beverly Reiser[4] built a series of "interactive poems" with the Amiga and Mandala. Using them was utterly unlike anything else I've ever interacted with on a computer – better in many ways than true, helmet-and-glove "immersive" VR. It was like looking into a magic mirror, and seeing yourself surrounded by a hitherto invisible reality.

The effect was magical in an almost literal way – an enticing avenue of development that the multimedia bandwagon seemed to roll on past without noticing. With the Amiga's demise (at least, as a mass medium) that avenue closed – but Mandala has continued as a "niche" product, and may now be due for a revival, as a system for building "immersive" arcade games and other kinds of "arcade experience." You can follow the story further at Vivid's impressive website: www.vividgroup.com.

**Beverly Reiser with interactive
poem at CyberArts, Pasadena, 1991**

Defining the new medium. "What *is* HyperCard?"

Developments that make the biggest impact often fail to fit into ready-made categories.

Before its launch, defining HyperCard *"was a full-time job for dozens of Apple product managers, marketing mavens, designers and copywriters."*[5] The puzzle continued to be a popular entertainment for years afterwards. Yet HyperCard's original purpose was quite simple.

HyperCard was created by Bill Atkinson, the man responsible for much of the original Macintosh interface, and it was a pure labor of love. Atkinson simply wanted to share the exquisite pleasure he got from computer programming with the rest of the world: *"programming for the rest of us,"* in his words. It seems John Sculley (Apple's CEO) allowed him to do it partly out of compassion and partly to promote a corporate agenda that was perhaps a little different from what Atkinson originally had in mind: "multimedia." The story goes as follows.

HyperCard's creator, Bill Atkinson. This picture comes from Bill's personal website www.natureimages.com with his permission.

Atkinson's "MacPaint" had been bundled, free, with every Mac sold – but Apple's marketing department decided in 1985 to "unbundle" it, to Atkinson's great distress. He was already at an emotional low after the extreme pressure and excitement of getting the Mac "out the door" and went into a profound depression. Then, during a night spent on a park bench, *"staring at the stars the entire night,"* he had something like a revelation.

I felt very small, but I also felt very proud. That was the motivation that got me going. This is coming from inside me. It's not coming for fame and glory. It's not coming from money. I've got enough of that. At that point, I turned around and asked what I could do and how I could contribute. I knew I was a really good programmer, and it suddenly dawned on me that I could teach a little of what I know.[6]

Atkinson went into a solitary creative frenzy, took the early results to Scully, won him over, and two years later HyperCard was launched.

So HyperCard was designed to introduce the world to the joys of programing: not specifically for making "hypertext" or "hypermedia," or "hyper" anything. In fact Atkinson didn't originally call it "hyper" card, but "WildCard." Yes, it could be *used* to do hyper-stuff (it was a computer programming environment after all, so it could do anything) but that wasn't its original purpose. As captains of industry so often do, Scully spied a brilliant solution, and applied it to a slightly different problem – with very interesting results!

A digression

HyperCard and Director: two different kinds of beauty

The differences between HyperCard and Director are fascinating. In many ways, HyperCard is far and away the better tool. Its language, "HyperTalk," is elegant, easy to learn, astonishingly quick and powerful, even witty. And HyperCard set a brand-new standard for computer-media work: a craftsmanlike "hands-on" activity rather than a plan-and-execute one. You develop your title in precisely the same "environment" the user will eventually see. You move between building things and testing them effortlessly, in moments, without even noticing it. This is quite different from the "code, compile, test" cycle you use in other programming and authoring environments: it's fast, fluid, and you see the effects of your actions instantly. It is the difference between creating a pot on a wheel, and running an economy.

HyperCard was widely imitated (by IBM with "Linkway"; by Microsoft co-founder Paul Allen's Asymetrix Corporation with "ToolBook"; by Bill Appleton with the excellent "SuperCard," to mention just three). It also had an enormous user-base (it was given away free) and inspired a mass of excellent books, which made it even easier to learn. Apple realized the importance of books very early on and invited Danny Goodman to write his HyperCard Handbook *– which appeared very soon after HyperCard itself and gave a whole army of non-programmers their "on-ramp" into the new medium. This was followed by dozens of other books (I especially recommend Harold Thimbleby and George Coulouris's* HyperProgramming*).*

HyperCard was limited by its lack of color (but there are plenty of solutions to this), its Mac-only status (but here too there are workarounds), and a confused development history: Apple changed its mind about HyperCard many times. Yet none of these problems stopped it from producing new media's first "blockbuster," the Miller brothers' "Myst" (which of course exists on PCs and Sony PlayStations as well as the Mac).

VideoWorks/Director, on the other hand, looks like a series of "kludges." Its language "Lingo" is nowhere near as elegant as "HyperTalk," and the mind-set you acquire by using Director for linear animation can make it difficult to switch to the Lingo way of doing things. Worse, Lingo had a very basic manual, and for years there were no third-party books that made things any clearer (although as time went on, MacroMedia's Director Forum on CompuServe provided a lifeline). Years passed before books like Peter Small's wonderful Lingo Sorcery *arrived.*

Yet Director swept the field. I think the reason is that it was guided by the single, practical goal of creating a new medium – rather than "easy-to-use" tools as such. Throughout its early history, MacroMind (Canter's original company) was as much a development company as a software publisher. They built games (like "MazeWars"), corporate training systems, presentations, and simulations – exactly the same kinds of things their users wanted to do. They were guided by the problems and opportunities they themselves found "at the workface."

The immediate need was animation: they provided it. When the Mac II came out people needed color: they provided that too, immediately. Then people needed color animations that ran quickly: they built a crude "VideoWorks Accelerator" that solved the problem by dumping a huge "streaming" file onto your hard disk; it was crude but it did the job till computers got fast enough to do it themselves. Then people needed interactivity: first, they made it possible to "jump" from one bit of the movie to another, then Erik Neumann quickly built a language of sorts (in TinyBasic) for VideoWorks – it was horrible but it got you there. Finally, Erik and John Thompson added Lingo in 1987. Infuriatingly crude and inconsistent at first, Lingo undeniably did most of the things you needed to do – and constantly improved.

They even had the "cross-platform" problem in hand, and tackled it early on with "player" technology (free software that lets you run the finished work from other packages – like HyperCard – as a "standalone," or even on other PC platforms, without needing the originating package). This started with VideoWorks – and ultimately gave us ShockWave, which lets you run Director-originated work straight off the Web.

The solutions they came up with always seemed to have this character: they weren't necessarily elegant, or even bug free, but they undeniably "did the job" – and did it well before anybody else got around to it. It seems very like the way modern rock-climbing technology developed: in the field, from bits and pieces, to deal with particular challenges. Later on, these "quick fixes" become refined and improved out of recognition but the mountain itself continues to be the source and proving-ground of new ideas.

Canter himself certainly seems to be of this philosophy. He left MacroMedia in 1990, when the company abandoned "content development." He pursues the idea of machine-independent, "scalable" multimedia that will run on everything from CD-ROM to interactive TV.

For more on Marc Canter and the Director story see www.venuemedia.com/mediaband/.

Now, back to 1987.

The "M-word" enters the language, and a bandwagon is launched

The "hyper" in "HyperCard" was clearly a bid to use WildCard as a means of annexing the whole Bush/Engelbart/Nelson dream for Apple. They felt it would be Apple's "next big thing."[7] Apple's new strapline enlisted the concept behind Vannevar Bush's memex: *The human mind works by association. So why don't computers?*"

Apple chose to promote this concept under the name "multimedia" – a word almost everyone who actually "does multimedia" hates! Not that the new "multimedia workers" had any alternative umbrella-term to offer. When you're doing the work, labels are irrelevant. Yet marketing required a succinct definition that would somehow encapsulate the raw excitement everyone felt.

Apple's marketing department particularly needed a word under which to sell some other new, exciting technologies: the Apple CD-ROM drive (launched the same year as HyperCard), then QuickTime (launched in 1989).

The CD-ROM and QuickTime   The CD-ROM drive was another Big Thing that nobody knew quite what to do with. Apple was out in front thanks to its association with Sony (makers of the Mac's $3\frac{1}{2}$" floppy drive, and other components).

Sony had spent millions co-developing CD-ROM with Philips, and was passionate about its potential as a data-delivery medium. It gave you access to oceans of text and images – but nobody had any clear idea how to market it.

As for QuickTime, this was hugely sexy – for the first time you could show video on a computer screen without any additional hardware: an intoxicating novelty. The quality of the video was not that great, but it would run at its correct speed whatever kind of machine you ran it on – on slow machines it would simply drop frames. And the video window could be resized – even while the movie was playing. Yet, again, what would anyone use this for? "Everyone will find their own uses" is not what marketers like to hear: they need a clear, defined "target audience."

Insofar as "multimedia" had a definition, it was that it allowed you to integrate text, graphics, and sound within a computer application. This had the unfortunate effect of implying that all you had to do, to create successful multimedia, was to integrate lots of those things.

The name, and attendant hype, came to cover, and to some extent to bury, the whole diverse family of "computer-as-medium" creations that had been in development and in people's minds since the 1960s – and launch a bandwagon that would, in the 1990s, devastate large areas of "Cyberia."

The M-word spread like a religion. Newspapers took up the story; other computer companies piled in. "Content owners" – book-publishers and film/TV companies – anticipated cleaning up on the grand scale.

The Multimedia Bandwagon rolls: enter Seedy ROM, Seedy Eye and Shovelware

Apple's espousal of the "multimedia" cause in 1987 was a turning point. From about that time, the interesting goings-on in the undergrowth would continue (and continue to be the main source of useful ideas) but against a growing background din as the corporates arrived.

The rhetoric was less about "exploring new territory" than "carving out new markets."

A few of those grand excavations bore fruit – but only after enormous effort and sometimes painful reappraisal (Grolier's Multimedia Encyclopedia, Microsoft's Encarta, and Dorling Kindersley's "Eyewitness" series being three notable examples). Mostly, all they did was scar the landscape. I won't describe the debacle in detail but briefly:

Philips's Seedy Eye disaster

From 1986 through to 1994 (or thereabouts) the Dutch electronics giant Philips (which, with Sony, invented the CD) poured undisclosed millions into its CD-I (CD Interactive) system, promoting it and subsidizing title development. It was not a bad system in theory (it was based on the elegant OS9 real-time operating system, which was far more compact, robust, and appropriate than existing PC operating systems). For several years CD-I was "the next big thing" – but it is now as if CD-I never happened.

Why did it fail? CD-I failed to produce anything that people flocked to buy; it had no equivalent of "Sonic the Hedgehog." And why was that? A convincing theory is that developing titles for CD-I was neither cheap nor easy. Its authoring tools were nothing like as interactive as HyperCard or Director. If you wanted to produce a CD-I title you had to do one of two things: pay thousands of dollars for a development setup (and then struggle with the fearsome authoring interface); or hand your "content" (the graphics, text, sound, etc.) over to Philips's own CD-I development people and let them "glue it together."

The paradigm was precisely the one conjured up by the "M-word" – the medium was all about integrating "assets" culled from other media. There was no notion that the interaction itself was anything more than a production-line exercise.

CD-I was surely a disaster – but not a public one, so not many lessons could be learned by the expanding multimedia community. Philips continued to be a massively profitable company (from sales of lightbulbs, kitchen appliances, and consumer electronics) and could write the episode off to experience.

The public, however, began to get the idea that "multimedia" was probably not worth bothering with.

The Seedy ROM fiasco

Major publishers like HarperCollins and Viking Penguin, and "book packaging" companies like Britain's Andromeda, entered the CD-ROM arena *en masse* in the late 1980s and early 90s. As "content-owners" on the grand scale, they expected multimedia to be their oyster. With very few exceptions they failed both commercially and esthetically.

The terms "shovelware" and "multimediocrity" entered the language. In spring 1992 Max Whitby (one of the original Domesday team, and one of multimedia's best-known pioneers) expressed disgust and disenchantment in an article entitled "Interactivity Sucks."[8] Could it be, he asked, that this brave new technology doesn't actually work?

Having spent a good part of my life in film cutting rooms … I should hardly need reminding how much effort and attention goes into constructing a coherent narrative path through a story. Yet in interactive media there is an unstated assumption that such careful preparation can safely be discarded.

In October 1996, Penguin and HarperCollins, and the British Marshall Cavendish, cut their losses and pulled out of multimedia altogether. One of the world's biggest multimedia companies, First Information Group, went out of business. The following year, Dataquest research suggested that a mere 4 percent of CD-ROM titles had been profitable.[9] The vast majority of CD-ROMs seemed to end up being given away with magazines as cover-disks, or bundled with CD-ROM drives.

Far from making a killing, it looked as if the big boys of "Seedy ROM" had killed the industry itself by glutting the market with inferior products. The French retailer FNAC even introduced its own quality assurance stickers, and an advertising slogan: "*Not all CD-ROMs are rubbish – just three quarters of them.*" The slump in sales that summer damaged high-quality producers as well as rubbish-merchants. The Voyager Company (Chapter

2.2) was brought to its knees. Dorling Kindersley sacked 50 multimedia staff. Even the Living Books company ("Just Grandma and Me," "Arthur's Teacher Trouble," and other delightful titles) shed staff and had to cancel projects. Bill Gates's Corbis Corporation, which had only just launched into CD-ROM publishing with a series of superb titles (see Chapter 2.3), now canceled development effort and pulled out of the business.

For companies like Viking Penguin it was certainly a setback – but not a catastrophe. Like Philips they could write it off to experience – maybe concluding, like everyone else, that multimedia was indeed a bit of a waste of time: an interesting diversion that they'd investigated, and found lacking. But it was an unqualified disaster for hundreds of their ex-employees. It also changed the "possibility landscape": CD-ROM was now a "no-go area" as far as many backers were concerned. The dozens of canceled projects undoubtedly included a few that would have led into new and important areas – which now may never be visited again.

Maybe it is as Voyager co-founder Bob Stein said. The transition to this new medium:

is going to take much longer than people talk about, and it may be a hundred years, two hundred years, before it settles out. This profound shift is more significant than the invention of the printing press, and the deep implications of it won't be known for some time. [10]

If multimedia is comparable to print then yes, we'd be crazy to expect it to mature in a mere ten years. But companies (still less individual authors and designers) can't wait even two years for things to become clear. So how to proceed?

While it's true that print took a couple of centuries to produce the novel, the novel is in many ways print's least potent achievement. Almost immediately after print was invented, it was helping people to transform their social landscape with a torrent of religious diatribes and political tracts; no-holds-barred satirical handbills and pamphlets; recipe and home-management books; almanacs, textbooks, manuals on seamanship, gunnery, and gardening; herbals; books on etiquette, horsemanship, courtship, penmanship, and swordsmanship; travelogs; books of martyrs and the lives of pirates; songbooks and penny ballads. None of those things came from the "great companies" of the day. Almost all of them came from little printshops – very often set up by the writers and illustrators themselves.

We probably shouldn't expect HarperCollins to have better luck with the computer than the Benedictine order did with the printing press. If this "new media revolution" really is at all similar to the print revolution, then we *should* expect to find the most interesting developments in the "social undergrowth." Once one lowers one's gaze from the lofty corporate pinnacles, that's exactly what we find.

Notes

1 To the mainstream business community, it was not at all obvious that the Mac would have a mass market – and for a couple of years it struggled. But, thanks to Paul Brainerd's desktop-publishing program, PageMaker (1985), the Mac gradually began to come good – and slowly but surely everyone was drawn into the graphical computing game.

2 Ray Dunakin's 32-bit shareware version can be downloaded from Ray's Maze Page: http://www.semitech.com/marc/ray.html. Another source (in Germany) is: ftp://ftp.gmd.de/if-archive/programming/worldbuilder/. It runs on all Macs, and has comprehensive tutorial files.

3 ... for more on whom, see Howard Rheingold's *Virtual Reality*.

4 Beverly runs Ylem – a San Francisco-based network for "artists using science and technology." The Ylem website (www.ylem.org) houses a Web-O-Tronic Gallery "carved out of cyberspace" – and an excellent archive. Much recommended. There's also a bi-monthly journal.

5 Jay Markham – the epilogue to *Interactive Multimedia*, ed. Sueann Ambron and Kristina Hooper, Apple Computer and Microsoft Press, 1988, ISBN 1-55615-124-1.

6 Quoted by John Sculley in "*Oddyssey – Pepsi to Apple,*" Fontana, 1988, ISBN 0-00-637284-8.

7 Apple had experienced two "Big Things" in the past: first Spreadsheets (with VisiCalc), then Desktop Publishing (PageMaker). Both were very Big Things indeed: each caused a quantum leap in the computer's acceptance in mainstream culture – but they were very different from "Multimedia": the concept in each case was simple, clear-cut, easy to communicate and gave a very explicit promise. PageMaker made it possible for anyone with a Mac to do their own print design. Spreadsheets gave you a magic piece of paper that did the sums for you. Multimedia's promise was terribly generalized: it simply let you do "anything."

8 In the British magazine *MultiMedia*, Spring, 1992.

9 From article by Emma Keelan, in *The Guardian Online*, 20 November 1997.

10 Bob Stein talking to The Edge: http://digerati.edge.org/digerati/stein/.

Section **2**

Eminent Cyberians

Introduction:
"Tomorrow's establishment is today's lunatic fringe"

"CYBERIA" HAS EMERGED from the dim realms of theoretical possibility to become a real, if rather earthquake-prone "possibility space" in which people could begin to make a living.

The big developments in computing itself were mostly unforeseen: the result of individuals getting their hands on the technology and carefully following their own intuitions. They weren't the result of big, military-style "assaults," all planned out in advance by great visionaries sitting in offices and passing orders down to "the troops"; that approach seems to have such a miserable record that we can say with some confidence "it doesn't work here." As the British commentator John Barker observes (of the astronomical amounts wasted on EC-funded "infrastructure" projects): *"All those billions… did not invent the World Wide Web. For that we thank a physics researcher at Cern [Tim Berners-Lee] who was trying to find a better way of emailing his colleagues."* [Inside Multimedia[1] #162, March 1998]

Now I want to show you that exactly the same thing is happening with the people who are using the technology as an expressive medium.

Few of the examples in this section were big-budget, high-profile projects. Some of them have become big money-earners, but mostly the success is measured by the influence they've had (a more scientific measure, I think). I also measure success by the personal pleasure that went into them – and the pleasure I personally get from them.

There is no end of wonderful examples that I haven't had time to investigate, and there are quite a few that I've researched, but had to omit for lack of time and space.

Who isn't here   I fail to tell you about Mark Schlichting – the man behind the justly famous "Living Books" (children's CD-ROMs published by Random House and Brøderbund). These include "Arthur's Teacher Trouble," Dr Seuss's "Green Eggs and Ham," and Schlichting's own favorite "Sheila Rae the Brave." It took me a while to discover Schlichting because his name doesn't appear on the products themselves. His story is (typically for this medium) unusual. John Peterson and Mark Gavini wrote a piece about him in May, 1993 (http://www.best.com/~siggraph/MeetingNotes/LivingBooks.html) that you might like to look at. Living Books suffered from the collapse on the CD-ROM market; Schlichting (in early 1998) was working on an online product for children called JuniorNet.

I haven't covered Rand and Robyn Miller (Cyan Inc., Spokane Washington) who gave this medium its first "smash hit" – Myst. But Cyan is fairly well known, and they have an excellent website http://www.cyan.com where you can pick the story up for yourself.

I wanted to tell you about Eastgate Systems – publishers of "serious hypertext" fictions, and of the "StorySpace" hypertext processor – but in the end their work was so rich I was quite unable to do it justice in the time. Instead, please visit their website at http://www.eastgate.com – where you can also subscribe to an excellent online newsletter.

No mention, either, of the work done here in England by musician Peter Gabriel's Real World company. This year (1998) they released a quite magical CD-ROM called "Ceremony of Innocence" – based on the book by Nick Bantock and developed by an intense young fellow called Alex Mayhew. You can see some of the work at Real World's beautiful website: http://realworld.on.net.

I also wanted to introduce you to the huge amount of fascinating "digital storytelling" that goes on on the World Wide Web – especially the work of Dana Atchley, Nina Mullen, and Joe Lambert at http://www.dstory.com. See also the "Hyperizons" online hypertext fiction site at http://www.duke.edu/~mshumate/hyperfic.html. But time ran out.

It would take the rest of this book, and then some, to list all the "Eminent Cyberians" who aren't here – but Janet Murray's *Hamlet on the Holodeck* (1997) should help. Her references are extensive and the book makes a great jumping-off point for independent exploration. To make it even easier she keeps an associated website at http://web.mit.edu/jhmurray/www/HOH.html.

Whatever … at least you should appreciate now that this territory is infinitely richer in interesting people and things than the average computer software catalog would have you believe.

> Before we move on, I want to put this "diversity" business into the context of an era that many people think has strong parallels with the present digital age: the early age of print.

Is this medium as "revolutionary" as they say it is?

This is Brian Thomas, in the sunroom of his home in Portland, Oregon. Brian is the man who started an unclassifiable multimedia phenomenon in 1988 with a set of HyperCard stacks called "If Monks Had Macs …" (described in the next chapter).

The picture is from his website: www.riverText.com, and the book he's reading is *The World Turned Upside Down* by the Oxford historian Christopher Hill (1972). Hill's book is about the English Revolution of 1641 – when the English Parliament challenged the king and his bishops, suffered defeats, then raised a "New Model" army (it had a new organizational model: men were free to debate their own beliefs and organize themselves) that swept everything before it and laid the groundwork for a more "people-friendly" kind of state. It was an epoch of enormous spiritual, political, and intellectual ferment, and I keep running into new-media people who are fascinated by it. Like our period, it owed a lot to a revolutionary technology: in this case the printing press. Press censorship had lapsed, and print was suddenly available to anyone with something to say, and the modest funds necessary to publish it. The Old Order was lifted right off its hinges in no time flat.

It looked, says Hill, as if the lunatics were taking over the madhouse – but those lunatics sound far saner to us nowadays than the seventeenth century's "responsible" minority do.

Is something similar happening today with personal computing and the Net? "Revolution" is one of computerdom's favorite words. "Empowerment" is its watchword. Does it actually amount to anything? If it does, where might it lead?

Empowering technologies empower unexpected people in unexpected ways, with totally unexpected results. In 1641 the vast majority of new voices weren't concerned with novels (which took another 100 years to get going as a mainstream art form). They wanted something much more exciting: freedom to live their own lives and think for themselves.

The (mainly wealthy, university-educated) Puritan Brotherhood lit the fuse of revolt – then found themselves thrust aside by surprisingly radical, articulate voices from the grass roots and the ranks of the New Model: Ranters, Seekers, Baptists, Quakers, Levellers, Diggers ... Many of their ideas now seem astonishingly modern: full democracy, non-violent protest, equality of the sexes, freedom to divorce, common ownership of land, universal education, and a national health service. Other ideas seem bizarre – especially a passionate, full-blooded spirituality that, nowadays, is supposedly only found among "exotic" and "primitive" peoples.

Just as the Ranters and Levellers sidelined the Puritan Brotherhood in 1640s England, so, maybe, cyberpunks and cyber-eccentrics will have sidelined Microsoft and the MIT Media Lab in a year or two.

The GNU/Linux operating system (Richard Stallman and Linus Torvalds) and the Apache software that probably runs your web-server are definitely "New Model" products that (in early 1999) are giving the "Old Order" a real run for its money.

History suggests very strongly that this revolution won't stop at a "revolution in home entertainment" or a "revolution in direct marketing." Having tasted its power, there are bound to be people, outside the mainstream at present, who'll use the medium to promote much more radical agendas. Or to do things that, to today's mainstream, seem trival, silly, or obscene. And they'll very likely have a much bigger effect in the long run than the Bill Gateses, Larry Ellisons and Nicholas Negropontes of today's elite.

Note

1   Inside Multimedia newsletter: http://www.phillips.com/PhillipsUK/im.htm.

2.1

Voices from nowhere

Making a statement: Jaime Levy; the Guerrilla Girls

"I've got a lot to say! I've got a lot to say! I've got a lot to say!

I don't remember it now. I don't remember it now. I don't remember it now."

The Ramones: I've got a Lot to Say *(1995)*

IF YOU'VE GOT SOMETHING TO SAY you can make a surprising impact if you say it on the computer monitor – without clever-clever programming or flash graphics. This can work even if you simply *feel* you've got something to say. (That sounds daft – but it's a basic principle of stand-up comedy and storytelling.)

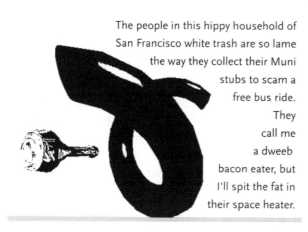

The people in this hippy household of San Francisco white trash are so lame the way they collect their Muni stubs to scam a free bus ride. They call me a dweeb bacon eater, but I'll spit the fat in their space heater.

Screen from Jaime Levy's "S.F. Hippy Scum" (1986 – done in VideoWorks) with her permission – online at http://www.word.com/ newstaff/blondeday/third/ jlevy/

I don't know much about Jaime Levy (but I believe "Jaime" is pronounced "Jamie" – not the Spanish way), and I can't really figure out what she's on about – yet I am impressed. I saw her at a conference in Pasadena in 1991 – selling "Cyber Raps" on floppy disk at $5 a shot. One of them was a long, angry diatribe that scrolled in a Director window to a loud techno soundtrack. Very simple – but it proved more memorable than some of the million-dollar Virtual Reality apps I saw there. One of her "Raps" is on the Web (see "SF Hippy Scum," above).

Hate seems to be a major interest – Nicholas Negroponte and *Wired* magazine are a couple of her targets – and she seems to thrive on it: she has an impressive career resumé and her studio's clients ("Electronic Hollywood" http://www.ehollywood.net/) include Tommy Hilfiger, and Jerry Springer.

For a while she was working on the *Word* ezine (www.word.com/). Then she worked for The Arnell Group, on a graphical chatspace system called The Palace Inc.: http://www.palacespace.com/. There (for a fee) you can join various online communities, in the guise of the "avatar" of your choice. These seem a bit wholesome. However, with Steve Speer, she's built her own palace "MalicePalace" (http://www.malicepalace.com/), whose intro says:

Come on into the Malice Palace and experience virtual pain. Don't you hate being ignored? You won't be here; come be abused by robots with artificial unintelligence. Set in San Francisco post-new-technology-industry-backlash (circa 2001), the environment depicts the net results of a rat race where survivalists eat hippies and computer nerds for dinner. Industrial jungle music by DJ Spooky will keep you dancing from room to room. The longer you stay, though, the worse the torture gets.

The animated "Pisser.gif" (on the left) welcomes you with a foretaste of what's in store.

The Guerrilla Girls

There is no doubt at all what the Guerrilla Girls want to say. They say it extremely well – and don't get distracted from the message by the seductions of computer technology. They write, design, and produce hard-hitting posters, put them on the Web, and that's it (http://www.guerrillagirls.com/). You can buy books of their posters on the site and "go to bed with a Guerrilla Girl."

They are all anonymous. They are:

feminist counterparts to the mostly male tradition of anonymous do-gooders like Robin Hood, Batman, and the Lone Ranger. We wear gorilla masks to focus on the issues rather than our personalities.

This is one of them, from the website:

… and this is one of their posters (from 1992):

I can't tell you much more because, as I said, they're anonymous.

Taking the piss seriously: downloadable salvation and sex from Robert Carr

Robert Carr's blasphemous Mac programs may seem either outrageous fun or utterly tasteless. I think both reactions are too superficial – as is this one (from Mark Frauenfelder, in *Wired* in 1997):

The programmers who write and distribute these programs give their products away. They aren't looking for money; they're attention-fishermen. The programs they write are like grotesque lures, which they cast into the Net in order to haul in as big a response as possible. (Mark Frauenfelder, Wired magazine ("Software Toys to Disgust and Amuse"))

"Attention fisherman" sounds dismissive. I'm not sure that it obviously applies to Carr (he is a recluse; answers email slowly and briefly; he lives somewhere in the environs of Boise, Idaho and does not fraternize with the software community) but who *isn't* an "attention fisherman"? Who *doesn't* want "as big a response as possible"? Carr merely declines to package his desire to communicate in the usual bright-eyed commercial veneer.

Taking the piss in 1520 – the cover of "Das Wolffgesang" ("The Wolves' Song"), one of the cheaply printed Lutheran pamphlets that fueled the Protestant Reformation in Germany and helped unleash the Thirty Years War. Reproduced by permission of The Folger Shakespeare Library, Washington DC

Carr is worth taking seriously – and so is his type of work.

The great Russian writer Mikhail Bakhtin argued in the 1930s[1] that "taking the piss" (or as he put it, "the parodic/travestying voice") is probably one of mankind's most important activities. It's certainly much more widespread than a survey of "art and literature" would suggest – and it has probably had a far clearer influence on society than "great literature" has: as you can see from the crude but effective example above. It's also endemic – as any parent knows, whose children came home with "Princess Diana" jokes after her bizarrely tragic death in 1997. But "old media" provide no forum for that kind of thing – they're too vulnerable to prosecution. On the Web, however, it's another matter.

Robert Carr's work

Carr says he works by day in a Kinko's copy shop in Boise and in his scarce free time maintains his "Lamprey Systems" website and develops such titles as "MacJesus – Your Personal Savior on a Floppy Disk," "Rupture the Rapture" ("Save the universe by destroying Christians with a railgun"), "F*ckem" ("move your penis through a maze while having sex with everything that it is physically possible to have sex with"), PGP 3 (Pretty Good Pornography), "Shock Da Monkey" (which, he alleges, was intended to be "*the heart warming saga of a sensitive young man coming of age in rural New England town*" but by a gross misunderstanding "*now involves using electrical shocks to coerce house apes to retrieve drugs and money from mine fields.*"), "Mormonoids," and:

XiST: X-Day Invasion Survival Trainer (1305K)

THE WORLD ENDS TOMORROW AND YOU MAY DIE!

Are you ready for the End of the World on 7:00 AM, July 5th 1998? What will you do when the Xist saucers appear above every major city on Earth and begin their campaign of worldwide destruction? Will you fry with the Pinks and the Normals or will you survive because you used XiST: X-Day Invasion Survival Trainer to prepare?

Lamprey Systems and the SubGenius Foundation, Inc. are proud announce the release of XiST: X-Day Invasion Survival Trainer – the only software guaranteed to help you survive X-Day July 5th, 1998 OR TRIPLE YOUR MONEY BACK!

SYSTEM REQUIREMENTS: Macintosh: A color Macintosh with at least 3 megs of free RAM. PowerMac recommended. PC: Because PC users are already familiar with surviving Hell on Earth, a PC version of XiST would be redundant.

DISTRIBUTION RESTRICTIONS: The X-Day Invasion Survival Trainer is intended for use ONLY by members of the Church of the SubGenius. Unauthorized usage by Pinks, Normals or Conspiracy Dupes may result in INJURY or DEATH; and is FORBIDDEN. (Lamprey Systems website)

... so it seems Carr is connected with the Church of the Subgenius: a long-running pseudo-cult whose pipe-smoking prophet, "Bob" (*sic*)

Dobbs, believes we all need more "slack" in our lives. Is Carr really Dobbs? The Church is to be found at www.subgenius.com, and has a mirror site at MIT: curious.

Carr's language and style, however, are very much more full-blooded and uncompromising than the Subgenius's. His targets are organized religion (especially the Jimmy Swaggart variety), *Playboy* magazine, "saving the universe," conspiracy culture, TV chat shows – things that, to many people, constitute the American Way of Life. He built his first pieces (Mormonoids, PornoWriter) in Bill Appleton's WorldBuilder (see Chapter 1.7) and graduated to HyperCard as soon as it appeared.

He is best known for "MacJesus," which he first released in October 1991 and has taken through a number of revisions since then. The current version (MacJesus Pro Gold) features "EtherealTalk™" – through which you talk to Jesus, and download miracles, prophecies, and sacred quotations.

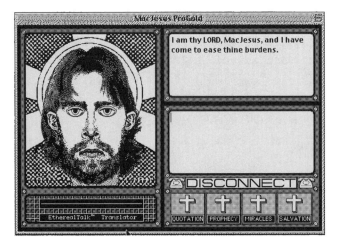

Main screen from MacJesus Pro Gold. Note the "EtherealTalk™" display at bottom left.

Carr's Jesus is a busy guy, impatient, foul-mouthed, sniffs a lot, and complains and even starts hurling abuse if ignored.

Conversations with Him are a bit like ones with Weizenbaum's "Eliza" (see Chapter 1.5). The program's "intelligence" can pick out some words from the text you give it, and give a sort-of intelligent reply; otherwise it just changes the subject. As with Eliza, these sudden switches are more or less in character.

Here's a sample:

Me: *Nice weather we're having for the time of year.*

MacJesus: *Fuck goodness and niceness everywhere.*

Me: *That wasn't very nice!*

MacJesus: *Nice guys finish last.* (*Shere Hite*)

Had I not used the word "nice" the second time, MacJesus would probably have changed the subject, giving me something like:

"*Tell me about your secret homosexual inclinations.*" or "*Considering your sins, I should nail your ass to a cross right now.*"

Carr's work is full of "cheap tricks" that more "serious" developers may like to study. They are very functional and hugely economical, as well as being fun. "EtherealTalk™" is an example. You see modem lights twinkle and get modem-noises as you connect to MacJesus – who then talks to you in squeaky high-speed gibberish (presumably "speaking in tongues"). Thus, Jesus can "speak" to you without the need for bulky audio files, or text-to-speech software – which not all computers have – and it provides a parody-bonus.

The parody is very consistent – right through to the licensing agreement and the "shareware details" screen: in the manner of a TV preacher's appeal for funds ("a love-offering of just $15" ... "One half of the proceeds received ... shall be placed under the control of The Jimmy Swaggart 'Scabs for Jesus' Love Crusade").

There are masses of detail and clever writing here.

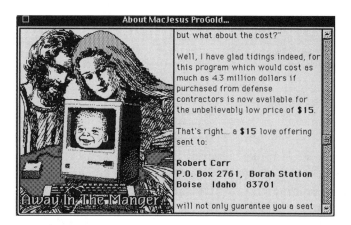

As far as I know Carr has never left Boise, Idaho – or had what you'd call a "career." He is a self-styled recluse. He does not communicate much – but whenever he does, what he writes is well crafted, and totally consistent with the persona he's created. For example, he says he is just an ordinary guy with "2.4 kids. The 0.4 is in the freezer." and sometimes signs off with "Babies: fun to make, fun to eat."

He says he's been offered legitimate multimedia work on various occasions but always refused:

I'm afraid that giving up editorial control and having to keep my work within a certain parameter of taste would take all the fun out of it. I think it's better to make my rent money by doing something completely separate from my software. (email to the author, 3 May 1998)

As with many artists, the work is to a large extent therapy.

Not being a redneck, Mormon or nazi, I was not your typical Idaho boy. Being "different" made me an easy target for a wide variety of commies, anarchists and dope fiends. My mid-twenties found me a brooding, hard-drinking Anarcho-Survivalist. Thank goodness for my first computer – a Mac Plus – which enabled me to get all the insanity and poison out of my head and into the real world where it belonged in the first place. (email to the author, 3 May 1998)

Carr has been featured in various magazines – ranging from *Mondo 2000* and *Wired* to *Business Week* – yet he makes no effort to capitalize on his fame and very few people even know what he looks like. He is his own man in way that's rare these days.

His website is currently http://www.lamprey-systems.com

Evidence of better ways to live: Brian Thomas and "If Monks Had Macs ..."

"If monks had Macs ..." became one of the very first real "hits" of the fledgling multimedia business – yet it was not a commercial product, and it seemed impossible to categorize. Ironically, this disqualified it from MacWorld's first HyperCard "SuperStacks" contest: the editor thought it was "too quirky." "Monks" started appearing in 1988 as a series of HyperCard stacks – released on floppy disks and bulletin boards. Thomas resisted "going commercial" for the first four years; it spread like a virus through the Mac community all the same. By 1992, Monks was the highest-rated non-commercial educational software program. Nowadays you can buy a Voyager CD-ROM version (from www.learntech.com/Voyager, or from Brian himself at http://www.rivertext.com/).

I think "Monks" established a genuinely new genre: the archive of evidence. As such, it is very close to Bush's idea of "trailblazing" – and it revealed something Bush hadn't anticipated: this kind of thing can have astonishing emotional force.

"Several people wrote to tell me that interacting with [The White Rose] was the first time they'd cried in front of a computer screen." (Brian Thomas, interviewed by HyperCard Heaven – see below)

What happens in "Monks ..."

"Monks..." opens on a "virtual monastery" with the Columbia River Valley in the distance; a fountain tinkles and unseen monks sing a

Gregorian chant. It looks as if it might be a precursor of "Myst," but no: from here on we're dealing mostly with text, supplemented with mainly 1-bit black-and-white graphics, and a small amount of music – from the "monastery jukebox." To our right a rotating four-sided bookcase contains the monastery library: 24 very diverse texts. My personal favorites are "Walden" and "The White Rose."

"Monks'" opening screen: the monastery garden and library

"Walden"

"Walden" is a treatise on the nineteenth-century "American Renaissance" visionary Henry David Thoreau, with extensive selections from his writings and excellent commentaries on them, written by Thomas. You can take a "virtual tour" of Walden Pond – in the woods near Concord, Massachusetts – where Thoreau built a hut for himself and learned to be a

writer. You can "explore" the hut, admire the view from its windows, and read what Thoreau said about it, and about his life there.

It seems Thoreau had the same frustration with linear writing that Ted Nelson has, and developed his own peculiar paper-based solution: a "multi-threaded" journal. Through "the miracle of HyperCard,"

From the "Walden" section of "Monks," with "Thinkertoy" navigation palette

Thomas helps you to create your own electronic multi-threaded Walden-style journal – and use it to "get yourself an inner life."

"The White Rose"

"The White Rose" is the story of Sophie and Hans Scholl – two students who launched a campaign against Hitler's Third Reich from within its very heart in early 1943, after the Stalingrad disaster (over 350,000 men abandoned to terrible deaths: one of this century's finest examples of "big picture" management in action). Both Scholls were quickly arrested by the Gestapo and executed.

Through their letters and leaflets, and the testimony of friends who survived, we get a sense that "a good life" that only lasts a few weeks may be far more satisfying than a long, compromised one.

Screenshots from the original version of "The White Rose." "Several people wrote to tell me that interacting with it was the first time they'd cried in front of a computer screen."

The Scholls' story is interwoven with the words of German artists and intellectuals who acquiesced to the regime, fooling themselves with vain hopes until the nightmare was palpable. It's very moving.

Other volumes are different again. We have a JFK archive, with "lost" eye-witness accounts from the original Warren Commission report, unpublished for 30 years. There's a hypertext version of *The Imitation of Christ* by Thomas à Kempis. There's a "virtual tour" of Pieter Brueghel's surreal painting *The Tower of Babel* – arguing (via a fascinating, fictitious "secret diary of one of the workers on the Tower") that "*Brueghel was an astute witness to the birth of a global economic system that now owns the entire planet.*"

"Monks …" would probably not please some interface-design purists. Navigation conventions vary from place to place. "Walden" has a "Thinkertoy" navigation palette that doesn't occur anywhere else. Some of the CD-ROM's contents are in Voyager's "Expanded Book" format – which gives you one set of rules for navigation – while other parts are still in the original, hand-crafted HyperCard format, and use a different set of conventions. Yet you find your way around fairly easily: a good example of "good-enough" design being quite good enough.

What's the idea behind "Monks …"?

As you can see, "Monks …" is anything but straight-down-the-middle entertainment, or education – or straightforward socialism, libertarianism, conspiracy theory, or even Christian mysticism. All of those themes are present. There's a world-view here that, as we say, "resists categorization." Whichever context we're in, whatever its content, I get a sense of being with someone who urgently desires you to bear witness to these things; for whom it all fits into some bigger picture – although it is hard to say just what that "bigger picture" is.

Brian Thomas and RiverText

According to an interview he gave to "HyperCard Heaven" (http://members.aol.com/hcheaven/interviews/thomas/thomas1.html), Brian Thomas started his career respectably enough, with a degree in English at Santa Barbara. But he went by choice into blue-collar work, at a large print-finishing plant, "*tabbing four-color separations of ads from Newsweek, Business Week, Sports Illustrated, and U.S. News and World Report.*" The work was "*desperate tedium relieved occasionally by a worker holding up – to a chorus of whistles and cat-calls – the color proof for an ad featuring a particularly bodacious babe.*"

One day in 1984 he came face to face with an ad for Apple's new Macintosh computer. "*Since I could barely communicate with some of the people who worked in the same room with me, it's unclear why I thought buying a computer would enable me to communicate with the world outside that room.*" Still, it seems he did communicate: he used the new Mac to produce "*fake company memos that satirized our muti-national corporation's contempt for us workers.*" Thomas quit the factory to explore the new subversive possibilities.

Early on, he made a "Reaganomics Pinball Game" with a piece of shareware called "Pinball Construction Set," which achieved a certain popularity. When HyperCard came out he was onto it immediately. "*HyperCard seemed to me to be for this age, like the parables of the prophets, a way to get people to consider a different view of the world.*" "Monks" was the result.

For two years, Thomas worked on it with a growing team of co-workers that included HyperCard scripting experts Philip Mohr, Richard Gaskin, and Kevin Lossner, and multimedia illustrator Bob Woods, releasing it a stack at a time. They called themselves "RiverText" (implying "*a more natural and purposeful hypertext*"). He says poverty finally persuaded him to "go commercial." Bob Stein (co-founder of the Voyager Company) was already a fan so Voyager was the natural choice.

Thomas hasn't become rich and seems to have no plans to do so. He moved from California to Portland, Oregon, and has worked mostly as a multimedia freelancer since then – on training and medical projects. However, he *is* working on a Windows version of "Monks ...," with the facetious working title: "If Monks had Windows ... they'd throw themselves out of them." Lately, he writes:

After living for almost a decade the life of ease that artists and other free-lancers are known for, I got really lazy. I got a job. I can't say exactly what it is, for I've signed a non-disclosure agreement. But I can assure you that is both legal and a lot like a Monty Python episode in which people pay good money to scream and argue with me through their telephones. It's my first white-collar job, my first cube, my first chance to "prairie dog." Each year our bosses hand out plastic coated wire figurines with "smiley faces" that they call "Bendies." They're meant to illustrate the company motto, "We're flexible." Others explain the mascot this way, "Bendie is slang for 'bend over'." When you walk through the cubes you see the flexible neon yellow Bendies in every conceivable contortion – banging their head against the computer monitor, sleep-walking, hanging from a noose, rolled up so that their head is up their ass, etc. (email to the author 3 May 1998)

It seems Thomas's inspiration is the chaos of everyday life and he seems to prefer observing it and commenting on it, to the self-delusion that comes so easily with the conventional career. It seems to give him a good life even if it doesn't make him rich – and what more can anyone ask?

It turns out he's not "religious" in any conventional sense – and not exactly conspiracy theorist either:

The great conspiracies are our conspiracies of silence and indifference. And, contrary to the standard media wisdom, that silence can hold not just 40, but 40 million people together.

The River Cafe website at www.rivertext.com

His "River Cafe" website expands on his ideas while still avoiding the convenient peg. There are "cafés" devoted to Simone Weil, Noam Chomsky, and Patti Smith.

Much (probably all) important art and writing has this "resists categorization" quality; yet older media seem to force it into categories. Put someone into a category and you discount them.

In this new medium – at its very outset – we have a work that has achieved "acknowledged masterpiece" status without anyone being able (or even wanting) to hang a label on it.

Peter Small: the secrets of the universe in black and white

Peter Small is a rather William Blake-like figure: his message is a cosmic one, fiercely expressed. His means of expression are utterly idiosyncratic, and he does absolutely everything himself. What copperplate gravure and watercolor were for Blake, the Mac and Macromedia Director are for Peter Small.

He arrived on the British "multimedia" scene apparently from nowhere in 1993, aged 50-ish, with an extraordinary, self-produced, self-published CD-ROM entitled "How God Makes God" (HGMG). He had sold his house in order to make it and it took him three years. It starts "*In the beginning, there was chance,*" and goes on to explain how chance works in every aspect of life from games, to investments, human relationships, natural selection, the evolution of emotion, quantum physics, and lots more.

HGMG appeared right at the height of the 1990s "shovelware" epidemic – and probably owed quite a lot of the enthusiastic reception it received in the British computer press to the way it so flagrantly defied the high-gloss, content-free approach that typified the era. Not only did it present the most daunting concepts imaginable – it did so entirely in 1-bit black and white, and used neither sound nor QuickTime. You're warned at the start: *"If you're hoping for an action-packed game you're in for a disappointment. However if you want to learn how to win at the game of life, read on."*

What "God" does

HGMG's subject seems so perfect for the computer-medium one wonders why so few other people have tackled it: chance. Random-number generation is one of the computer's most basic functions. (It's not *true* randomness – but Small explains why that is.) Where a book merely explains about chance, here you can experience it for yourself, hands on.

For example, you're given an explanation of a system for winning (modestly) at roulette, then you try it for yourself – and discover why "systems" don't in fact work. You can experiment with dice and coin-tossing – and of course run much bigger experiments than you'd be able to do with real dice and coins: thousands of throws in seconds – limited only by your computer's clock speed. You learn about Erwin Schrödinger's famous "cat" thought-experiment[2] – and try it for yourself.

From these basics you learn how chance gives rise to Life, the Universe, and Everything – including such basic, human issues as money, emotion, religion, the odds against popping a champagne cork so that it goes down the barmaid's cleavage, and how to decide whether a prospective husband is worth marrying (in actual cash).

The Interface of "God"

"God's" interface is a bit clunky, but it works (in a mysterious way naturally).

Computability explained by speech-bubble technology in "How God Makes God"

Small's problem was that he had something like 90,000 words that he wanted to get across. There was no way he could do it with sound – even reading it very fast and recording it at the lowest quality setting. He decided to present the whole thing as a comic book, using speech bubbles.

Then there was the graphics problem: he couldn't afford to

commission an artist and couldn't draw himself. So he spent a few days in the secondhand bookshops of London's Tottenham Court Road buying old Victorian and Edwardian annuals. From these, he culled a wonderfully idiosyncratic cast of ready-made, copyright-free characters and scenery. There's a man and woman in a Sherlock Holmes-vintage railway carriage; a pair of seductive, Burne-Jonesish beauties with flowing hair and heaving bosoms; small-time crooks, drunks, and horse-fanciers in the snug of a Holborn tavern; distinguished statesmen with pince-nez spectacles and starched collars in the smoking-room of a Pall Mall club, etc. ... a cast of thousands, all acquired for a few quid.

There was still the problem of how to produce the hundreds of animated comic strips he needed, without running out of disk space. His solution was to make Director itself do the animations, at run-time. He built himself a special authoring interface in Director in which he specified precisely where everything would appear and when. When you run the CD, a Lingo "animation engine" assembles the animations from his "kit of parts," on the fly. This way, each piece of artwork could be used over and over again – and he was able to control the action very precisely.

Menu screen, and the start of one of the "conversations" in "How God Makes God"

The final sequences have an amusing superficial crudeness – but they are also highly cinematic: well-paced, with wittily used close-ups, cutaway shots, fades, dissolves, and pull-backs. It is a shame that so few other developers have tried this technique.

About Peter Small

Peter Small's background is at least as odd as his "God." He has alluded to an unusual education among British government scientists, a career in the fashion industry, followed by another career as a professional gambler – all of which (and such books as Douglas Hofstadter's *Gödel, Escher, Bach*, Richard Dawkins's *The Blind Watchmaker* and Andrew Hodges' biography of Alan Turing) led to a consuming interest in the workings of evolution and randomness – and thence the computer.

He has never made much money from "How God Makes God," but the techniques and ideas he developed while making it have made him quite famous – at least, among people who use Macromedia Director and ShockWave. His book *Lingo Sorcery* has revealed the power of object-oriented Lingo to thousands of new-media workers, and its successor, *Magical A-Life Avatars*, introduces extremely powerful techniques that used to be considered strictly the province of theoretical computer science: for example, genetic algorithms and "Hilbert space."

And although his ideas push towards the boundaries of computer science, he still clothes them in the same stock of Edwardian images he acquired for the making of "God."

Notes

1   The relevant essay is "From the Prehistory of Novelistic Discourse" – in *The Dialogic Imagination* Trans. Emerson and Holquist, University of Texas at Austin, 1981).

2   The central riddle of quantum theory is that very small particles seem to be able to exist in two states simultaneously – and only "choose" which state they are "really" in when they are observed. In 1935 Erwin Schrödinger suggested that if a single atom of radioactive metal were to be used, say, to trigger on its decay the release of poison gas in a closed box containing a cat, the cat would technically be neither alive nor dead until the box was opened. "How God Makes God" explains this much better than I can do, of course!

2.2

Voyager: Cyberia's first viable community

THE VOYAGER COMPANY'S 12-year history (1985–97) is, almost exactly, the period during which "Cyberia" emerged from the sea of conjecture and became something like solid, habitable ground. Their 1988 "Companion to Beethoven's 9th Symphony" is generally agreed to be the title that proved to the world that Cyberia could support life. For most of the 1990s, they were almost the only evidence that it could produce anything worthwhile – its "white tower" in a morass of what Ted Nelson dubbed "multimediocrity."

Voyager's achievement is remarkable on at least five counts, any one of which would have marked them out as exceptional:

(**a**) Their 12-year run was probably the most unstable period in new-media history (e.g., constant upheavals as rival computer platforms, tools, and delivery-media standards jostled for acceptance) yet they thrived on it, while "big players" came, fell flat on their faces, and went.

(**b**) Not only did they survive, they achieved almost universal critical acclaim for almost everything they did.

(**c**) They explored territory that looked unpromising to many eyes – and proved that it was rich. The titles they produced were often ones nobody would have expected to succeed – yet they not only succeded, but became "canonical examples" that the rest of the industry would follow.

(**d**) People loved working there.

(**e**) They achieved all this with a very modest resources. The Steins weren't rich, and their company was always tiny compared to others in the field. At its peak, it had 100 staff but most of the time far fewer. Many of its landmark titles were done on shoestring budgets of $5,000 or so.

Voyager seemed to defy "commercial gravity": something we would all like to do. How did they do it? Their achievement deserves a book of its own and this account is woefully brief.

Voyager's origins

Bob Stein in 1997 (courtesy of *Wired*).

Aleen Stein at Milia, Cannes, 1996.
(Author's photo)

Aleen and Bob Stein met in the 1970s; both were grass-roots radicals.

Bob, an education MA from Harvard, had abandoned a PhD to work for a left-wing publishing collective. I have not been able to talk to Bob but he has the reputation of an inspiring and visionary leader – if impatient, and easily caricatured as some kind of ultra-left-wing maverick. I suspect most accounts of him do not really do him justice.

Aleen (then Aleen Holly – married with two children) had been a student and postgraduate at U.C. Irvine and was working as a journalist. She had been instrumental in setting up a student community at Irvine where she discovered she had "a passion for creating communities," and was good at it.

Aleen joined the protest movement against the bombing of Cambodia by the US in the late 1960s. By 1970 she had become a leading light of the west-coast Women's Liberation Movement. She started a PhD in anthropology, spent six months in Hong Kong, fell in love with China ("my second, adopted culture"), formed a west-coast chapter of the U.S. – China People's Friendship Association and led its first women's delegation there in 1974.

They married in 1978, moved to Chicago to work for Bob's book collective, but became disillusioned and moved back to LA. Aleen found work in the film industry and Bob took work as a waiter and scoured the public libraries for ideas.

He homed in on the new laserdisk technology. He researched it and put together a proposal for an "Encyclopedia of the Future" (based on *Encyclopaedia Brittanica*) which he took to Alan Kay's research lab at Atari: then a "mecca" of interactive development with a coterie of talented Kay protégés that included Brenda Laurel (whom I mention a lot in Section 3).

Kay liked the approach and he liked the Steins – and hired Bob as a consultant. After years of struggling on the edges, here was a wonderful new community that appreciated them, shared their passion for human empowerment – and had the means to accomplish it.

Building a community

From here on, the Steins' West LA home became a regular feature of that community. It embraced all manner of people, from all manner of backgrounds – including of course remarkable computer folk like Jim Blinn (then at Caltech) and Bill Atkinson (the man responsible for key parts of the Lisa and Mac interfaces, and for HyperCard). The home was full of the latest computer gadgets and games, and children: Morgan and Alita Holly, Murphy and Katie Stein. They shared the work of parenting and home-making and tried to keep the borderlines between home and "work" fluid. It sounds a hard way to live – nothing like the orderly way of conventional business – but it seems they all thrived on it. All four children became enthusiastically involved in the business as soon as they were capable of doing so, and made big contributions to it.

It seems Voyager owed a lot of its success to the exceptional degree to which it was a community. This was achieved by a quite deliberate, hard-won vision of what life and work are about.

Aleen describes the company they built as

a creative family which people took tiny wages in order to be part of it, where children (employees' as well as ours) and dogs and cats felt comfortable, where home style lunches were served every day, people came in to eat breakfast, sat around the living room eating lunch together, stayed over for dinner (usually cooked personally by me), and worked long into the night. We had progressive employee policies ....We had employees who stayed 8 or 9 of the company's 10 years. (email from Aleen to the author, February 1998)

The Voyager community eventually became a worldwide one, with all kinds of celebrities dropping in on a daily basis: poets, writers, film directors, academics, TV producers. This was naturally good for business – but all comers were welcome. When I visited in 1991 I was given exactly the same warm welcome as the much more celebrated John Perry Barlow (ex-Grateful Dead; founder of the Electronic Frontier Foundation), who was also visiting that day.

It was evidently an unusually delightful place in which to work. I asked Colin Holgate, one of their longest-serving programmers, what were the high points of his time there. He replied that he couldn't remember any particular high points because *"Voyager was such an active place that there was often a constant high, because of the amount of energy rather than because of particular achievements."*

Voyager's original HQ, overlooking the ocean at Santa Monica. It was wrecked by the earthquake of 1993 – just after the company had completed its move to New York. (Photo by Julia Jones)

Working, first, from the Steins' home and then from an old UFW (Union Foreign Wars) hall on the beach, close to Santa Monica pier, and finally from New York, this community produced a bewildering quantity and variety of work: from the laserdisks of the Criterion Collection, to the Beethoven disk (and other similar titles developed with Robert Winter) to the "Expanded Books," to avant-garde art, to popular culture ("Baseball's Greatest Hits"), to "fun stuff for kids," to agit-prop (a CD produced to support the Philadelphia death-row activist and writer Mumia Abu-Jamal, in 1996), to film, to "unclassifiable classics" like Brian Thomas's "If Monks Had Macs ..." and Pedro Mayer's "I Photograph to Remember."

An agenda: de-mystifying media, restoring context

The Voyager oevre looks anarchic – yet it evidently wasn't: nearly every one of the 250+ titles paid for itself, usually in less than a year (Voyager couldn't afford long payback times). Also, those titles, even though they're so diverse, have a highly recognizable common "feel."

Voyager's work was bewilderingly diverse – yet there is a common thread. "Salt of the Earth" (left) contains Paul Jarrico's film, the story of its making (by blacklisted film-makers during the McCarthy purges in the 1950s), and accounts of the original events (a Mexican miners' strike). Rodney Alan Greenblat's "Dazzeloids" takes the rise out of media super-heroes. Here, Yendor Talbneerg applies the Brain Fun Stimulation Device to a child whose brain has been scrambled by watching too much TV. "Brain stimulation" was Voyager's goal. "Bring your brain" was their slogan.

Aleen has said that the overriding desire was to provide great stories – whatever their form. There was also a desire to promote an overall "cause" – a questioning kind of sensibility – rather than one-off "winning products"; and a very strong desire to use the computer-medium to restore vital information about the human context of art and events – information that traditional media shed as a matter of routine.

Restoring context: from Criterion to "Beethoven" to "Expanded Books"

Film was, naturally, ever-present in their thoughts and an idea took shape at the very beginning, for using film as a way of "bootstrapping" the medium.

For most people in the early 1980s, laserdisk seemed just a classy way of delivering videos – nice but not revolutionary. The Steins' idea was to use the medium to explore films, providing additional background material and out-takes on the same disk, take users below the surface of a film, reveal how it was made, the people who made it, and the context in which it was made.

"Context" is crucial to understanding – yet "old media" shed it as a matter of routine. Out-takes end up on the cutting-room floor, a writer's first drafts go in the bin, sets are dismantled. The audience gets a beautiful treat (hopefully) but no idea how it got there. It becomes "part of the scenery," which leads us to think that it was bound, somehow, to be that way – and never suspect it was made by people like us.

"Restoring context" became a guiding theme through most of the work they did subsequently. But first they needed material on which to apply the idea.

In 1984 the Steins managed to buy the US laserdisk rights to two classic movies, *Citizen Kane* and *King Kong*, for $10,000. They teamed up with a former Warner Brothers VP called Roger Smith and launched the disks as the Criterion Collection. After a shaky start – during which Smith dropped out – Bill Becker and Jonathan Turrell of NY-based Janus Films came on board, provided some capital and in 1985 they joined the Steins in partnership – calling the new company Voyager, after the US space-probe.

Voyager's Criterion Collection became one of the very first commercially viable uses of the new medium and it established principles that the multi-media industry (which came later) would take years to discover. Within a few years it had over 100 titles – ranging from European and Japanese classics, to early Hollywood, to recent box-office hits. You had the whole film, plus scripts, storyboards, out-takes, alternative cuts sometimes, commentaries, background information, and interviews. For example, in the Criterion version of Steven Spielberg's *Close Encounters of the Third Kind* you can have the special effects explained to you by Spielberg himself and Douglas Trumbull (the special-effects director). When "summoned" they appear in video-windows above the film itself, as if watching it with you.

Criterion went out of the limelight when Voyager moved into CD-ROM development but it was always one of the company's most profitable ventures (and will probably become even more profitable in future, as Criterion moves over from laserdisk to DVD distribution). It was also an invaluable source of ideas, experience, and creative insights.

Curtis Wong, who worked on many Criterion titles, said that there was probably no other place on earth where he'd have been able to spend so much time with so many great directors, cameramen, and sound engineers, and have them explain their work to him in minute detail. It was "the best education in storytelling anyone could wish for."[1] The insights he and his fellow-workers obtained became part of the "Voyager cultural heritage."

Later on, Voyager would develop the Criterion principle on CD-ROM with film-based titles like Richard Lester's "A Hard Day's Night," Jon Else's "The Day After Trinity" (which covers the same events as "Critical Mass" – Chapter 2.3) and Paul Jarrico's McCarthy-era classic "Salt of the Earth."

Enter HyperCard; Voyager takes off

By the time HyperCard came out, in 1987, the Steins were well ahead in their understanding of the medium. While a wave of "let's-do-everything" enthusiasm began to sweep the land, they'd moved on to a philosophy of careful observation and "incremental innovation," which would prove both more robust and more exciting.

Their first HyperCard products were add-on "stacks" that could control audio CD and laserdisk players. They used the stacks to develop their laserdisk publishing – but also sold them as tools in their own right. "Empowering tools" were always part of the Voyager vision – resurfacing again, in 1991, with their "Expanded Books" project – and again at Bob's present company, Night Kitchen,[2] with a cross-platform authoring tool called TK3 (see www.nightkitchen.com).

Robert Winter becomes the first multimedia star

They already had one particular user in mind: a young music lecturer from UCLA called Robert Winter, whom they'd first met in 1982, with an infectious passion for explaining music.

A *Wired* interview[3] reveals that Winter discovered his passion for music rather late. He had started a science degree, then had a "road to Damascus" experience one evening when a fellow-student started playing Mozart on the common-room piano. He switched to the music course and within a year, incredibly, he was playing Mozart in public himself. From then on he wanted to share his revelation with the rest of the world. Winter became a hugely popular teacher at UCLA. His enthusiasm spilled over into a series of public lectures – one of which the Steins attended. Sometimes these featured a volunteer orchestra, other times nothing more than a piano, some slides, and lots of stories and charisma. Winter knew nothing about computers, and didn't understand what Bob Stein meant when he called him "a natural multimedia personality."

Bob took one of Voyager's new audio stacks, with a Mac and a CD player, round to Winter's house some time in 1988 and showed him how it could be used to select any phrase of music on a CD instantly. For Winter, this was a revelation: "*I knew then and there that this was my medium.*" From then on he was a new-media convert.

Six months later Stein and Winter demoed the "Beethoven stack" at the TED conference.[4] It was a sensation. Alan Kay declared it "*The first CD worth criticizing*"; Microsoft's founder Bill Gates, who was also there, said "*we've finally seen what CD-ROM was made for*" – and licensed a Windows version. (Strictly speaking, this first version wasn't a CD-ROM – just a standard music CD with a "companion" set of HyperCard stacks on a floppy disk.)

"Beethoven" put Voyager, and multimedia, into the limelight. There were reports of tough, military types being moved to tears by it. The general verdict was that it was an "emotional experience." For the first time, people said, they "really understood" the ninth – even though they'd loved it for years.

How does "Beethoven" work?

There is nothing technically or graphically stunning about "Beethoven": it's just a collection of black-and-white HyperCard "stacks" with lots of text, and a simple question-and-answer game. The "star of the show" is the symphony itself: a very good recording (by the Vienna Philharmonic). There's not much in the way of graphics, and those are just 1-bit black-and-white. There are awkwardnesses: there's no at-a-glance "visual map" of the symphony; you can't follow the score continuously as the music plays; you can't call up a piece of information without stopping the music.

 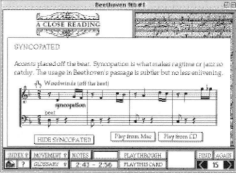

Title screen and a "close reading" screen from Winter's Beethoven disk

However, you *do* get a well-written commentary all the way through (the "Art of Listening" option), and tools to explore any part of the symphony on a "drop in" basis (the "Close Reading" option) that reveal its structure, its themes, how they work, where they came from, and the ways they evolve and interact with each other as the symphony unfolds. And of course we get the story behind the symphony: the long "fallow period" that preceded it; Beethoven's deafness – which meant he never actually heard the music he'd created (and the fascinating one-sided "conversation books" that he used for communicating with musicians when arranging the ninth's first performance). We learn about the hopeless love-life and the tragedy surrounding Beethoven's nephew Carl (whom he adopted, loved, but seems to have overburdened with impossible expectations – leading to the boy's near suicide). By the time we hit "An Die Freude" (the choral Ode To Joy) in the last movement it has become a personal thing.

It is powerful. But you could also say that Winter's "Beethoven" is just a small improvement on the idea of sleevenotes. Indeed I think both Bob Stein and Robert Winter have said as much themselves. In a way it's not as good as sleevenotes: you can read sleevenotes in greater comfort – relaxing in your favorite chair while the music plays from your hi-fi. So why did (does!) the CD produce such a strong response?

If this is only a "small improvement," it seems to be of the "small step for a man, a giant stride for mankind" variety. The very simple act of putting the music into the same physical space as the story behind it achieved what millions of dollars'-worth of bleeding edge wizardry had hitherto failed to achieve: sock a real, live human audience in the aisles.

What happened to Robert Winter?   Winter was utterly hooked by the medium. He went on to produce interactive essays for Voyager on Mozart's *Dissonant Quartet*, Stravinsky's *Rite of Spring* and Dvorak's symphony *From the New World*. He packed more and yet more information, explanation and archival material, and ultimately himself (in a QuickTime video window) into his productions. Then he set up his own company, Calliope, where he produced "Crazy for Ragtime," and this seems to have been a flop – perhaps because he opted to do it with heavily hyped but unwieldy authoring technology called Script-X, which was a definite flop. Another interpretation is that Winter simply didn't have the money to market the work properly. He continues his career at UCLA.

From "Beethoven" onwards, Voyager was "the first name in multimedia" and never failed to come up with exciting new stuff. The range of work can seem bewildering – yet very often one can see that the underlying agenda was the same: restoring context.

Expanded Books

The "Expanded Books Project" did this *par excellence*. The project started when Apple produced its first laptop machine: the PowerBook. Within hours of the machine arriving in the Voyager offices they were testing it as a reading medium.

"Expanded Books" weren't intended to bring about the "hypertext revolution" but simply to give "a better interface to books than you get with solid-state ones" (as Colin Holgate, lead programmer on the project, put it). A key feature here was that you got, not just a book – but a host of associated material as well.

One of the first titles was veteran mathematics writer Martin Gardner's *Annotated Alice* – his definitive version of Lewis Carroll's two "Alice" books: *Alice in Wonderland* and *Through the Looking Glass*. It explains Carrol's thinking, and the background to the writing of "Alice." Naturally, Gardner, who lived nearby, was welcomed into the Voyager fold, became an immediate convert – and dug out all sorts of additional material that hadn't made its way into the printed version of his book.

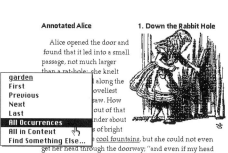

Thus, the Expanded Book version became much more definitive than the printed one – and this trend continued as the series progressed.

What are Expanded Books?   Expanded Books are HyperCard stacks containing the entire text of published books – with some very useful added features – notably the ability to click on any word at all and almost immediately find all other occurrences of that word, wherever it is in the text, and jump to it. Then you can "mark" text (by underlining it) and mark pages with paperclips or by turning down the corner, and make notes – all immediately retrievable. One of the most amazing things about the Expanded Books was that they were made entirely in HyperCard. The swift searching makes that seem implausible – but Voyager's programmers (chiefly Colin Holgate in this case) had an unparalleled grasp of HyperCard, and could make it do amazing things.

Later, the Expanded Book concept was itself expanded – to accommodate the authors themselves! In the "First Person" series, people like HCI guru Donald Norman, biologist Steven Jay Gould, and Artificial Intelligence pioneer Marvin Minsky would appear right there on the page (in QuickTime format), amid the text they'd written, to give you even more of the background – and their subsequent thoughts.

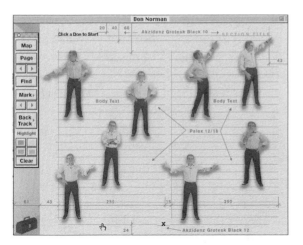

Donald Norman critiques his own book, in "Defending Human Attributes."

Here's something Colin Holgate wrote to me, about how Norman's "First Person" CD came to be made – it gives a nice insight into the way things happened at Voyager:

I had seen Don Norman on Apple laserdiscs about seven years ago. I didn't have any idea why he was being asked to describe the Mac interface as if it were a pencil, but he seemed to know what he was talking about. Then, one day at Voyager, there was a reception going on because Martin Greenberger's UCLA Round Table event was on. That's a meeting that he organises for gurus to gather around a table and spout off at each other. It was held about 600 yards up the beach from Voyager, so the attendees didn't mind dropping down for some free food and drink.

When I came into the room, I noticed Don Norman, and recognised him from the laserdiscs I had seen. I went over to him and said "hi, I recognise you from some Apple laserdiscs, and I was wondering who on earth you were?." He told me he was Don Norman, and that he was an author. This got my attention, because I was programming the Expanded Book Toolkit at the time, so any chance to get an "author" involved was worth grabbing. I casually mentioned who I was and what I was working on. I said "I should show you sometime," to which he responded "how about now?." So, we trotted off downstairs to my desk. We could just about get to it, because Steve Riggins was showing off Poetry In Motion that he was working on, and he had a small crowd around his desk.

I showed Don the Expanded Books, and a little bit of how the toolkit was coming along. He was quite excited by it. He also looked in on Steve's work, and was quite excited about that too. I said to him "you know what's funny?," he said "what?," I said "how long have you been in this line of work?" He answered "ten years." I asked him "here you are, and there are two things in one room that you think are exciting. How often does that happen?" He said "you're right!"

By the time he left my desk, he had agreed to e-mail me the text from his upcoming book Turn Signals are the Facial Expressions of Automobiles. *He did so a couple of days later, and I threw it into an Expanded Book template, and e-mailed it back to him. That was probably the first time a book had been in an electronic form before it was in a hardback form. He proceeded to demo the book wherever he went.*

A couple of years later, Bob and one of the producers at Voyager saw Stephen Jay Gould speak at the TED conference. They came up with the idea of a first person series, where the author would appear in person alongside the text they had written, and that having Stephen Jay Gould explain something in person might help you understand it more than just the written words do. Once the idea was fine tuned, the next step was to think of suitable authors. Marvin Minsky was an obvious choice, and Don Norman was a natural contender too.

I'm not sure how much that fact that he knew about the Expanded Books affected Don's decision to let Voyager do his CD-ROM, but I like to think that it helped. (Personal email to author, 1998)

The CD that Colin made (with producer Melanie Goldstein) is called "Defending Human Attributes in the Age of the Machine." As well as Norman himself, it contains the entire text of all of his books on Human Factors (*Psychology of Everyday Things*, *Things that Make us Smart*, *Turn Signals* …) and a "gallery of undefinable things," and a workbook, to "test your own design IQ."

Taken together, the Criterion Collection, the film-based CDs, "Beethoven" and its successors, and the Expanded Books all share a strong concern to reveal authorship and context – the human stories behind the things we admire.

The broader strategy: building not just products, but a cause

But not all Voyager titles are like that. What about the "Amandastories," "Silly Noisy House," Rodney Alan Greenblat's "Dazzeloids" and "Wonder Window" – or Pedro Mayer's "I Photograph to Remember"?

According to conventional wisdom small companies should concentrate their efforts so as to make the biggest possible impact. In multimedia, even big companies do this, putting large budgets into just a handful of carefully researched titles. Voyager could not even stick to one genre. The approach looks suicidal: a heroic, broad-front assault on a totally unknown market, by a handful of under-resourced enthusiasts. Yet it is not as eccentric as it sounds. New technologies can make just such a "broad-front" approach very successful.

In the early part of this century publishers like Random House had seized on new printing technology (hot-metal typesetting) to create entire libraries of the world's greatest writing at low cost for the new reading public. The Random House Library represented not just a conservative view of "the classics" but an exciting, catholic, eclectic, wide-ranging taste; a sense that "the public deserves a chance to get acquainted with these works." It didn't matter if many titles merely broke even – setup costs weren't huge, and anyway the mere presence of so much richness made the name of Random House one that you automatically gravitated towards. Earlier, in Britain, Dents had created a similar phenomenon with their "Everyman" library. This was the model: "If it deserves to be published, and we can afford to do it, let's get it out there."

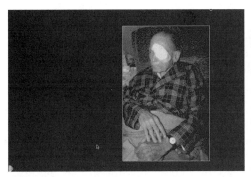 

Pedro Mayer's "I Photograph to Remember" (1991) was a sensation – yet it offers very little "interactivity," and has a most unpromising subject: an old man dying of cancer. It is Mayer's photographic record, narrated by him, of his parents' lives and deaths. "IPTR" established what has become a standard convention: the well-paced "essay" based on "primary evidence," accompanied by music and narrated not by a voice-over artist but by the person whose story it is. Few had suspected that something so simple would have such power in the computer-medium. You can follow Mayer's story at his website "Zone Zero" (http://zonezero.com).

The "broad front" approach began to work: bookshops began to have sections devoted to Voyager titles while other companies, which produced just one or two titles, were finding it hard even to get a presence in stores.

There are two secret ingredients to making this approach work: technology, and trust.

Technology: don't waste time inventing it – exploit what's there

Many CD-ROM publishers of the "shovelware" era insisted on building their own, proprietary software tools. With the sole (I think) exception of Mark Schlichting's Living Books company they paid a high price. Voyager on the other hand grabbed ready-made tools and ran with them: first HyperCard, then Director, then anything else that came along that would help them do the job.

Later, it was said that Voyager had insufficient technological expertise. Amy Virshup, writing in *Wired* in 1997,[5] speaks of "*only two in-house programmers.*" Speaking as someone who's worked on projects that were bulging with in-house programmers, I can see that that might have been a good thing. Programming isn't like chopping wood – where the more hands the better. It's more like coal-mining, where extra hands can really get in the way. Then, as Colin Holgate says:

Even when there were six programmers, I could still understand someone thinking that the technical expertise was light, because we were doing amazing things with higher level tools, instead of average things in C or C++. (Email to author)

Higher-level tools meant that a lot of the programming did not, in fact, need to be done by programmers. Producers would do a fair amount of scripting – and content-authors did lots. Aleen felt it was vital that artists should "get their hands dirty": get involved in actual coding and thereby develop a sympathy for the medium. In 1992 she expressed grave doubts about Philips's CD-I production process, which required authors to deliver up their "assets" (graphics, animations, and sounds) to the publishers, and entrust the assembly-work to the tender mercies of unseen "techies." But much of an application's charm lies not in the "assets," however beautiful they are, but in the nuances of interaction, and these are apt to be lost if the author is no longer involved. She was right: CD-I was a commercial and esthetic failure.

Trust: it's not what you do, but the way that you do it

Trust is the glue that holds society together – but it's quite rare for a commercial organization to get a very good handle on it. There's much more to it, for example, than not selling rubbish. Random House, Dents, Penguin, and innumerable successful smaller publishers are ones that people gravitate towards because there's a certain kindred-spirit feeling about them. You have the feeling that "they're my kind of publisher." Once you've got that feeling, you're likely to consider, if not buy, almost anything they offer, even if it's not something you're particularly interested in. "If they like it, maybe it's my kind of thing too!"

It is very hard to say how that "kindred spirit" feeling comes across, or what it's made of (and in fact large organizations spend billions trying to quantify it, with research and "customer care" programs, etc.) but Voyager definitely had it. People would try almost anything that Voyager produced, whether it was music, film, or "fun stuff for kids," simply because it came from Voyager. "Voyager" was the hallmark of a certain kind of sensibility. Where does it come from?

I think it goes right back to the phenomenon I mentioned right at the start of this book: the "invisible handwriting" that things seem to inherit from the people who made them. It can be the "handwriting" of one designer (like Alec Issigonis, who designed the Mini) or of a culture. This sounds almost metaphysical – but it is a real, acknowledged commercial fact:

Three examples   In Britain there is a retail chain called Marks & Spencer that started life selling underwear. People learned to trust "Marks and Sparks" so completely that they will now buy almost anything from them: sandwiches, wine, ready meals, and even personal pension plans. If you ask people why they trust M&S they refer to the consistent quality and the no-questions refund policy – but also to the fact that they are well known for treating their staff decently, and a large element of "don't know, I just like them."

Then there's Richard Branson – who set up the Virgin record label back in the 1960s. He subsequently found that people would prefer to buy many other things from him, so he now offers them an airline, a railway, and – yes – personal pension schemes and investments. People trust him. Why? He is an old hippy (albeit a rich one) and he treats his staff well. Branson in fact believes that this ethical, humanitarian dimension is the bedrock of successful "branding." In a recent lecture (for the BBC's *Money Programme*) he pointed to several other present-day multinationals founded on caring principles, including Cadburys (founded by Quakers) and Lever Brothers (pioneers of enlightened worker-housing and health).

Yet another example: British "building societies." Building societies were started in the early nineteenth century by working people who needed somewhere decent to live. The banks wouldn't help, so they organized an alternative financial system of their own. As time went by, building societies became prosperous and, in fact, indistinguishable from banks in almost every way: same besuited staff, same flashy offices, same interest rates, same awful financial jargon. But people continue to trust building societies implicitly – whereas they implicitly distrust banks. Are they perhaps buying a "culture"? There is no other clear basis for this preference.

The Voyager community at its peak – 1991 or 1992.

Voyager's main "product" was not laserdisks, or CD-ROMs, or any particular genre, but Voyager itself: a community whose values were manifest in everything it did. The lesson for any would-be new-media powerhouse is that there is great value in having a culture that people like, respect, and want to be a part of.

The Voyager legacy

The Steins lost control of Voyager in 1997 after two major setbacks: their divorce in 1995, and the 1996 "Seedy ROM slump" – compounded, tantalizingly, by the new responsibilities that came with a large influx of investment: in 1994 Aleen had secured a $6.7 million investment from the Von Holtzbrinck family (the German publishing family that owns *Scientific American*). This required developing a more structured and accountable way of working – and the huge internal stresses and external crises made this impossible.

The Voyager name and titles continue under the ownership of Learn Technologies Interactive. (LTI was founded by Luyen Chou, the author of "Qin – Tomb of the Middle Kingdom" – the exploration game that's been described as "more Myst-like than Myst".) Bob continues to develop tools under the name Night Kitchen. Aleen formed her own company, Organa, in 1996 – which published Domestic Funk's award-winning "PAWS" (a crazy cartoon "dog simulator") and "Lulu" (Chapter 2.4). Criterion continues as a separate company.

I have judged Voyager a success – yet no sooner did Voyager stumble than Cyberia's observers were pronouncing them a failure. What does one have to do, to be a success? Everything ends. The only way to judge success, I think, is the scientific one: has the organism we're discussing produced progeny? Voyager's progeny are legion. Something like 600 people worked there at one time or another; millions more have used Voyager titles, picked up at least something of the "Voyager way of doing things" through their finger-ends, and introduced it into their work. The "disapora" of "Voyager graduates" has spread ideas, insights, ways of working and thinking forged at Voyager throughout the industry.

A philosophy: People and stories first, technology second

Voyager's work is a celebration of human diversity. The Steins were very wary of grand theories about new media. Bob "the visionary" seemed very well aware that visions deceive – you need to keep revising them.

Voyager succeeded not via some arms-length, Grand Unified Theory of interaction, but on thousands of small, carefully considered decisions, always measured against the ultimate goal of bringing the user/reader into contact with the subject matter.

The approach was to "work away at the edges" of the medium, looking for stepping stones and handholds that might lead into interesting new territory, using available technology wherever possible. These "little steps" have led us all into some surprising places: nobody would have predicted that a heavyweight study of a Beethoven symphony would be the medium's first "hit," or that its next hit would be about an old man dying of cancer (Mayer's "I Photograph to Remember"). Both titles became reference-points for new-media development.

Mostly, "available technology" meant HyperCard. This allowed them to accomplish far more, more rapidly, than companies that insisted on coding everything in "proper" languages like C and C++.

On the downside, this made them dependent on Apple, whose HyperCard would never become cross-platform despite frequent encouraging rumors. But that was a risk that came with the territory, and it's hard to see how they could have done things differently without drastically restricting their ability to "push the frontiers."

Aleen was adamant that technology itself was not the issue. The prime requirement was good content that people wanted to know about. "Beethoven" was not dreamed up by someone sitting in front of a computer and thinking "what can we do with this?." The computer application is only one manifestation of Winter's work. The same went for most of their other artists: they were typically people who already had great stories to tell.

Do radicals make the best capitalists?

There is a notion that radicalism and idealism are incompatible with "hard commercial reality" – but there are plenty of examples that suggest the opposite is the case. This kind of radicalism is all about paying attention to people, seeing what needs to be done, and getting on with it – instead of waiting for some "important person" to wave a magic wand.

I think conventional wisdom has got things the wrong way around: to get anything meaningful done, you need to be a radical.

Notes

1   Conversation with the author at Milia 1996.

2   "Night Kitchen" was the name Bob and Aleen chose for their very first company – preceding Criterion and Voyager. I presume it comes from Maurice Sendak's famous children's book of that name.

3   Interview with Ray Sawhill in *Wired* 2.12: "A Crazy Shade of Winter" see http://www.organa.com/Outerspace/Core/wiredwinter.html.

4   "TED" = "Technology Entertainment Design" – a prestigious annual conference organized by writer Richard Saul Wurman, usually in Monterrey. See http://www.ted.com/.

5   See http://www.wired.com/wired/4.07/features/stein.html. Virshup's article describes the fraught "endgame" of the Voyager story.

2.3

The power of "primary evidence": Curtis Wong develops the Voyager vision at Corbis

I MET CURTIS WONG WHEN I visited Voyager in 1991; he was making a new Microsoft Windows interface for the Criterion laserdisks: you could create "buttons" of your own to activate particular parts of the movie, and put sequences of them into your own little "control panels." It was not spectacular stuff but as neat as you could wish – even given the limitations of Windows: at that time still very much the Mac's "poor relation"

Curtis Wong, on the Corbis stand at Milia, Cannes in 1996. (Author's photo)

appearance and behavior-wise. Compared to the other things being made there, his seemed, to me, the "Cinderella" job, and he, with his calm demeanor, an obliging nominee for it.

Nearly five years later, in 1996, I was at Milia – the Multimedia festival that's held in in the south of France at Cannes every February. On the Corbis stand a CD-ROM called "Critical Mass" grabbed my attention. There was something about it – clarity, simplicity, the graceful way things unfolded on the screen perhaps – that

115

seemed both excellent and inexplicably familiar. Then I spotted the name "Curtis Wong" amid the closing credits and thought "hang on – I know that name." I mentioned this to the Corbis functionary and he replied, "As a matter of fact Curtis is our main man. That's him over there."

So I reintroduced myself. He said that "Critical Mass" was not strictly his but Lisa Anderson's work – his own role was executive producer. Then he showed me his own favorite new work, the CD called "A Passion for Art" (about the Barnes collection of impressionist art in Philadelphia).

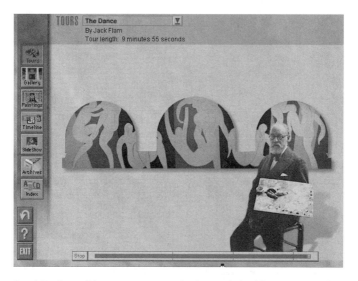

Henri Matisse with *Les Danseuses* – the intensely problematic piece that marked the turning-point between his early naturalistic and his later "découpage" period. Completing it, he felt "a new world" opened up for him . This shot comes from an "essay" that, like the work itself, is essentially a collage: it pieces the story together from fragile and priceless scraps of evidence, drawings, letters, and receipts, drawn together by Curtis from numerous non-public sources. It is not narrated by a professional voice-over artiste, but by art historian and Matisse expert Jack Flam (the nearest Curtis could get to an authentic voice).

This contains a poignant "essay" about the creation of Matisse's *Les Danseuses* (The Dancers): a frieze commissioned by Barnes for his Philadelphia home, fraught with nearly tragic problems, but through which Matisse discovered the "découpage" ("cut-out") technique for which he became so famous. It is a narrated, linear presentation using still photographs and a beautiful slow-paced sound track. It seemed very simply put together, but it packed a very particular kind of emotional power. I said, "This is so like 'I Photograph to Remember'." "Well," said Curtis, "I worked on that one too." He had helped Robert Winter and Pedro Mayer on the audio that's such a feature of "I Photograph." I now realized that what I'd thought were two quite separate phenomena ("I Photograph" and "A Passion for Art") were in fact one: and the unassuming chap in front of me was a major part of it.

Later, Curtis explained his approach like this:

The importance of authorship is something that was part of the culture of Voyager.

When I came to Corbis to start their interactive group, I wanted to create another model, that of the producer as author. A Passion for Art is exactly that. While I could have chosen to use an art historian as author, I preferred that role myself as a representative member of the audience. What did I want to know/see from such a title? Why should I care about this art? As an average person who didn't know a lot about art I wanted something that would reach out to me. In working with the art historians on this title I would try to get them to tell a story with words people not in art circles would understand … and always bring it back to stories about people and their struggles, which are the common themes we all can relate to. (From an email to the author, summer 1997)

Curtis had left the Voyager Company in 1995 to establish a multimedia production unit at Corbis – the company Microsoft's Bill Gates set up to create a massive commercial archive of artworks and images from all over the world. Corbis is regarded by many as rather predatory – it has acquired exclusive electronic rights to entire galleries of the world's greatest art – but it must have been a dream come true to be able to work with such a wealth of primary material. Corbis's CD-ROM production venture didn't last long – it ended in 1997, after the "Seedy-ROM slump" – but while it lasted, Curtis created an ethos there that some found "more Voyager-like than Voyager."

"Critical Mass" (produced by Lisa Anderson, with art director Cecil Juanarena) tells the story of the race to build the atomic bomb at Los Alamos, New Mexico, in World War II. This is of course one of the most ambivalence-fraught episodes in modern history – perhaps in history, period. The great text account of this endeavor is Richard Rhodes's *The Making of the Atomic Bomb*: a massive, 900-page work of scholarship – and this was the starting-point for "Critical Mass." But where Rhodes *refers* to original source material, Anderson and her team were able to *show* it, and make it "hero" of the situation.

Respect for "primary materials": The menu screen for "Critical Mass" is an obvious (but attractive) collage. All images are from 1944/5 and presented as honestly as possible. The way they're assembled makes it quite clear to the user that Bohr, Oppenheimer, Feynman, and Bethe never actually posed together like this (although they all stood in this hut at one time or another). "Rollovers" are used well here. At the moment the mouse is over the young Richard Feynman.

Clean (and obvious) 3D graphic reconstruction of the site. In the background we hear the faint sounds of power-tools and typewriters. I've visited Los Alamos myself, and found this simulation surprisingly evocative of the actual place – even though all the buildings have now changed.

We are able to see the actual letters the Hungarian physicist Leo Szilard wrote to US President Roosevelt, urging him to take action – with Roosevelt's own marginal notes. We hear the actual voices of the people who were involved: the "legends," like Richard Feynman and Niels Bohr, and of many "bit-part players" who worked as secretaries and lathe-operatives. We get images and sounds from the popular culture of the times: the naive euphoria of the postwar atomic age (e.g., the front cover of a comic-book, *Dagwood Splits the Atom*; a little-known Bluegrass band, the Buchanan Brothers, singing a surprisingly good hit single called *Atomic Power*).

Pride of place on screen goes to original source material. Where no original exists, the image used is clean and simple, with no pretence to be anything more than it is: a menu perhaps, a title, or a visualization.

The "collage" style that comes so naturally to multimedia is a help: because radically different graphic styles can coexist happily on the monitor screen, you can use them to flag different kinds of information and differentiate them clearly: photo images for original materials, flat 2-D imagery for interface artefacts, 3-D Studio graphics for reconstructions (the images of the original Los Alamos site, by Russell Phillips).

Carefully controlled combinatorial explosion

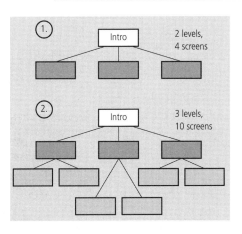

Combinatorial explosion. Even in this simple example, just one more layer of information gives you over twice as many screens to design.

"Critical Mass" is, I think, a good example of a "controlled combinatorial explosion." These explosions are a major hazard for anyone developing many-layered hypermedia, especially websites, where the temptation is to create so many links you end up with far more work than you can ever do justice to – and give the user terrible navigation problems into the bargain.

The "Critical Mass" team managed to restrain the natural desire to link everything to everything else without, somehow, making the application seem restricted. They have overcome the problem by making the "rules of use" clear to the user in the very first moments. If, when you move the mouse-pointer over something, it sprouts a "rollover" title, or changes its appearance, you know it's "hot" and can be clicked. You learn this unconsciously because the main screen (above) is packed with "rollovers." Having learned this rule, you don't bother clicking anything that doesn't produce a rollover effect. Without this, "Critical Mass" could have seemed very restricted: for example, text information doesn't include hyperlinks. We can't "find all references to Richard Feynman" – however, we have learned not to expect such things. Instead we have a collection of very good, linear accounts of Feynman's life

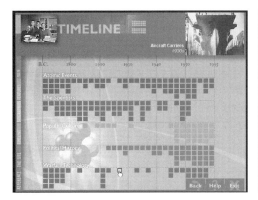 

From the "top level" we can go to the "timeline" (left), and thence to a particular item of "archive" information (right). Critical Mass could be accused of some "interface inconsistency" – this is a different method of navigation from the one shown in the main screen – but this isn't really a problem: the application is only three levels deep and we can always see how to get back where we came from. The second screen here is a "combinatorial explosion hazard," sensibly contained. (Which British aircraft carrier was this? What was its story? It could be the *Glorious* whose sinking in 1940 was a landmark in the information war – which led to the computer. A project can easily get sucked into hyperspace by questions like these!)

and work (ditto Bohr, Einstein, etc.). And because the layering isn't too deep, we can fairly easily find other references to him for ourselves.

By restricting the amount of hyperlinking, the team could break the job down into a set of fairly self-contained modules, to which sub-teams could devote their full attention.

Simplicity also, perhaps, allows the navigation interface to be less strictly regimented and standardized than it would need to be with a "deeper" structure. For example, we have at least three kinds of "menu": the "rollover collage" (main menu screen: the office); the "pan-and-click" 3-D reconstruction of the Los Alamos site (above), and the more abstract, diagrammatic menu through which we search the archives.

Most of the examples discussed in this book were done on shoestring budgets. I regret that I don't know what the budgets were here, but I assume money was not a problem. I think these two works are rare examples of what good teams can achieve when they have all the resources they need, a creative leader who understands them and their needs, and a strong, well-articulated vision to work towards.

Both titles were built mainly in MacroMedia Director, with various sophisticated additions that were programmed in-house – and although Corbis doesn't supply them any more, they are still available from Hoffman Associates (http://www.h-plus-a.com).

2.4

The "book as hero" in Romain Victor-Pujebet's "Le Livre de Lulu"

WORK THAT'S DONE FOR LOVE, for an audience of one, can often have truly universal appeal.

"Lulu" came out in 1995 and has taken large parts of the world by storm. (But not the US – a failure of marketing has, so far, denied it to US users.) I think it is the first new-media title that you could strictly call a "children's classic." As well as finding it downright beautiful, I find the same pure emotion and crazy but totally self-consistent logic you find, for example, in *Alice in Wonderland*. Like other children's classics, adults are knocked out by it too.

The story begins: "There was once ... in a book, a princess called Lulu."

On the face of it, "Lulu" appears to be a children's book translated to CD-ROM – like Mark Schlichting's "Living Books." You have pages that turn when clicked, text that reads itself to you, and pictures that come to life in delightful ways. It also has wonderful, haunting music – by Olivier Pryszlak.

Ceci n'est pas un livre

In fact, "Lulu" is not a book: there is no "real" Book of Lulu, and its author, Romain Victor-Pujebet, insists there never will be one. Instead, it is a play on the whole idea of books, the people who live in them, and the passionate yet impossible attachments we often form with them.

"The book is more than just an interface, it is the third hero of the story!" (Romain, interviewed by Jim Gasperini for Interactivity *magazine)*

Lulu's world only exists when the computer is on, and you are separated from it by the thick glass of your monitor screen. You cannot put it into your pocket and imagine you possess it. That is Romain's message: we cannot physically possess what we love.

The fun here is suffused with a poignant sense of unattainable beauty – underscored at every turn by subtle interplay between the reader and the characters of the tale. You can make Lulu dance and many other things,

"Le Joli Château" has numerous hidden treats. The mouse-pointer has become a butterfly, and the scene changes from night to day, through all four seasons, as you click.

but she does not acknowledge you. Standing on the stage of her home-made theater to recite a poem, she appears to look you straight in the eye – but in fact she's addressing her own, completely imaginary audience. One relates to Lulu as through a one-way mirror: an unseen intruder.

The word "magical" comes easily, but here the word is almost technically correct. Victor-Pujebet started with an illustrative style that he found in a nineteenth-century book (the illustrator, alas, was unnamed – but he or she clearly was under the inflence of the great Gustave Doré). In itself, this creates a feeling of a "lost world of perpetual summer." The animations capitalize on this: the ones featuring Lulu herself are blue-screened live-action sequences (of the ten-year-old Emilie Cornac). The technique of illustration + live action is not new (first used in the Walt Disney *Mary Poppins* and since then in countless TV commercials), but I have seldom seen it used so appropriately. In this context they seem like ghosts of another reality emerging from the page.

A quick synopsis of Lulu's story may give you a better idea of how Romain uses multimedia to play with these ideas.

What happens in "Lulu"

The lonely little princess Lulu lives in a beautiful castle, in a beautiful book. She's two-dimensional, but perfectly normal in every other respect.

One day a spacecraft containing a robot, Mnémo, crash-lands in the château's grounds. Mnémo is on an errand for his young master, Prince Megalo Polo, who lives on a distant planet. The errand is to find something called "warmth" (a tricky concept for a robot). Lulu agrees to help him and off they go, out of the book, into space.

But "space" is three-dimensional: an impossible place for two-dimensional Lulu, who suddenly rolls up like a poster. Mnémo crash-lands back into the book – but the "warmth-detector" has not been switched off, and they find themselves in the hottest part of the tale: the chapter set in the Sahara Desert. Lulu soon suffers terribly from thirst ("Mnémo! J'ai soif!," she calls, from the book).

Lulu and Mnémo reunited at the North Pole.

Mnémo hurries ahead, into the text, to fetch water from the rainforest in Chapter 6 – and finds himself "lost in the intricacies of plot." They search for each other through deserts, jungles, exotic lands, and finally the North Pole. Finally it is Lulu who rescues Mnémo, frozen in the ice – and Mnémo realizes that the "warmth" he has been seeking is "human warmth." And he has found it, of all places, in a book.

The problem remains: how can two-dimensional Lulu make the journey into "space"? Mnémo thinks he can achieve this by "extrudomorphosis": a process, he explains, invented by the Italian Renaissance painters to allow otherwise flat, paper characters to enter the 3-D world. This fails – tragedy – but then Mnémo realizes that there is a solution after all:

The day I found the ending to the story, I just jumped in the air, I was so happy! Of course ... he [Mnémo the robot] will take the book with him. Only the solution will be that he will have Lulu with him in the book. You see, he is looking for warmth, which he discovers in Lulu. But he must leave her to return to his planet. She is sad. But because he has her in the book, he can take her with him [...]. The whole attitude of Mnemo changes through the book, and in the end he discovers that he can find the warmth he is seeking in the book.

(Romain, interviewed by Jim Gasperini in February 1997 for Interactivity *magazine).*

The story behind the story

Romain Victor-Pujebet, at Milia (Cannes) Feb. 1996.
(Author's photo)

Victor-Pujebet had no multimedia credentials at all, or even a computer, when he started on "Lulu." He had led a pretty adventurous life as a photographer and musician, in Paris, New York, and traveling throughout the Americas and Africa. Then, when his daughter Lola was born he moved back to France and settled in Castres, near Toulouse, and devoted himself to fatherhood full-time while his wife Lila worked – although for much of the time they were living on welfare. "Lulu" first began to take shape in a series of scrapbooks that Romain made for Lola, to help her learn to read.

When Lola was three he bought her a computer – a secondhand Mac – and started making toys for her in HyperCard. The collage style Romain had used in the scrapbooks seemed perfect for the computer. As he played with the Mac, "Lulu" began to evolve. They made a "strong demo" in HyperCard. Then Romain began the thankless task of finding a publisher. And all the publishers insisted on changes that, for him, would have ruined everything.

These editors, they take children for stupid. They said we must highlight the words, like in Living Books. But for me that misses the pedagogical side. It becomes just a visual thing. I had spent years on the process of teaching a child to read. So I did not want to do it, I would not compromise on that issue.

(Romain, interviewed by Jim Gasperini in February 1997 for Interactivity *magazine)*

Eventually, in appropriately fairy-tale fashion, Romain encountered a fairy godmother: Aleen Stein. She'd just left Voyager and was setting up her own company, Organa. Aleen recognized his vision and found the money. An eight-strong production team, DadaMédia, was set up in Paris, and the whole thing was finished in six months, in MacroMedia Director.

I learned the story in 1996 – and I'd heard a very similar tale the previous year from fellow Aleen protégés, Alan Snow, Nick Batt, and Dave Furlow (Domestic Funk Productions). During 1993 and 94, they took the demo of their "PAWS" dog-simulator around to all of the publishing houses. "What is it like? Carmen Sandiego? Living Books? Reader Rabbit?" said the publishing execs. "Well, it isn't like anything really," they replied – and the corporate eyes glazed over. "Well," said the execs, "Could you make it teach spelling, or French? We might consider it then." Then they met Aleen Stein. She liked "PAWS" just the way it was; it became the first offering from her new Organa publishing house; took the Milia d'Or at Cannes in 1995, and is now firmly established in the small canon of long-running multimedia masterpieces.

After "PAWS" won its Milia d'Or, various publishers asked the team, "Why didn't you show us this?" – to which they often had to reply, "We did."

> D'une voix sourde, Mnémo ajouta dans un murmure :
> – Moi, c'est dans un livre que j'ai ressenti pour la première fois une vive émotion. Tu comprends ça, Lulu ?...
> – Veux-tu dire que c'est uniquement dans le livre que tu as découvert l'imagination ? la fantaisie ? les intrigues ? les sentiments ? le rêve ?

The payoff: "It was in a book that I felt genuine emotion for the first time."

Romain went on to create a series of CDs for the French publisher Flammarion, including "La Reine des Neiges" (Hans Andersen's *Snow Queen*), "Robinson Crusoe" and Prince Megalo-Polo's spiritual ancestor, "The Little Prince" by Antoine de Saint-Exupéry.

Lola, now 13, is working with with him, as co-scenarist, on yet another (undisclosed) product.

You can find out more about Lulu (and Domestic Funk's "PAWS") at http://www.organa.com. Wayland Multimedia sells an English-language version of Lulu at http://www.wayland.co.uk.

2.5

The Nationwide Building Society and its "Interact" project

Sometimes, you have all the best people, a great project, fabulous resources, and nothing happens!

Jeremy Bullmore, Chairman, J Walter Thompson London
(talk given to staff in 1979)

All my examples so far were made either on their authors' own home turf, or in multimedia companies, where working regimes are very different from the ones you find in the traditional "world of business." My final example – the Nationwide Building Society's "Interact" project – was built in just such a world, and I worked on it myself (from 1994 to 1997).

The context: old radicals in new suits

Nationwide does not look like a revolutionary organization – but its origins are radical. It's a building society (Britain's biggest). As I said earlier, building societies were set up in the early nineteenth century, when British industrial towns were disease-ridden refugee camps. (The building societies' precursors were in fact "burial clubs.") People desperately needed housing; banks would not help them, so people organized their own co-operative system where they pooled what money they had for their mutual benefit.

Building societies became a complete alternative financial system within a few generations, and through some apparently inexorable process, they came to resemble banks in almost every way (same kind of management hierarchy, buildings and financial jargon – and very similar interest rates). Yet they retained enormous loyalty: surveys show that people still overwhelmingly trust them – and overwhelmingly *dis*trust banks – even though they look so similar.

The shop in Toad Lane, Rochdale: where the co-operative movement started

In the "greed-is-good" 1980s mutuality went briefly out of fashion. Many societies abandoned it and became banks – but Nationwide resisted this, with solid backing from its members, and a CEO (Brian Davis) who's committed both to mutuality and to the redeeming powers of computers.

Nationwide, then, is the main bastion of a powerful and well-loved idea, and you get a sense of this when you visit their offices: people seem to be better treated than they are in most banks I've dealt with, racial and other minorities seem better represented, and staff seem to feel much more "part of the show." Their managers tend to be people who've risen from the shop floor and know the business in detail – not mandarins hired from outside. The founders' handwriting is still discernible under the corporate gloss.

Everything you ever wanted to know about money. Including things you didn't know you wanted to know

"Interact" is a touchscreen system to help people understand things like mortgages, loans, insurance, banking accounts, savings plans, investments of various kinds – the Mysteries of Money.

Money is great stuff to have in your pocket. But "Money" – the subject, with a big "M" – makes people's eyes glaze over. Why is that?

"Money" behaves in very counter-intuitive ways. It is "n-dimensional": any decision can involve any number of variable and interdependent factors. Yet the whole thing has very distinctive "behaviors" that only a few lucky people manage to notice, become enthralled by, and turn into an unending source of pleasure and wealth. It has a strange kind of beauty. As I remarked earlier, Benoit Mandelbrot's great discovery – fractals – came out of work he was doing on the behavior of financial markets. Somebody, somewhere, has called money "mankind's first abstraction."

Over the top: the "waterfall"[1] approach

Most of Nationwide's computer projects till now had dealt with reasonably well-understood "terrain": payrolls, interest payment, etc., where a hierarchical technique *can* work quite well. The technique that's used is known as the "waterfall" or "cascade": the project is broken into a number of stages (from analysis and specification to implementation); when a stage is completed the work "cascades" down to the next, and so on until it reaches the users, debugged and ready to run (hopefully).

Nationwide applied this method very thoroughly. They put some of their best programmers and managers onto the job, hired the very best specialists they could find (including an excellent team from Andersen Consulting) and put a good man in charge: Mike Rehberger – a new-technology expert and something of a visionary, who also knew Nationwide's business from top to bottom. Andersens built a good-looking prototype, produced a detailed master plan that specified everything and left nothing to chance, and the whole thing swung into action.

Within a couple of months it was clear that it wasn't working: test-users weren't impressed by the early efforts, and the first milestones remained obstinately anchored to the far horizon.

The "waterfall" has a giant flaw. It *seems* to deliver software that works – but only because most software has a "captive audience" of users who have the time and the will to *make* it work. Either they've paid good money for it and are prepared to spend a few hours mastering it, or their employers are paying them to master it. You can assume some kind of "learning curve." But Interact was designed for "discretionary users": non-computer-users mostly, who expected to be able to use it immediately. They had no "duty" to learn how to use it. At the user interface, instead of a learning curve Interact met a "learning brick-wall".

Working "under the waterfall" is no fun

My job was to design interfaces for various modules specified by the overall plan (savings, investments, etc.). I was to "produce concepts" – on paper at first, discuss them, get them agreed with everyone, then pass them to the graphic designers, who would then hand the finished graphics to the programmers, who would finally give them cybernetic life. Everything could be checked and debugged on paper, nobody's efforts would be wasted, nothing would be implemented that wasn't 100 percent rock solid.

I found that my ideas were impossible to implement. This was puzzling because I wasn't suggesting anything I hadn't already done myself, in Supercard or Director. Why couldn't we use Supercard or Director here? They were not deemed powerful or stable enough for a serious software project like this. There was also a (fairly understandable) fear that easy-to-use tools would open the door to "spaghetti code": a mare's nest of handlers and variables, and different programming styles, that nobody would ever be able to maintain.

But without an easy authoring environment it was very difficult even to design a screen "button," and see how it would look and work *in situ*. You had to get a programmer to stop what she or he was doing (which might take anything from half an hour to a couple of days), load your button-graphic into the special database, then load the whole Interact application, and finally test the button. Having actually got it "onto the system" it was tempting to let it stay there whatever it looked like.

Because it was so difficult to see how components would behave in action, people would try to judge them in isolation, as flat immobile artwork. Work would be scrapped or revised to death before anyone had a chance to try it on the computer. A mounting sense of anxiety and pressure began to pervade the place: here was a team of over 20 highly experienced people, costing God-knows-what per day, producing work that was not so much "state-of-the-art" as "state-of-the-ark" – and not very much of it either.

The Metaphor becomes an albatross

Then there was "The Metaphor." Computer interfaces that use "real-world metaphors" are supposedly easier to use than more abstract ones: the Apple Desktop being the classic example. Interact used a "branch metaphor." On the opening screen we would see a typical Nationwide branch, in a typical main street. You would be able to "go inside" by touching the doors, then move around to the different departments: mortgages, savings, insurance, etc.

The "branch metaphor" – Interact's original opening screen

It seemed to make sense: people would find the interface easy to use because they already knew what a building society branch office was like, but it became like an albatross around our necks.

First, there was the "consistency" problem (described incisively by Ted Nelson – Chapter 3.6). Whenever we wanted to add a feature, we had to find a way of representing it that was consistent with "the metaphor": some object you might, perhaps, expect to find in a building-society branch, which instantly suggested "home insurance," "30-day notice lump-sum deposit account," etc. Unfortunately there is no object on Earth that resembles any of these multidimensional things – and a building-society branch is the last place you would find one if it did. They are clean, tidy places containing very little that you can recruit into a computer interface: desks, blotters, computer monitors … and that's about it.

Then, there was the problem of "things that want to be everywhere." If you're taking out a mortgage, for example, you usually need insurance as well, and perhaps an investment too. Should we make the user "go" to a different part of the "branch" for each bit of the mortgage, or allow "insurance devices," etc. to be omnipresent (adding yet more clutter to already crowded "virtual rooms")? Explanations needed to be everywhere – yet the metaphor confined them to "virtual books" that lived in a "virtual bookcase" in the "virtual foyer." These were beautifully produced – but when they were needed, they were "out of sight, out of mind." You could neither leaf through them as easily as real books, nor carry them around with you.

We seemed to be trying to re-create reality, not very well, while preserving its worst impediments and adding some extra ones of our own.

A paradigm shift

Statistics (in Thomas Landauer's book and elsewhere) suggest that projects that run into problems like these usually bury themselves, and are erased from the corporate memory with no useful lessons learned – but here things began to change. Eventually we achieved an utterly different, much more successful approach for Release 2 – which was also very much quicker and cheaper. Briefly, it hinged on two things:

1 Making "user-focus" central to everything that was done.

2 A quite different team structure.

Release 2: the small core team and the "deliverable minimum"

Release 2's main feature was to be a module that explained about pensions and investments, and showed you how much money you might make over different periods of time – allowing for inflation, regular saving, etc. It was very much more complicated than anything we'd attempted before. Yet the job was done in a fraction of the time (less than four working months), by a tiny team, and became Interact's most successful feature: it accounts for over half of Interact's usage and produces more than twice as many "sales leads" as all the other features put together. It was also an immensely enjoyable working experience.

Instead of the "waterfall," we used a sort of "core-and-satellites" approach. The "core" was just two of us: a remarkable programmer called Chris McEvoy, and myself. The "satellites" were the people who dropped in to help us from time to time, as and when we needed them, and got on with their own work when we didn't: Nationwide's legal experts and financial sales people (to explain things to us), John Cato (who managed our usability program), one of Andersens' programmers, and two graphic designers.

A good manager really helps   We had a marvellous project manager called Julie Cutts: the perfect example of what Tom deMarco and Tim Lister say (in *Peopleware* – see Chapter 3.8) about managers. Their job is: "not to make people work, but make it *possible* for people to work." She knew the organization inside out, and what it was for: she had been a branch manager herself and dealt personally with thousands of its customers. Julie was the perfect sounding board and reality check – and she made sure we met our deadlines, not by "kicking ass" but by making sure she, and we, knew exactly what we were doing and why.

Our solution didn't follow any "real-world metaphor" – nor is it any great shakes graphically, but it conveys a lot of information, and it works: even for people who have never used a computer before. There were plans for a more beautiful interface in Release 3 (shown below).

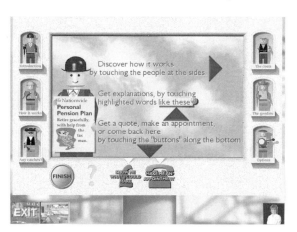

Interact's "Investments" system – introductory screen

First, we spent two weeks working out what we could realistically achieve in the time: a "deliverable minimum." This would just give text information, with a few animations to explain difficult concepts like "compound interest" and "market risk," and a simple calculator-style interface for working out what a particular investment might make over a particular number of years. We could start work on this right away – it would nearly all be needed by our "maximum option" as well.

The "deliverable minimum" gives you a safety net

Our "maximum" goal was something that would give people a physical sense of the way money can grow.

People need "Thinkertoys"   People don't save enough because they don't think the puny amounts they can put aside will make much difference. What they don't realize is the "magic of compounding": the interest you get on interest you've already earned. Growth that seems insignificant at first gets progressively more dramatic as time goes on.

Supposedly, we learn all this in elementary mathematics – but somehow we remain unconvinced. Figures on a page don't do the trick. Graphs are better. Dynamic diagrams (drawn before your very eyes) are very much better. But the "holy grail" would be something that lets you play with compounding and experience it in some physical way. A "mind tool" in Richard Gregory's sense (see Chapter 3.4) – or what Ted Nelson would call a "thinkertoy."

You can probably think of a several ways of doing this, and so did we. I won't bore you with the details but "legal compliance" requirements put paid to most of them. We had to show so much statutory information that the interface kept ending up like the control panel of a nuclear power station. For example: we had to show growth at three "illustrative" interest rates simultaneously, each getting equal emphasis.

This almost floored us – but we had our "deliverable minimum" to fall back on (the calculator-style interface) so there was no need to panic. After the sixth or seventh attempt had bitten the dust our project boss, Mike Rehberger, said, diffidently, *"I keep getting this silly idea about electricity meters. You know: they have a disk that spins as you use electricity? Do you think we could have something that's a sort of cross between that and a one-armed bandit?"* – and that did the trick.

As you can see (opposite), the interface we arrived at is a sort of sideways one-armed bandit where strips of little pictures (from clip-art) move along to represent your possible "payout" as you change your "input parameters" (how much you're investing, over what period, etc.). The "Lego" people (who supply background information) live in little "niches" at the side, *somewhat* like the statues of saints around the West Door of a medieval cathedral. This is what we call a well-mixed metaphor. It can be improved, but it works!

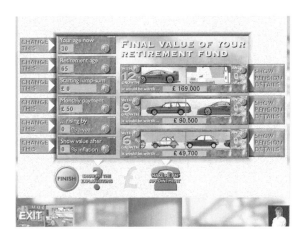

The "one-armed-bandit-cum-gas-meter" interface

Building from the bottom up

We weren't able to use a ready-made authoring tool like SuperCard or Director but Chris had already started to build us an authoring environment of our own ("McThing") in VisualBasic. It started as a simple hypertext system – with a simple markup language of his own invention. I was able to write my explanations, with hot-text "popups" and background graphics, and try them out quickly – just like doing HTML (and in fact he later made an HTML interpreter so that you could use the same information on the Web).

As the job progressed, he extended the language so that I could summon the "one-armed bandit" from my pages, put values into it – and then give it messages to present to the user ("Sorry – you can't invest more than £6,000 in this particular scheme," etc.).

McThing was built precisely for the job in hand, so we could work fast; it developed as the job developed – and we could hand parts of the job to temporary helpers easily if we needed to: there wasn't much for them to learn, and not much to get wrong. If we discovered that we needed another feature, and it was do-able, Chris would come in early and write it.

As we developed the device we'd get other members of the team to try it out and give us their impressions; every two weeks we'd clean up the loose ends and submit the whole thing to usability testing: a one-day session where half a dozen members of the public, selected

The planned Release 3 interface, in which Emma (a Nationwide employee) is your financial-planning crash-dummy and guide. She "morphs" to any age (or sex) you require.

at random, would be asked to use the system to solve some particular investment question, "thinking aloud" as they did so. These sessions were videotaped and analyzed, resulting in a list of things to be fixed and improved that got gratifyingly shorter as the weeks went by.

The system was good enough for "signoff" after six of these usability cycles, two weeks (I think) before our deadline. We'd expected signoff to be quick and simple – but we'd hadn't noticed just how much ground we'd covered! Around a dozen different people's different, specialized areas of knowledge were in there, in this one, simple-looking device – and every single one had to check it.

The unexpected bonus: "so *this* is what we do!"

The main reason why financial products are so complicated and anxiety-inducing is you can't see them. Building the system, we had to figure out how all the invisible components of these invisible products worked, and how they influenced each other. This knowledge had to be complete in every detail, and work together consistently in every possible situation. We got the information, piece by piece, from a dozen or so specialists – but few if any of them had ever been able to see exactly how it all fitted together. Our system made the whole, complex thing physical and visible – and this was a revelation.

Even people who'd been selling investments, going through the figures with customers for years, were surprised to *see* exactly how much of a dent 2 percent inflation makes over 15 years – and what a colossal improvement it makes, if you increase the amount you save by just 5 percent each year. It was as if a mist had lifted. Later on, when the system went into Nationwide's branches the staff there loved it too: they could now see and understand these mysterious products for themselves, see their relevance, and share their new-found understanding with their customers. They didn't feel like dummies any more.

This simple-looking device seemed to have an unexpectedly empowering effect on Nationwide's people – by turning a largely theoretical product into a physical thing that you could look at, discuss, and play with. It gave them a common focus: they could see what Nationwide actually did.

The catch. The "small team" isn't as small as it looks. It takes time, before you can work that fast

This kind of efficiency doesn't come *simply* by using a small team: its members must be multi-skilled. Chris is a phenomenal programmer; he can write his own low-level graphics routines when he has to; he has also worked on stuff for nuclear power stations – so he knows all about complicated "mission-critical" interfaces. He is also a usability expert, and knows about an enormous range of other things. I can write, draw, do adequate graphics and 2-D animations with reasonable competence. Effectively we were doing the work of five or maybe ten – but with none of the "communication overhead."

But is it really so rare, to have people who can do a lot of different things? Perhaps not. Most of the people in our team had other skills. Some were musicians, all of them could talk and explain things pretty well; some of them painted and took good photographs in their spare time.

Dana Atchley, Lisa Mullen, and Joe Lambert's work at the "Digital Diner" in San Francisco (see www.dstory.com) shows that total amateurs can discover a surprising amount and diversity of talent within themselves when suitably encouraged and supported – and produce very effective work. Not everyone is a great artist or a great programmer – but work does not always need to be great. A "good enough" job is infinitely of more use than no job at all – and if you want things done professionally later on, a rough-but-effective working model makes the professionals' job a lot easier.

Also, the short timescale is a bit misleading: we had already spent a year working together, during which we'd been developing ideas and learning about the Money business. We had also developed a very high degree of mutual trust.

Rapid development is often like that. My classic case (mentioned in my introduction) is the way Alec Issigonis developed the Mini: it took him and a team of eight people just eight months to put the first protoype on the road – but they had already worked together on other cars for several years, and developed strong mutual understanding, trust, and friendship.

It's like growing plants: if the root system is there, the plant will grow rapidly, apparently from nothing.

"Good-enough" can be quite good enough

We'd have liked to do far more – but that is almost the test of a successful project: your head fills with more and yet more great ideas that would make it better and better – and you can see exactly how you would do them.

Nationwide's biggest asset is Nationwide itself – and here, we barely scraped the surface. We learned plenty of fascinating and important things about the Society, its history, and its place in the world. Some of this went into the system, and now it's there to stay, where everyone can see it. Had we been making a brochure or a video it would have become buried again, in the same sea of old information we ourselves had to wade through. It would have been nice to get the whole story in there – it's just as important to the Society's customers as its interest rates, probably more so. As I said, it's a business built more on trust than on facts and figures.

But perfection is a tricky target in this medium. Maybe perfection is a questionable target anyway. With old media, there's always that drive to get things perfect (at least visually) – and it can usually be done. A TV commercial is only so long. A brochure only has so many pages. But the computer-medium has elastic sides. There's no limit to the effort you can pour into it.

It seems we need a way of working out how good "good enough" is. Perhaps Interact has done its best work simply by turning its products into things *all* its staff can understand and talk about – and letting *them* be the "medium."

Notes

1   Thomas Landauer critiques the "Waterfall" at greater length in *The Trouble with Computers*; so does Bruce Tognazzini (*Tog on Interface*).

Section

Working in Cyberia

"Unleash your creativity!"
Copyline on a software box I saw
sticking out of the bin the other day

Introduction:
Do we really *have* to "get real"?

WELL, THAT WAS ALL VERY NICE. I've talked mainly about the kind of work most of us would love to do: work done purely for the love or hell of it, or at least with supportive colleagues and bosses. But most of us spend most our working lives knuckling down and doing "bread and butter" stuff, for money, for busy, anxious, and sometimes downright horrible people. It's supposedly a necessary evil – we must grit our teeth and get on with it. If it helps, we can encourage ourselves with the dream of someday escaping its evil clutches and "doing our own thing."

This distinction between stuff you do for love, and stuff you do for money is a fundamental problem. Why should there be a difference? Life really should not be like that – although one can be accused of being "naive" and "unrealistic" for saying so.

Yet with very few exceptions even the most cold-bloodedly "commercial" project relies, ultimately, on people actually *liking* what you've made. Ultimately, everybody wants "good stuff." Yes, they want to make money – but they'll only get their money if some humble, real-world person actually goes "wow – I like that!" – whether "that" is a CD-ROM like "Lulu" or a life-insurance quotation system or a medical database. Or for that matter a chair, a car, or a carrot. Plus, things that are nice do a much better job than things that are nasty – and it's extremely difficult to make things nice in nasty conditions.

It is all blatantly self-evident. William Morris said it all more than a century ago and legions of management consultants and professors have restated it since then. Yet creative workers of all kinds are put through hell on a regular basis, whatever their status or salary. You can find yourself in a supposedly fabulous job, with good pay, beautiful surroundings, and brilliant colleagues, and having the very worst time of your life. When that happens, you feel extra-specially awful in a way: here you are, one of the lucky few, doing work that everyone says should be "fun" – and hating it.

From a manager's point of view it's often another kind of hell. The more "creative" the job, the harder it is to predict when it will be finished, or what it will be like when it is finished. Cost estimates and delivery dates can slip by an order of magnitude.

What's the problem? There are two sides to this.

First, there's the way creative work is so often managed: on Henry Ford, production-line principles. The job is broken down into well-defined activities, each delegated to a specialist who does that job and nothing else. You are trained and hired to do graphic design or typography or programming. Then you're given one of these "atomized" tasks – and it often seems impossible or nonsensical. The overall aim is to produce something that someone else will find useful, and enjoy using: a requirement that transcends job-titles – only that is not deemed to be any of your business. I shall argue that you must make it your business, for everyone's sake.

A second reason is the way we simply don't talk, or even think, about creativity intelligently. It's widely assumed that there's something "ineffable" about it. Either you've got it, or you haven't – and if you haven't got it you'll never get it, so why talk about it. Or it's a fragile thing that mustn't be looked at too closely in case you kill it (like Erwin Schrödinger's cat – Chapter 2.1). Whatever it is, it's something you simply "unleash" (like it says on the software box). Creative work is seldom easy – but ignorance of the creative process guarantees it will always be difficult.

All of this is a very great shame because creativity is now very much better understood in many quarters than people generally realize. There's a wealth of practical wisdom and even solid, scientific evidence available on the subject – but before I present it to you, I want to give you an example of the traditional, "let's not talk about it" approach in action. There's nothing very unusual about this example, apart from the fact that it was faithfully recorded in full, embarrassing detail.

3.1

Crying all the way to the bank: Microsoft's "Sendak" saga

MICROSOFT PROBABLY SPENT AT LEAST $2.5 MILLION between 1993 and 1995 on "Project Sendak." This was to be a CD-ROM series based on Dorling Kindersley's Children's Encyclopedia, for children aged 7 to 11. No existing CD-ROM encyclopedia catered for this age group and the grand plan was to "capture" the market before anyone else did, and make Microsoft the sole source of "cradle to grave" interactive reference materials. (It was called "Sendak" after Maurice Sendak: the author and illustrator of *Where the Wild Things Are* and *In the Night Kitchen* – although any resemblance to Sendak's work disappeared early on.)

In December 1993, while researching for this book, I paid Microsoft a visit. Tom Corddry, who was then head of consumer multimedia, told me about Sendak and introduced me to several members of the team. I liked them all, they said many things that made sense, the examples I was shown looked delightful, and I looked forward to seeing the finished thing. A year and a half passed. Then in mid-1995, a book appeared entitled *I Sing the Body Electronic*[1] by Fred Moody. Moody, an eminent computer journalist, had spent the whole of 1993 and 1994 with the Sendak team, attending all their meetings and recording everything. His book gave a candid, "fly-on-the-wall" account of the whole Sendak saga, and it revealed that the project had been an absolute vale of tears from start to finish. All the charming people I'd met were in there, having an utterly dreadful time. In fact the day of my visit had been one of their very worst – which just goes to show how good people are at putting a brave face on things.

I imagine Microsoft, and Moody, had hoped that the book would be the 1990s equivalent of Tracy Kidder's *The Soul of a New Machine*.[2] Instead he found himself writing the definitive account of "creative hell." He felt repeatedly that he was *"observing an object lesson in how not to develop a product. … everyone connected with Sendak was so miserable, so angry, and talked so incessantly about frustration and disappointment."* In fact, the whole culture at Microsoft seemed typified by *"endless mistakes in judgement, blind alleys, power struggles, bitter personal battles, hospitalisations from stress, abrupt resignations."*

Absolutely everybody in Moody's account comes across as a victim, with all their enthusiasm beaten out of them. The one who suffered most was Bryan Ballinger, the illustrator whose work inspired the project in the first place, then found himself sidelined – and finally condemned for having a "bad attitude." Ballinger was off ill on the day of my visit.

Moody doesn't claim to be an expert on "the creative process," but a number of things really smacked him in the eye:

- Everybody on the team was young. Few had worked anywhere other than Microsoft, or had much life experience outside Microsoft.

- He was amazed how little they understood or even cared about their "target audience." None of the team knew much about children. Child psychologists and teachers were only involved briefly, long after the project was started, and then their advice was largely ignored. The needs of Microsoft (and especially of the feared, remote Bill Gates) loomed far larger.

- There was no coherent creative team. The lead programmer wasn't involved until the project was well advanced – and even then he didn't work physically alongside the rest of the team. In the crucial early stages there was nobody on the team who knew anything about programming. The vast amounts of text required for the product were farmed out to an unseen army of freelancers.[3] Those lucky enough to work "on site" were divided into warring camps: management (or "suits") and the "creatives."

- The "creatives" were divided into two camps: programmers and "designers" (i.e., graphic designers). Each viewed the other with suspicion. They enjoyed no sense of solidarity or shared purpose.

- None of the team felt it was "their project," or at least not for very long. People who thought they were in charge would find their plans countermanded behind their backs, by distant superiors. Most of the time the project was like a cushion that "gives you the impression of the last person who sat on it."[4]

▪ There was no clear leadership. In an organization like Microsoft a creative team absolutely needs the protection of a good leader. They were effectively working on "the client's" (Microsoft's) territory so they were wide open to intervention at every level. The obvious candidate for this role was Tom Corddry: he seemed to have all the characteristics of a good advertising-agency creative director, and in fact he had been one before Bill Gates hired him – but he was so overburdened with other responsibilities he became almost as distant from the action as Gates himself.

It sounds an extraordinary situation but it's not. I've "been there" myself often enough in the past, and Moody received emails and letters from plenty of other multimedia workers who'd also had exactly the same experiences. In fact, it seems they are much more likely to be the norm than the exception.

The really unusual thing about the "Sendak" episode is that it got documented in detail, while it happened, by one of the best writers in the business – and published. (Bill Gates had personally signed a release, allowing Moody to publish everything. "*It hangs on my wall to this day, the most valuable autograph I own,*" says Moody [private email to the author].) Episodes like these are usually buried quietly, and only resurface as anecdotes, told around the bar by case-hardened veterans, and in the statistics for work-induced stress.[5]

But what was the outcome? Who won? Was all the suffering worth it in the end? Is this creative life just, basically, hard?

I phoned Computer Warehouse for a copy of "Explorapedia" and when it arrived my dismay was complete. It was one of the most dispiriting multimedia experiences I'd ever seen – the more so because I'd met, and liked, some of the people involved. But was that just my own, quirky reaction? What did the market make of Explorapedia?

As he finished the book, Moody still couldn't quite believe the evidence of his own eyes and ears. Perhaps, he thought, "Sendak" was really a triumph and the apparent grief and lunacy were just manifestations of some higher wisdom that he, an outsider, was bound not to understand. It was certainly true that great technical problems were tackled and beaten, and the product went "out the door" pretty much on time. So you could conclude that grief comes with the job: no pain, no gain. You trade creative control and personal happiness for money, and the glory of "having been there."

It's a highly credible analysis: a lot of creative work seems to get done that way. Film, television, theater, advertising, engineering ... creative industries regularly devour their creators.[6] Some veterans of those industries wear their divorces and alcoholism with pride, as old soldiers wear their scars.

And it's an easy idea to sell. These episodes have a "rite-of-passage" quality about them. The new wave of "creatives" who come to work in multimedia are young, inexperienced, and easily persuaded that "this is how it has to be." The persuaders are very convincing: they are older, they look "successful," they control companies, they have made money, so it seems they must be right. But the dénouement to this sorry tale shows that they are not necessarily right.

Explorapedia was a flop.[7] Two years on, Fred Moody reckoned the first disk (of a proposed four-disk series) sold 50,000 copies in its launch year. Assuming Microsoft received $40 for each copy sold (unlikely) that would give a return of $2 million – not enough to cover development costs. Explorapedia was intended to produce $8.9 million in the first year, rising to $20.6 million in 1997. The second disk did even worse: selling something like 20,000 copies. Disks 3 and 4 were formally canceled in mid-1996. Fred comments: "It was no Encarta, that's for sure."

So: is there a better way to do things? Yes there is.

Voyager, Living Books, Corbis, Brøderbund – most successful producers in fact – do things very differently. Microsoft itself can do things differently – at least, with some of their applications software packages (e.g., their award-winning C++[8]).

There is no shortage of information about better methods. There is even a vast "management guru" industry that promotes them (see Tom Peters' *The Pursuit of Excellence*, etc. and the meters of shelfspace devoted to that kind of book in your bookstore). Every year this industry sells millions of dollars'-worth of books and courses to industry. Microsoft, I presume, is a regular customer.

With so much knowledge and wisdom available, why do "Sendak sagas" persist?

Perhaps the problem is that the "Henry Ford regime" perpetuates itself, despite management's best intentions, through "management culture" itself – which promotes the perception that people cannot manage themselves. It separates the people who do the work from the people who make the decisions, and turns both camps into parodies of themselves. Otherwise decent useful people are removed from the task they know, put into suits, sent on courses, and told they're responsible for the work you do. They're bound to feel insecure and behave strangely: the only person who can possibly be responsible for the work you do, is you.

Insecure managers become obsessed with control, and turn into "suits." "Creatives" respond in a variety of ways: some become despondent and introverted, perpetuating the myth that creative people are like that. Others respond by making a virtue of their lack of responsibility: the fluffy/anarchic creative stereotype. In no time at all you have two tribes that even have completely different languages and dress-codes, and share nothing but fear and anger. It's no wonder our world is so full of what Donald Norman calls "psychotic artifacts."

So is there a way of getting rid of these silly, tribal divisions? There is, and it's right there in the management literature under "personal empowerment": one of its major themes. But you mustn't wait for managers to empower you – they're too busy and insecure already. The best approach is quietly to empower yourself. But before you can do that, you need to understand what you're doing – which is a surprisingly novel thing to do.

Peasants rarely intellectualize what they do, they just do it – and then succumb to the same fate as today's overstressed "microserfs": bossed about from pillar to post by the people who have nothing to do *but* intellectualize the world – which they inevitably do in the simplistic way of people who don't make anything themselves.

Notes

1 *I Sing The Body Electronic – A Year With Microsoft On The Multimedia Frontier*, Viking Penguin, 1995, ISBN 0-340-58652-4.

2 Tracy Kidder's *The Soul of a New Machine* describes the building, in 1980, of one of the first 32-bit "super-mini" computers: Data General's Super Eclipse. Here, too, a (mainly) young team was handed an almost unbeatable problem to solve, against a seemingly impossible deadline, and suffered mightily. They, however, succeeded. Highly recommended reading and fascinating to compare with Fred Moody's account.

3 Typical of these (although he didn't work on this particular title) was Paul Roberts – author of a savagely entertaining piece called "The Future of Writing" (*Independent on Sunday*, 29 September 1996 – but first published in *Harper's Magazine*). In his account, there is in and around Seattle an extensive archipelago of electronic hacks, making silly money writing 60 100-word gobbits a week on every subject under the sun for "edutainment" CD-ROM titles – and hating it. "Multimedia is the epitome of corporate production, of breaking projects into elements and doling them out. As such, the average writer is effectively, if not intentionally, sealed off from the larger narrative, and quickly learns not even to think about how the texts will be used or where the writing is going, because it doesn't matter."

4 The simile is borrowed from the British Liberal prime minister David Lloyd-George's description of his aristocratic Tory opponent Lord Derby.

5   For example, see the statistics in Juliet Schor's best-selling *The Overworked American* (Basic Books, 1992) and the late Andrea Adams's *Bullying at Work* (Virago, 1992). In Britain alone, 270,000 people take time off work every day because of stress-related mental illness (Health Education Authority, 1995).

6   Fred wrote to me: "When I finished writing this book, I read a biography of Faulkner and was stunned to see nearly identical scenes in Faulkner's experiences in Hollywood. I think that problem remains the rule in the movie business to this day ... has gotten worse, in fact. And I do hear a lot from people that the Sendak experience is "their" experience as well – particularly in the software industry."

7   The figures given here are Fred's own informed estimates, which he kindly sent to me in July 1997.

8   One of the very best books on "the creative process" is by the man who led the C++ project, Jim McCarthy: *The Dynamics of Software Development*, Microsoft Press, 1995, ISBN 1-555615-823-8.

3.2

Get yourself a theory, and make it a good one

❝In my view creative individuals possess no extraordinary characteristics –
basically they do what we are all capable of doing❞

Robert Weisberg: *Creativity: Genius and Other Myths*

A "THEORY OF CREATIVITY" is no idle luxury – it's a "survival essential."
Why? First: theorizing is fun, and fun is essential to sanity. Second: good
theories simplify complicated things – and this is a very complicated business indeed, where we need every shred of simplicity we can find. Third:
everyone else has a theory anyway – and they'll use it to define your job
for you, unless you can come back at them with something more convincing. Moreover, their theories are diverse and contradictory.

Here are some of the more popular "theories of creativity" you'll run into,
if you haven't run into them already:

▦ The most popular notion is that creativity = decoration; it is something
you sprinkle onto the product like fairy-dust, after the hairy-handed
ones have done the "real work."

▦ Running a close second comes the idea that creativity is the quick
"flash of inspiration" that (allegedly) produced Coleridge's poem
Kubla Khan. Somebody has a great idea, then it is simply a matter of
"knocking it into shape" – a mechanical business that can be delegated
to the workers.

▦ Then there is the notion that there are different kinds of creativity, such
as computer programming, knitting, writing, graphic design, fine art,
and corn-dolly making. Entrepreneurs look at their proposed project
and make shopping lists of the creative specialists they think they will
need: a few animators, a couple of graphic designers, a writer, etc. and
give each one responsibility for some small part of the title.

▨ Then there's the notion that some tasks are not creative at all. Some people put programming and researching into that category. They think those jobs should be delegated to unquestioning, efficient employees, who do not need to know, and should not even want to know, the "big picture."

▨ This goes with the notion that "the creative bit" is different from other work, and "creatives" are different from other workers. They are more temperamental, less practical, mysterious, unreliable, etc. Therefore they can be treated like children (although you shouldn't treat children "like children" either).

▨ Finally, and flatly contradicting all the ideas above, there's a widespread belief that "we're all creative." The most macho manager will assert this, and exercise his "right" to have a creative idea once in a while, and use his (almost always "his") managerial power to enforce its adoption, whatever the consequences. If it ends in tears the explanation is simple: the minions are stupid.

There are grains of truth in all these ideas, so there is plenty of scope for creatives to be piggy-in-the-middle, unless they have a really strong theory of their own, which encompasses all of them. So here's what I believe to be the best, most solid general theory of creativity available. It fits in with my own and other creative workers' experience "at the coalface" and most of it is underpinned by very good, thorough research.

The ground rules: everyone's creative; everyone's creativity is different; "creativity in a medium" is *very* different

It starts with three basic ideas.

Creativity is universal – but you're most creative at what you do most

Robert Weisberg (in a book called *Creativity – Beyond the Myth of Genius*[1]) shows that creativity is not a rare, elite activity but much more widespread: it's what everyone uses, all the time, to make sense of the non-stop flow of experiences we encounter in life.

Weisberg drew together a mass of research and experimental data covering numerous aspects of creativity: in science, art, music, chess-playing, writing, etc. He found that it contradicts almost all "accepted wisdom" on the subject. For example: the idea that people always work best in teams (when the proposition is actually tested, it turns out they often work better on their own); the value of "lateral thinking"[2] and "brainstorming,"[3] and the notion that great ideas "come in a flash" (as in *Kubla Khan*: it seems Coleridge made that one up. Also, the "fact" that Mozart wrote his greatest music straight out as clean, uncorrected first drafts turns out to be false).

Weisberg supports the idea of "everybody being creative" – so, he asks, "why can't we all write great poems?" The evidence is: good poets are good mainly because they spend their lives writing poems; the rest of us don't. Of course, you can spend your life writing poetry and never achieve greatness – but that doesn't disprove the rule. It's like winning a lottery: not everybody wins, but nobody ever wins without buying a ticket first.

This seems to bring most of the argument over creative judgment down to a more solid and sensible level. If you are a programmer or a graphic designer, you have probably spent much of your life programming or designing. Yes, the boss is creative too and, yes, he can have opinions and feelings – but he may not have spent his whole life doing what you do. You're entitled to claim credit for that.

Everybody's creativity is different

People's brains have increasingly well-understood features that deal with vision, language, spatial awareness, emotion, face-recognition, and a thousand other things – and there is great diversity in the way these areas develop between individuals. Even identical twins' brains have differences – due to the different ways they fold into bulges and valleys ("gyri" and "sulci") as they grow. Nowadays one can even see some of these brain areas at work, via new kinds of brain scan.

The American neurologist Howard Gardner proposed in 1983[4] that we all have "modular minds" and "multiple intelligences" ("logical/mathematical," linguistic, musical, etc.). Some modules are better endowed with brain material in some people than in others. For strong evolutionary reasons, most people have very good "linguistic intelligence": we take to language like ducks to water. The baseline for linguistic intelligence in people is around the "genius" level. Some people's musical, mathematical, or "bodily-kinaesthetic" intelligence is similarly well endowed – we call them "natural" musicians, mathematicians, tennis-players, etc. Naturally, they tend to spend lots of time on these activities (they enjoy them!) which fits with Weisberg's observations. But just as "wild children" who spend infancy deprived of language never acquire it properly, so "natural" musicians, mathematicians, and athletes can be prevented from realizing their potential – or even that they have it.

The enormous diversity in brains means we all notice, understand, and do some things more easily than others – and in different ways from other people. Diversity gives us so many differences – and therefore so many potential areas of excellence – that we probably aren't even aware of most of them.

The underlying, shared set of "brain modules" lets us appreciate other people's insights, peculiarities, and precocious skills – and emulate them by hard work. As we do this, our own brain peculiarities can shed yet more new light on the subject.

The diversity of brains means there can be no "correct" way to understand anything (although we do, collectively, develop a common view of the subject, and its general rules).

We have to watch for our own – and other people's – unique abilities and insights. Everybody really does have something to offer – but it physically cannot be precisely the contribution we expect. If we try to prescribe the precise kind of "creativity" we need for a particular job, we will not find it – and miss the outrageous wealth of talent that's right under our noses.

It takes special skill to be "creative in a medium"

I mentioned the strange, and revolutionary, phenomenon of "media" at the beginning of this book. Using media is where most would-be "creatives" come unstuck: not because they're not creative, but because they don't really understand what a "medium" is, or does.

This isn't surprising because few people had realized what "media" were, until Marshall McLuhan made the word famous in 1964.[5] Many people find McLuhan's work stronger on enthusiastic assertion than scholarship, but he did us all a huge service by drawing attention to the fact that we're surrounded by things other people have made – and that these things radiate messages from their makers at us 24 hours a day, whether the makers intended that or not: "*Every human artifact is a 'medium' of human communication.*" (*Understanding Media*)

"Media" obviously includes such things as books, films, and computers. Less obviously, it includes things like buildings, lunchboxes, doorknobs, and your computer's case and keyboard. Each of those things does far more than just "do a job" (and this is reflected in the price). It also advertises its purpose in subtle, elegant ways. It also speaks volumes about the person or people who made it (we'll talk about that later).

To summarize:

- A "medium" is some physical thing which you manipulate, so as to create a message that can be "read" by another person, at some other place and time.

The "message in a bottle" analogy   Using a medium is rather like putting a distress-message into a bottle, as opposed to jumping up and down on the shore and shouting "help, help!" at passing ships. Vital information that's self-evident when you stand on the shore will not be evident from your message, unless you explicitly put it there. Just writing "help, help!" on a piece of paper won't do. You also need to tell the finder where you are, and convey the urgency of your situation. If you're really "creative," you'll also give the finder a vivid (and appealing) picture of who you are and why you're worth rescuing, and you'll express all this so as to engage their emotions as well as their reasoning mind.

- A medium is quite different from its message – and this brings "constraints" into the picture: every medium has inclinations of its own (sticks are inclined to split, clay is inclined to flow, computers are inclined to give yes/no answers). You have to find some way of getting the message across in spite of the medium's inclinations – and preferably of turning them to your advantage.

- Communicating via a medium is very different from communicating face to face. It seems to take a different kind of creativity: stand-up comics don't automatically make great comedy writers; great actors aren't always great film directors, and vice versa. The problem is: you're trying to influence another human being who isn't standing there in front of you and whom you may in fact never see.

- Media are pervasive – cities are made almost entirely of "media" – but that doesn't mean they're instinctive or easy to use. Electricity is pervasive too, but that doesn't make us all Faradays and Maxwells.

So is this kind of creativity something that relatively few people have?

Maybe and maybe not. Maybe it requires a particularly well-endowed "media module" in the brain (bringing Gardner's "module count" to 9 or 10) – but whether it does or it doesn't, it's something you can only be good at if you do it a lot. And whether you do it a lot or a little, you need to know how this kind of creativity works if you're going to be an effective part of a multimedia development team.

Notes

1 *Creativity: beyond the myth of genius* (1992) is an expanded version of Weisberg's earlier work, *Creativity: Genius and other myths* (1986).

2 "Lateral thinking" was made famous by Edward DeBono (in *New Think*, Basic Books, 1968). The idea is that you have to "break free" from old habits of thought (especially rational thought) and allow the non-rational part of the brain to take charge. A whole "creative training industry" was founded on this idea from the 1960s onwards.

3   Brainstorming was the brainchild of Alex Osborn (the "O" in the advertising agency BBD&O) and it was sold with "patriotic fervor" to big business in the 1950s. Weisberg shows that it was never tested "head-to-head" against other methods – and when such tests were finally carried out, they showed that the old-fashioned method of sitting and thinking by yourself got better results. Like lateral thinking, brainstorming is no holy grail – but if you accept that, it can be a helpful tool: see Victor Papanek's experience of using the method in *Design for the Real World* (1992).

4   See "Frames of Mind – the Theory of Multiple Intelligences." Gardner's work inspired Steven Mithen's account of brain evolution (referred to in the Introduction). He believes we have eight (but perhaps nine) distinct "intelligences": logical-mathematical, linguistic, musical, spatial, bodily-kinaesthetic, interpersonal, intrapersonal, "naturalist" – and possibly "existential" intelligence as well (highly developed in religious and philosophical thinkers).

5   Marshall McLuhan's books include *The Gutenberg Galaxy* (1962), *Understanding Media* (1964), and *The Medium is the Message* (1967) – all re-released in 1997 by Penguin, in conjunction with *Wired Magazine*. McLuhan's central argument is that "media change us" – and this is nothing like as self-evident as he makes out. A better case, I think, for the radical nature of "media" is made by a Jesuit professor from Missouri, Walter J. Ong, in *Orality and Literacy – The Technologizing of the Word* (London: Methuen, 1982). Another highly readable source on the world of man-made things, and the things they say, is Umberto Eco's *Travels in Hyperreality*.

3.3

Audience: Who are you making this for – *and where are you taking them*?

> **❝**While you are designing a program, continually remind yourself that you are designing for an audience. Think about them, think about their problems, and concentrate on how you're going to communicate your ideas to them**❞**

> Bruce Tognazzini: *Tog on Interface*

IT IS ALL ABOUT GETTING PEOPLE from A to B via the most efficient route.

"A" is where they are now (the kitchen, the sofa, a blazing building, or the "styles" dialog of Quark Xpress). "B" is somewhere they might like to be (the fire-escape, or the resolution of some real or fictional mystery). The route can be as short as hitting the emergency handle, or as long as *War and Peace* or the Mahabarata. It must get them to "B" before they're burned alive or bored to death.

All media-users start at some particular "A." Old media give them only one "B" and only one route to it – but the media-makers still mess up more often than not (usually because they become so entranced by their one particular kind of route-building that it becomes an end in itself). Computer media can offer enormous numbers of "Bs," and even more enormous numbers of routes to them. The problem looks intractable and usually is … *if* you insist on looking at the problem instead of the people.

The answer is what writers and performers call "paying attention to your audience," and software designers call "user focus" or "user-oriented design."

The computer has made "user focus" a life-and-death issue

As a medium, the computer often carries far more responsibility than, for example, a book can ever carry. Computer displays are used in aircraft cockpits, air-traffic control rooms, in the control rooms of nuclear power stations, and in systems where the user's allowed to part with hard cash, there and then, online.

If a novel's "user focus" is wrong, the author just goes back to the garret and carries on starving. If it's wrong in a flight-control system, people die. Hence, whole university departments and companies are now devoted to the subject, under the banner of Human–Computer Interaction (HCI).

HCI sources   I've already mentioned the doyen of HCI, Donald Norman. Another excellent authority is Harold Thimbleby. His book *User Interface Design* is rather more challenging reading than Norman's but I find it hugely rewarding. Also, if you can, try to get to one of the annual CHI conferences, run by the Association for Computing Machinery (the ACM: http://acm.org/).

The HCI community has produced no end of good guidelines and techniques for testing "user focus" – however, one very interesting thing, for me, is the way they endorse things that artists, authors, and other "media creatives" say about their work. These have a very intuitive feel, and I've based this chapter on them.

Lessons from Adland

Advertising has more in common with the new computer-medium than you might think. If the thought appalls you, remember that in the past, new media have not always built their greatest successes on the best of the old media, but on its trash. The first novelists didn't take the Bible and work on from there. Insofar as they drew their inspiration from other media at all, it was from scandal-sheets, almanacks, and unscholarly, sensationalistic travelers' yarns: the ephemeral street-trash of the day. Film owes less to Shakespearean drama than to vaudeville.

First, an important truth about advertising: the best things don't need it.

The best things are their own advertisements

The British retail chain Marks & Spencer (mentioned in Chapter 2.3) hardly spends anything on advertising. Its "body language," the quality of its merchandise, and its reputation say everything that's necessary. This built-in language is the property of every M&S employee and item of merchandise – not the creation of some bunch of hired "experts." You get the message constantly as you walk around the stores, handle things, buy things, and ask questions of the staff. A 72-sheet poster or TV campaign would be a waste of money: pushing on a wide-open door.

You can call this "intrinsic advertising" – and it's everyone's favorite kind (except the advertising agencies').

The best computer creations are "M&S-like" in that they, too, explain themselves, and the values of their creators, without needing additional explanation.

That said, "intrinsic advertising" follows all the same rules as "extrinsic" advertising (the stuff you see on posters and TV).

Advertising is "multilinear"

Advertising (considered as a "medium" in itself) is much less linear than other old-established media. An advertising campaign can't presuppose a passive, attentive audience that sits down and follows the whole thing from start to finish – the way they do a book or a movie. It's something we dip into, the same way we dip into websites – not necessarily at the beginning, and not necessarily for very long. People may only see the last commercial in the series, or only see the point-of-sale materials. They almost certainly *won't* read every single word of an ad.: they'll "skim" it, reading a bit here, a bit there. But however much or little they see, they need to get the whole story every time, even if only in a short, potted form.

The story has to make sense to us at whatever point we join it, however little time we can spare, and if we *can* spare the time, it must be capable of development over any length required – and in any number of ways.

Advertising has developed ways of telling stories multi-directionally. The sub-head, the star-burst, the multi-part mailshot, the campaign that works in everything from a 30-second TV commercial, to a 48-sheet poster, to a 24-page brochure, to a beermat. These forms prefigure computer media by giving us lots of routes into the same story, and allowing *us* to decide how long we'll spend there.

Veterans of advertising often say that doing ads is like taking your audience on a journey. Each time, it's a slightly different journey – but it's always through the *same landscape*. One may conclude from this that the *landscape*, in fact, is the story – not the particular path that you take through it. There are lots of "paths through Adland" – just as there are through Cyberia.

How (some) people stay sane in Adland

A lot of advertising people do not stay sane – but those who do often gain some very good insights.

Like many people, advertising workers often have to do things for which they've no natural enthusiasm, for people they'd never want to be seen dead with. They have to do this over and over again, to deadlines, with lead-times that can range from a few days to a few months, with almost any size of budget, for the whole range of anxious, self-important, devious, uncomprehending people one finds in life: the perfect formula for "creative hell" and "suit wars" on the grand scale.

Advertising is a precarious business that just can't afford foul-ups so, from sheer necessity, it has found ways of containing the pressure and even, for a small but reliable fraction of the time, producing things that are quite good. (If you want to follow this up, treat yourself to some of the excellent books on creativity that have been written by ad-men.[1])

The brief. If you haven't got one, invent one

Advertising life revolves around "the brief." It may not be great, but at least it is always there. In other walks of life, people are often asked to start work with no brief at all. There's an assumption that "we all know what we're supposed to be doing so just get on with it." Later, it always emerges that our ideas were all rather different – so work has to be scrapped, time is lost, money wasted, and everyone's unhappy.

If nobody has given you a brief, write your own, then make sure everyone else reads it. This will reveal any misconceptions early on. If they don't read it, and raise objections when they see the work, they're the ones who'll have to explain themselves, not you.

A basic brief tells you five things:

▦ Who your audience is.

▦ What you are promising them.

▦ What you want them to do about it.

▦ The "one great thing" or "singleminded proposition": the message that will make them sit up and go "Wow!"

▦ What your constraints are (i.e., how much time and money you've got, and what media).

What differentiates good briefs from woolly ones is "focus." It gives you the best chance of doing the job well (and profitably) if you get it, and an important feeling of virtue if you don't.

Mrs. Herbert's website   A colleague and I were asked to quote for producing a website for a company that produces freeze-dried herbs and spices: Herbert's Herbs. (Not its real name.)

Their brief to us was "put us on the Web": this is not untypical. They had some ideas: nice color pictures of all their 287 products, recipes, a "virtual tour" of their factory, and the company's history. When we asked "who is this for?" (define the audience) they said "for Mrs. Herbert – she's seen Bonko Herbs' website and wants one too."

The five-item brief was quite an exciting novelty for them and they were really impressed. We agreed that the "audience" should be professional chefs – the most lucrative market. They're busy people so we would promise them easy ordering and scheduled doorstep delivery so that they'd never run out of things, plus a monthly special offer (e.g., fresh saffron direct from La Mancha every April), and an online newsletter, relevant to chefs, which would be delivered to them by email. We would want them (a) to register for the newsletter online (capturing their details for future automatic mailings) and (b) to buy stuff – by email or online, preferably using an online checklist to make a "standing order" for regularly used items. The "One Great Thing" would be something like "that's all my herbs and spices taken care of for good!"

Item 5 of the brief was the killer, of course: the constraints – notably the budget. They wanted to spend just £10,000 (about $15,000).[2] You can make quite a lot of colorful web-pages for that amount of money but it was barely enough to set up a long-term operation, which is what our proposal entailed, even on a shoestring. Another constraint worked in our favor: the medium's limitations. At that time (early 1997) most people in the UK still had slower (14,400k) Internet connections that didn't cope well with "graphically rich" websites like they'd asked for. Our proposal (to use email as the main means of communication) would work just fine with slow modems – as well as creating a regular channel of communication: a long-term relationship between Herbert's and their customers.

Our proposal "won on points" – we got a long letter of appreciation – but they decided to give Mrs. Herbert what she wanted anyway. Ho hum. But so far (December 1998) no website has appeared.

> Without a good brief, the tendency is to produce something "generic" (a website that looks like the last website you saw and liked – whether appropriate or not). As soon as you get specific, the job starts to define itself and acquire a character all its own. Furthermore, you've reduced the scope for misunderstandings with the client, and between the members of the team. You can go through these five stages with any kind of project.
>
> Finally, I should add that there's no single "right answer" to any brief. As I said above, the analogy is exploring a landscape: there can be infinitely many ways across it and you can never be totally sure you've chosen the best one. The important thing is to get across. The brief identifies landmarks that help you do that.

The JWT-square: a device for losing yourself and becoming your audience

It is not enough merely to know who your audience is. You don't start getting useful ideas until you find yourself looking at the world through their eyes and empathizing with them. There's a knack to doing this – like riding a bike. Advertising people can take years to master it – but this idea may help you get the hang of it sooner than you otherwise might.

The "T-square" is a very simple, back-of-an-envelope idea I discovered when I worked at the J. Walter Thompson advertising agency (JWT). I believe it was first described by James Webb Young, JWT's creative chief, in Chicago, during the 1920s. Young wrote the *Technique for Producing Ideas*, of which more below.

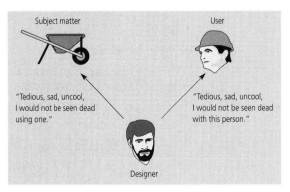

The "V-sign": how *not* to look at your audience or subject matter

The T-Square has three components: you (the creative person), your audience, and the thing you are offering to that audience. At first, it looks like this – a letter V, known as "the V sign":

You look at your subject matter (or the product you've been asked to sell) and maybe you find it boring. You look at the audience, and they fill you with disgust: you have nothing at all in common with them. You conclude that you have been given a lousy job. These reactions are no use at all to the creative process; to be a professional you must learn to shed them as effortlessly as you shed your coat the moment you arrive at your desk.

As a professional, you're interested in the *relationship* between your audience and the "product".

What it boils down to is "promise": what the subject matter is offering, and to whom. Your job is to make that promise crystal clear: not just logically, but emotionally and, ideally, in a physical way too.

The "T-Plan." You become interested in the way the audience relates to the subject.

An aside about physical communication.   This is where electronic media should be walking all over all other media. In advertising, it has always been difficult to get physical interaction going – yet that's the aim. Ads urge you to test-drive the car, often with a special offer, or "try this in your own home without obligation." Ads that carry actual, physical free samples always seem to outperform other ads – however cleverly written or beautifully illustrated.

It's well known that neither *telling* people things nor showing them things is anywhere near as effective as *letting them try things for themselves*. There are well-understood reasons for this – which I'll explain in the next chapter.

On the computer, you can offer far more physical interaction than you can with a page of print or a 30-second TV commercial – but most Web design still seems to be based on an assumption that printed ads and brochures are the acme of effective communication. Good admen know that they are nothing of the sort – just the best they can manage with the media they've got.
This is not to say that any old physical interaction will do. It has to be relevant.

> Whatever you create, it must be a "lightning rod" between the subject matter and its user, carrying its promise straight to their hearts. I believe this principle holds good for all kinds of creative workers, from the most abstract painter, to the engineer designing a car radio, to someone who "designs" a good party for their friends, to someone who designs on-screen buttons.
>
> It is the art of being in three places at once: in the audience's head, inside the "product," and at your desk.
>
> ### *"Physical thinking"*
> You can't do this kind of thing solely from your desk. Least of all if it's a nice tidy one, in some squeaky-clean corporate HQ. When I worked in advertising, my art director and I would always try to get into the audience's shoes, almost literally. We would buy, and read, the papers and magazines they bought, watch the TV programs they watched. As an absolute minimum, we would walk around the shops where the products were bought, try them out, study the people who bought them, and try to see them through their eyes. Many managers hated us doing this: we were not at our desks, "working," but it always paid off. After these outings there was never any question of mental block – ideas would come thick and fast, and they'd be neater, more surprising, and also more "do-able" than the ones we'd had while simply sitting at our desks.
>
> After all – why pummel your brains trying to imagine a situation, when you can just walk out onto the street and experience it?
>
> ### *John Cato's "Active Visualization" technique*
> John Cato (Chapter 2.5) has formalized this "walking about" technique with the "active visualization" workshops he runs for big business. Managers, programmers, and secretaries work together as equals in these exercises.

He gets everybody involved in the project into a comfortable room, and asks them to share and discuss everything they know about their customers. Then he asks them to *become* those customers. They think themselves into a particular imaginary customer's shoes: age, sex, job, family, interests, everything. Having done this, John asks them to ask themselves "what would I really, really like, when I walk into one of our branches?." (Or pick up one of our products, or whatever.) The answers always contain surprises. Then he asks them to go into one of their own branches, and competitors' branches, to make a specific enquiry as if they were customers. Even bigger surprises follow and it nearly always turns out that the original project brief can be improved.

James Webb Young's "Technique for Producing Ideas"

Once you've got your brief, the brain-pummeling starts. Whether you have a whole application to design, or just a code module, there's a strong urge to go about it in the same way: get stuck in and keep going till you've finished. A simple technique can make the work more fun – and get better results.

Paul Arden – the brilliant Saatchi & Saatchi art director – was once asked "where do you get your ideas?" He replied "Ah. I have a little book." The book was James Webb Young's *A Technique for Producing Ideas* – and it really is a little book: A5 format, and just 62 pages, in big type. Webb wrote it originally as a lecture for the Chicago University Business School.[3]

Young's "technique" comes in fact from two famous mathematicians (Henri Poincaré and Jacques Hadamard) via the English philospher and educationist Graham Wallas. Young's version is, however, nicely succinct. Briefly, he says that there are five distinct stages to getting an idea:

1 **"Browsing."** You submerge yourself in the detail of the subject you're dealing with, with no attempt to form it into any kind of story. This is the first hurdle at which most projects fail. Young says: "*Gathering raw material ... is such a terrible chore that we are constantly trying to dodge it. The time that ought to be spent in material gathering is spent in wool gathering. Instead of working systematically at the job of gathering raw material we sit around hoping for inspiration to strike us. When we do that we are trying to get the mind to take the fourth step in the idea-producing process while we dodge the preceding steps.*" Remember the importance of "physical thinking": find, and handle if possible, the actual things you're talking about, go to the places where they are used, go and talk to people who know about them – on their territory, not yours: people's environments are rich in information.

2 **"Chewing it over**." You try to wrestle this material into some kind of an answer. You search for patterns, trying one piece of information against another. Young observes that: "*you feel the information all over, as it were, with the tentacles of your mind.*" You jot down any ideas that come to you – however weird or embarassingly weak they may seem. Eventually, you reach a brick wall (but this is where professionalism comes in: like the long-distance runner, the professional creative keeps on going till he or she really hits the wall).

3 **"Incubation**." You walk away from it and do something else entirely, to give your unconscious mind a chance to do its stuff. Preferably (and this is interesting) do something that will stimulate your emotions. His exemplar is Sherlock Holmes, who would drag Watson off to a concert, just when the case seemed to be most in need of decisive action.

4 **"Illumination**," or the "bolt from the blue." You come back to your desk and the idea hits you, "out of nowhere." As long as you've faithfully performed the preceding three tasks to the best of your ability, this will happen.

5 **"Verification**." "*In this stage,*" says Young, "*you have to take your little new-born idea out into the world of reality.*" You have to show it to people. Often, you find that it isn't as great as you thought, but other times, "*a surprising thing will happen. You will find that a good idea has, as it were, self-expanding qualities. It stimulates those who see it to add to it. Thus possibilities in it which you have overlooked will come to light.*"

Now, what does all of this mean for your working practice in new media? Is it as useful for programmers and animators as it is for advertising copywriters and art directors? Programmers who have tried it say it is. It helps you divide a job into stages in a way that (a) reduces the sense of pressure, and (b) seems to gets better results. The technique is "scalable": I have found that you can divide a one-day job this way, as effectively as you can a one-month job. If you have a tricky-looking problem dumped on your desk to be completed by the end of the day, it is beneficial to feel you don't have go into brain-pummeling mode right away – and that it will be better if you don't.

On a longer project, you may have to renegotiate "milestones" to accommodate the process – especially the "browsing" and "incubation" stages. It's not uncommon for clients and managers to ask you to "come up with concepts" in a couple of days – although the total duration of the project may run to six months or a year. They fall, as so often, into the mistake of thinking that because ideas "come in a flash," you don't need any time to produce them. Poincaré (one of Young's sources) puts it well: "*sudden illumination [is] a man's first sign of long, unconscious prior work.*"

You have to apportion time for each stage of the process. The "five stages" can't be skipped, but as I've said, they are also "scalable" to fit into any time-frame. So, if you really do have just one day in which to get your idea, then it's a good idea to apportion exactly the same proportions of your day to browsing, "chewing it over," and incubation, and make a firm appointment with your subconscious mind that the "lightbulb over your head" will come on just after lunch.

When you break the vague, mystical idea-getting process down into these stages, you remove a lot of the anxiety that gets in the way of getting good ideas. You spare yourself the rod of expecting to get a "great idea" in the first five minutes. And you benefit from "full-bandwidth" data-gathering.

The "Procedure" also exposes two common errors:

Some fallacies that the five-stage technique exposes

- **The "test-from-the-word-go" fallacy**. User-testing is absolutely vital in computer work, but the "testing it on other people" stage is Stage 5 – not Stage 1 or Stage 2. Yet some software professionals believe you should start testing from the word go, and "iterate" your way to a successful product. The technique is called "iterative design" or "rapid, iterative production prototyping" (RIPP) – and it's basically a good one: by getting the product in front of people early on, you expose flaws in the system before they become a problem – and learn extra things about users' needs while you still have time to make changes. So testing should, indeed, start early on – but not before you've created something *worth* testing. *No amount of "iteration" will turn a cardboard box into the Taj Mahal.*

- **The "give us a dozen really quick ideas for tomorrow, and we'll all thrash them around" fallacy**. This comes of the belief that ideas come quickly – and from excessive faith in the power of "brainstorming." By all means have brainstorm-sessions – they're fun, which is good – but use the session's output as "input" for the creative process proper. Don't let yourself be too tightly bound by the results.

With brainstorming, quantity of ideas is held to be better than going for a few quality ideas – but Robert Weisberg's sources (see above) found that this simply isn't proven.

Don't agree to deliver ideas too quickly – unless the project timescale really is a short one. Most of the ideas will be non-starters. The "Church of Lateral Thinking" says that doesn't matter: bad ideas can trigger good ones – but again, the research doesn't bear this out. And what's worse, the client or manager may "buy" your weakest idea – and then you'll have to implement it. Try to avoid dumping a sheaf of half-baked sketches on the boardroom table, and letting the management or client finalize the design in a one-hour "pick'n'mix" session. As they swan off to their next meeting, you'll be left with a mare's nest of inconsistencies that no amount of fretting will resolve.

You may sense a hint of creative, deliberate uncooperativeness here, but if you're not prepared to defend your own "creative space" nobody else will do it for you. At the end of the day, what managers, clients, and everyone else wants from you is some magic: a vision: a great idea that the users will love, that their bosses will love, that will win awards, and that the rest of team will love at first sight, be proud to work on, and bust a gut to deliver. For that, a little firmness is a very small price to pay.

Some good general rules

If you aim to please everybody, you'll please nobody (the "Beatrix Potter Paradox")

In advertising I discovered that if you try to aim your message at "everyone" you'll fail, whereas if you are brave enough to aim it at a single (hopefully representative but inevitably idiosyncratic) individual, then you may, paradoxically, set the whole world alight.

The classic example is Beatrix Potter, who wrote *Peter Rabbit* for Noel Moore, the young son of a friend.[4] She had no idea of offering it to the world, let alone publishing it in 83 languages, turning it into a film, a ballet, and a multi-million-dollar merchandising operation.

Likewise, in 1963, Larry Roberts designed the Internet mainly for himself, his friends, and academic colleagues, whose needs and tastes he knew well: a community of a hundred at most. Ditto, Tim Berners-Lee, who designed the Web around his own and his colleagues' needs at Cern. Ditto, Romain Victor-Pujebet, who designed "Le Livre de Lulu" for his daughter Lola.

Even if you are already in the mass-market business (in fact, especially then) it is vital to focus on the particular needs of particular people. That is, in fact, how Henry Ford arrived at the design of the Model-T, and how the Japanese carmakers (especially Honda and Nissan) invaded the world's markets in the 1970s and have held them ever since.[5]

And anyway, nobody ever needs to reach "everyone in the world." One percent can make you quite adequately rich.

Finally, you'll find that the work and ideas come far more easily as soon as you start to visualize a real, live person for whom you're doing all this. The idiosyncrasies, tastes, and fears of that individual will suggest ideas to you that you would never have thought of otherwise.

Constraints come with the territory: you must learn to love them

All creativity, without exception, involves an intimate dialog with the constraints of the situation and the medium you're using. Violins and oil paint, for example, are vastly more constraining than computer code.

If you come across people who boast that their ideas are just too big and wonderful for today's pathetic technology, remember that. Technology is and will always be pathetic, until the day when it can do "the creative bit" itself – and thereby make human beings redundant: creators and audiences alike.

Code's constraints

Everybody who works in the computer-medium needs to understand computers. This sounds reasonable – yet in many places it's assumed graphic designers don't need to know anything about coding, and sometimes they even boast of their ignorance.[6] In the "Sendak saga," graphic designers neither understood coding nor had programmers on hand to help them. This led to major problems. They didn't know what was difficult and what was hard. They invested months of effort in interfaces that would prove almost impossible to implement – and neglected options that would have been easy to do, had they known of them.

A lot of artists balk at learning anything about code because they think it would take them forever to do anything useful. Yet even a modest knowledge of code can be enormously useful: it gives you a sense of what is, and what is not, "do-able."[7] You then begin to realize that code can give you some excellent "free rides." Code is counter-intuitive: things that are difficult for a human are easy for a machine, and vice versa. For example, it can calculate things that make your hair stand on end, in no time flat.

Cash constraints

Budget is a major constraint – so you must know exactly what is in the kitty, and what you can do with it. Some managers don't like creatives to know what is in the kitty. Money is one of the few things they have control over, so they cling to the purse-strings for security. But if the budget is $10,000, and you have a $100,000 idea, you will either have to dump it, or (and this is worse but more likely, because you'll have run out of time) you'll have to water it down, and it will look pathetic. It is always better to do one thing well than ten things badly.

Time constraints

Your final constraint is time and the same observation applies here as to money: a one-year idea is usually better than a one-month idea, but again, many managers and clients don't really understand this. Deep down they are convinced ideas "come in a flash," while you're in the bath, shopping, etc. Some managers lie about how much time is available. They know that on past performance you'll keep on going right up to the deadline, so they figure it won't make any difference to you (and will spare themselves a lot of anxiety) if they bring the deadline forward by a couple of weeks. If they understand the process, they don't do this.

Emotional response is the key to success

The final item of the brief is the "One Great Thing." This is the toughest item of the four to pin down. It is, remember, the thing that will make the user/reader sit up and say "Wow! That's exactly what I want!" It is not just a logical proposition; it carries a big emotional charge as well – which can make it very difficult to put into words. Even a spreadsheet interface has an emotional appeal: it can give a feeling of power, and convey eagerness to help the user. The more "artistic" the work, the larger will be the emotional component of its message. You may never encapsulate it perfectly – which is why it needs to be revisited many times in the course of a project. Painters, whose work operates 100 percent at the emotional level, repeatedly stand back from the canvas and asks themselves: "What is this saying?"

The presence or absence of this "emotional charge" is the clincher.

Notes

1   For example, *Ogilvie on Advertising* by David Ogilvie (founder of the Ogilvie, Benson & Mather agency in New York), *The Craft of Copywriting* by Alastair Crompton (the man who invented "the inch war" for Ryvita) and above all James Webb Young's *A Technique for Producing Ideas* – which I refer to later in this chapter.

2   What should a website cost? At the "top end" budgets are comparable to ones for TV commercials: $100,000–$5,000,000 according to anecdotal evidence. But whereas TV commercials have a "lower limit," websites don't. Many websites are built for next to nothing, by clients themselves, or by students keen to get some experience. When pitching against that kind of competition it's essential to be able to make a strong case for spending money – and a good brief helps you do that.

3   Incidentally, the book's success illustrates the point I made earlier, about things that start out addressing a fairly small audience, and end up being adopted by the world in general. Webb, in an afterword to his third edition, expressed delight at receiving correspondence from "poets, painters, engineers, and even one writer of legal briefs." Which is echoed 35 years

later by Fred Brooks, in his afterword to his 1995 edition of *The Mythical Man Month*: he was delighted to receive "reviews, citations and correspondence from lawyers, doctors, psychologists, sociologists, as well as from software people."

4   See Margaret Lane's *The Tale of Beatrix Potter*. Allen & Unwin 1975.

5   For more on this, see Desmond Pilcher *Winning Ways* and Theodor Levitt *The Marketing Imagination*.

6   This is possibly more the case in Britain than in the US, where the "code is cool" school of thought is much stronger.

7   Web developers Vineel Shah and John Musser say (in *Director Lingo and Shockwave*. Wiley 1996), "When you've been through the emotion and drama of giving birth to a program, you'll be amazed how easily you start to relate to your programming staff."

3.4

Emotion, interaction, participation, carnival

THE COMPUTER-MEDIUM CAN GIVE people enormously rich emotional experiences. The examples in Section 2 give some indication – but there's much more, which I'll come to in a moment. First I want to tell you a little about this subject of "emotion." In the past few years it has become *the* "hot topic" in brain science – it's central to the new awareness of the power of "unconscious processing" that I've referred to elsewhere. The findings have big implications for what we do (covered in this chapter), and how we do it (in the final three chapters, when I come to "ways of working in Cyberia").

Emotion is a tricky thing to bring into a business meeting but – as the Buddhists say – 90 percent of what we consider rational thought is rationalized emotion. We all know very well that disregarding people's emotions usually leads to disaster. Art is nothing without emotion. Most educators agree that engagement of emotion is vital to learning. Science is now proving that these claims are if anything too modest.

Emotion is far more important than anyone thought

A neurologist from Iowa, Antonio Damasio, has explained[1] why emotion is essential for rational thought. Once the links between emotion centers in the lower brain and the reasoning part of the "higher brain" are cut (by a tumor, bullet, or lobotomist's scalpel) people cease to function rationally – even though they can continue to score well on intelligence tests.

He (and Joseph LeDoux, below) shows that emotions are hard-wired to body-states – their purpose is to trigger appropriate behaviours quickly: much more quickly than the more recently evolved conscious brain can.

Damasio shows that intuition is part and parcel of emotional/bodily activity. Science is just as emotional a subject as art: when asked what role intuition played in their discoveries, 79 out of the 83 Nobel laureates questioned replied that it was absolutely vital.[2]

In New York, Joseph LeDoux[3] has shown that even sea-snails and fruit-flies have at least one emotion: fear. (They don't have *feelings* of fear though – that requires consciousness, which requires a large brain.) Fear is their (and our) most essential piece of "survival software." Emotion was there long before reason – and is linked in much stronger, quicker ways to our muscles and hormonal system than the conscious, rational mind is, and largely sets the mental agenda. "*Consciousness, and its sidekick, natural language, are new kids on the block – unconscious processing is the rule rather than the exception throughout evolution.*" (*The Emotional Brain*, p. 71.) LeDoux and his co-workers have proved that emotions are the mind's main engines, dragging the conscious mind, and rationality, along in their wake.

This is an emotional medium!

If emotions and body-states are so closely related, a medium that engages us physically should have a big "emotional edge" – and so it does.

It's often said that computer games "lack the emotional richness" of older media. Yet some kind of emotion is aroused, and very strongly, both in games and in "serious" applications software. Games are notoriously addictive to some people, and so is applications software. People play with their favorite applications in a way they wouldn't with, say, a typewriter, drawing-board, or calculator. Why?

In 1980 Robert Plutchik[4] worked out a set of eight "primary emotions" (found in animals): sadness, disgust, anger, anticipation, joy, acceptance, fear, surprise. He arranged them in a circle (like a color wheel) and showed how other, more subtle emotions arise by mixing adjacent ones: for example, fear + surprise = alarm; joy + acceptance = love.

Experienced programmers often speak explicitly of "the *joy* of programming" – but there seems to be more to it than joy alone. Using Plutchik's system we can surmise that programming, computer-gaming (and even spreadsheet-twiddling) engage no fewer than *three* adjacent emotions: anticipation, joy, and acceptance. Three emotions engaged at once is very good going! When the machine acts up, even more emotions pile in: fear, surprise, and anger. No wonder this stuff is addictive!

The very people who claim the computer lacks "emotional richness" call programming "unhealthily obsessive behavior" – oblivious, apparently, to the fact that love, anger, and grief can also be "unhealthily obsessive."

If we can understand the way emotional involvement works for the "geek," the compulsive desktop-tweaker, or the office spreadsheetaholic, maybe we'll be better able to achieve other kinds of emotional involvement.

A uncommonly powerful emotion: the sense of "being in control"

Perhaps the problem people have with "compulsive computer use" is that the particular mix of emotions involved is not terribly common in everyday life.

It is a "sense of power" or "being in control": words tarnished by history, where they usually mean "abuse of power" and "control of other people." But the feeling of control is not necessarily evil. Throughout most of history it's been a feeling very few people could enjoy – with the interesting major exception of sailors: who were always believed to think and behave differently from land-dwellers. Machines began to make the "joy of control" more accessible: first with industrial machines, then motorbikes and cars, now with computers.

Most programmers can describe the specific point in their lives when they discovered what they could do with code – and their accounts are usually very similar. This is Carl Alsing, who wrote the "microcode" for Data General's Super-Eclipse in 1979, recalling his "midnight programming" sessions in the basement of his university in the 1960s:

"I'd run a little program and when it worked I'd get a little high, and then I'd do another. It was neat. I loved writing programs. I could control the machine. I could make it express my own thoughts. It was an expansion of the mind to have a computer."
(Kidder (1981), p. 90)

Power, play, and playfulness

As I said above, the emotions that go with exercising power are tarnished by history: they are associated with sadism: "absolute power corrupts absolutely." But corrupt power can also be described as perverted playfulness.

Play seems to be a matter of exploring "possibility spaces."

Play, in the pure sense of simply controlling and manipulating things, in a safe environment, for no particular purpose, is crucially important for humans. For a very good explanation of this, see child psychologist Donald Winnicott's *Playing and Reality*: he treated many people who had been deprived of play as children and consequently became unhappy, dysfunctional adults. Play restored them. Many believe there's far too little outlet for playfulness pure and simple in the adult world, and always has been. Many people also believe that the computer is an ideal remedy.

Ted Nelson says: "*If the computer is a universal control system, let's give kids universes to control.*" (*Dream Machines*, p. 131)

Mark Wieser (of Xerox Parc) says: "*Our computers should be like our childhood: an invisible foundation that is quickly forgotten but always with us, and effortlessly used throughout our lives.*" (*ACM Interactions*, November 1993[5])

Controlling a computer program is not as good as controlling your life – but Winnicott's point (I think) is that the experience of safety and control, wherever you get it, helps you "get a life."

What sorts of things can we offer people to play with, and exercise power over? At the moment we can enjoy power over drawings, 3-D models, numbers and text – not a lot perhaps but it gives millions of people a lot of pleasure. Maybe it also helps their mental and (dare I say it) spiritual health – I do not know that anyone has even begun to explore that possibility.

Computers also *promise* control over your investments, your time, your "busy schedule," your company payroll ... they sometimes even promise that they'll let you control your own computer. But the amount of *useful* control they really deliver to organizations is surprisingly modest (to learn how modest, see Thomas K. Landauer's *The Trouble with Computers*).

As Landauer says, one part of the "trouble with computers" is that people use them for satisfying but unproductive tasks (report-writing, "spreadsheet-twiddling," etc.). This may be very good for them – many workers have very little control over anything beyond their computer terminal – but maybe it would be even better to provide "playthings" expressly designed for pointless play, where they can just experience, and get the hang of, "being in control." Perhaps something rather valuable is going on here: equivalent to the way small children play with pots and pans. Good, "serious" utensils are often the best playthings.

The challenge of pointless playthings

"Pointless playthings" are not as easy to create as you might think – which may explain why there are so few of them around. Also, in this serious world of ours it is very hard to make a commercial case for things that are simply for playing with – it has to be an accompaniment to something "serious." Even children's software has a serious agenda: teach them basic math, or reading. Software publishers are extremely wary of products that have no such agenda: as Alan Snow and his team found when they were trying to find a publisher for "PAWS," and Romain Victor-Pujebet found with "Lulu."

Some real-world playthings offer inspiration: sandpits, toy gyroscopes, yo-yos, hula-hoops, spinning tops, paper airplanes, skipping ropes, puzzles of all kinds... . The great British neurologist Richard Gregory treasures such things. He believes they've done just as much for human progress as any number of "serious," task-oriented devices.

In his book *Mind in Science* Gregory showed that our progress as a species can be explained almost in its entirety as the consequence of "mind-expanding encounters" with new "hands-on" devices that people have added to our everyday environment – from the simple lever and the "clep-sydra" (a pipette-like device used in ancient Greece for drawing wine and oil from large containers) to the wheel, the wheel-brace, the pulley, clock-work, the steam locomotive, and the computer itself.

He shows that *tools become mind-tools*. Levers and pulleys extended our mental vocabulary and "leveraged" mind itself. It's our ability to make new devices to do new things, that allows us to *think* new things – and allowed the human mind to "bootstrap" itself into the present age. The philosopher Daniel Dennett finds Gregory's idea so apt that he thinks we should consider ourselves "Gregorian" organisms.[6]

There is not a lot of point in re-creating yo-yos and skipping-ropes on the computer: the real thing gives an almost infinitely richer experience. But "low-res" worlds can offer experiences that are impossible to provide with real matter. Pioneers like Myron Krueger (mentioned in Chapter 1.5) and Carnegie-Mellon University's Hans Moravec (in his book *Mind Children*) have long been preaching how Virtual Reality will allow whole-body experience of and interaction with processes (like gravity, relativity, and quantum physics) that at present we can only be told about – especially if the VR system provides "force feedback."

The under-appreciated market for pointless games

Games are the obvious "pointless playthings." But most computer games are not "pointless" in the strict sense: you have a recognizable goal: shoot the baddies or win the race. But there are notable exceptions – and these tend to be very successful indeed. "Tetris," by the Russian programmer Alexei Pazhitnov in 1985, was a spectacular success. Here, irregularly shaped tiles fall down from the top of the screen, and you have to guide their descent so that they fit into position with their fellows. It is notoriously compulsive, and spawned a host of imitators on every computer platform from the Mac to the GameBoy – and it is hard to see how you could provide this experience otherwise than on a computer.

Some people, as usual, were worried that "Tetris" was addictive – while having no apparent objection to children being addicted to skipping-ropes, spinning-tops, and books.

"Tetris" was a phenomenal success. So was "Sim City" (the "urban planning simulator" built by Will Wright for Maxis in 1987) – although it does depart from the "pure play" ideal in that you do have a goal: a *viable* city. Mattel's "Barbie Fashion Designer" seems a fairly pure, goalless, and very successful piece of fun.

Recent research suggests that the majority of computer-gamers in fact prefer the "pointless" variety: a study by Media Metrix in 1998 found that the vast majority of game-playing activity was not with goal-oriented blockbusters like "Quake" and "Riven" but in the more trivial "parlor games" provided by Microsoft's Entertainment Pack.[7]

"Pure fun blockbusters" are rare, but non-commercial examples are plentiful. All that they seem to lack is commercial justification: many of them offer "brief encounters" that are enjoyed and fully explored in minutes: they do not justify a whole CD-ROM. And their "user-benefits" are not obvious – even though they are so powerfully justified by mind-science.

Maybe "delivery media" are the problem here. We need media that allow small things to be distributed cheaply, yet profitably. This, maybe, is where the Web and "micro-cash" will help. Ted Nelson's "Xanadu" (mentioned in Chapter 1.4 – with its automatic royalty-payment) would be the ideal delivery medium.

Roy Stringer – the self-taught interactivist genius who heads the Liverpool-based multimedia company Amaze Ltd – has made a number of beautiful "pointless playthings" over the years (see http://www.amaze.co.uk).[8]

The hero of PAWS – a typical piece of pure, pointless fun by Alan Snow. (By courtesy of Organa Inc.)

The essential charm of Alan Snow's work (e.g., "PAWS") seems, at heart, to be "pointless play." His test-pieces show this in its purest form – it seems almost a shame to have to dress them up and pad them out to fill a CD-ROM.

In its last days, the Voyager Company started to produce a series of "pure play-things." Bob Stein was demonstrating one of them at Milia in 1996: a set of kids' building blocks that you could play with while talking on the phone: a nice development of the under-explored pleasure of "doodling."

The "computer art" world has produced no end of wonderful experiments – mostly "installations" that make rare appearances at art exhibitions and festivals. Early examples include Myron Krueger's GLOWFLOW (1969) and METAPLAY (1970). Recent examples include Char Davies's "Osmose" (a VR environment that you navigate as if scuba diving, using a sort of "data life preserver), "Configuring the Cave," by Australian artist Jeffrey Shaw, who works at ZKM in Karlsruhe in Germany (see www.zkm.de), and English artist Jane Prophet's "Swarm" – a virtual environment that has a related website and "playspace" at http://www.technosphere.org.uk.

Play with a purpose

It's easier to justify giving people the "fun of control" if you have a serious, didactic purpose. On our Interact project (Chapter 2.5), we were able to allow people to "play with money" to a limited extent: for example, they could develop a sense of what compound interest actually does, in an intuitive way. This has proved to be both the system's most popular, and its most commercially valuable, feature. Other parts of the system that just give "straight answers" to questions ("what will my mortgage cost?") are less popular, and produce less in terms of "sales leads."

And of course when people use Excel "seriously" (as opposed to fiddling around with formatting) they are playing "what-if" games.

You would think educational software would be full of "virtual toys" that give this kind of playfulness and emotional reward – but relatively little of it seems to. After more than a decade, it is still dominated by "drill"-type question-and-answer exercises. Presumably this is because awareness of the "power of play" is still poorly understood in the commercial world – but that is sure to change.

Are tools and toys, not film or TV, new media's closest living relations?

Where should we look for models of playful media? Film offers no precedent. Nor does radio, TV, music, the printed book, or painting. In the context of "art," the computer really seems to be something new and unprecedented. But in a wider context it isn't.

There are in fact media that have always allowed us to be "part of the action" – only we never thought of them as "expressive" or "artistic" media until the Russian "Formalists" and "Constructivists" took notice of them early this century (mentioned in Chapter 1.3). These are: machinery, toys, and tools. Our modern world is full of them and what's more, says Richard Gregory, so are our minds.

Are "classic emotion" and interaction compatible – and if so, how?

The "fun of playfulness" is extremely powerful. But what about the "classic" emotions addressed by literature, music, drama, and film: anger, sadness, grief, love, compassion, joy, delight, etc.?

We saw earlier that certain computer applications provoke a highly recognizable emotional response: tears – in Brian Thomas's "If Monks Had Macs," Robert Winter's "Beethoven," and Pedro Mayer's "I Photograph to Remember."

However, those *do not seem* to be as "highly interactive" as games, spreadsheets, or compilers are. There is very little point-and-clickery. Much of "I Photograph … " is absolutely linear. You could also say those examples "cheat" because they've borrowed their emotionally arousing material from other media: stories that you can also read in books, and recorded music that you could enjoy more conveniently on your hi-fi or personal stereo. I have argued that the computer adds a great deal to their emotional force – by "restoring context." But how does that work? Just piling on the background information does not guarantee powerful results. Plenty of rubbish is produced that way. Is a different principle at work here? If it *is* a different principle, it makes life complicated for would-be designers of successful multimedia. How can we have "interactive" things that aren't terribly interactive – yet go down a storm – and highly interactive things that go down like lead balloons?

Brenda Laurel offers a particularly helpful idea in her 1991 classic, *Computers as Theater*.

Musing about this problem (what is "interactivity"? how much "interaction" do you have to have before you can call something "interactive"? etc.) she proposes:

There is another, more rudimentary measure of interactivity: you either feel yourself to be participating in the ongoing action of the representation or you don't. (*Computers as Theater*, p. 20–1 (my emphasis))

This has the ring of good common sense, and it squares pretty well with real-life experience.

In real life (be that the school playground, at work, wherever) we are *not* constantly interacting in a physical way: often, we are perfectly happy just to observe (although we can get bored in that role). More important than having the ball at all times is the sense of being involved in the game. You can even feel well and truly "part of the action" just by "being there" – as everyone who has ever been at a good football match or a rock concert knows. Hence:

Optimizing frequency and range and significance in human choice-making will remain inadequate as long as we conceive of the human as sitting on the other side of some barrier, poking at the representation with a joystick or a mouse or a virtual hand. (*Computers as Theater*, p. 21)

Laurel's book is a thorough, and fascinating, development of that idea.

Computers are "communities of agents"

One of her key ideas is that we should think of computer systems as communities of "agents." This is not quite what people usually mean when they talk about "software agents." One of Laurel's "agents" is you, the user. The others are the "entities" that make up the system you're using: tool-palettes, menus, routines that open, find, and save files, apply "filters" in Photoshop, etc. For her, the computer is like a theater with an audience of one, who is free to participate if he or she so desires.

This is a powerful idea, and we can easily see that the Mac interface perhaps owes a lot of its charm to this principle: the menu items, folders, disk icons, and "trashcan" can be seen as as a quaint little community of "helpers": not colossally intelligent ones to be sure, but that adds to their charm – highly intelligent ones might be rather intimidating. These are more like cartoon-film characters.

"Complicity" between the user and an "agent" in Mark Schlichting's Living Books. This is the screen you get after you've chosen to "quit" the program ("Do you *really* want to quit?"). The character at bottom right nods mischievously as if to say "Go on – do it!" – urging you to ignore the forlorn "please don't" character on the left, who is shaking his head anxiously.

A sense of "community" triggers rich emotional response: we are social creatures. As I have said, we do not need to be consciously aware of the things that cause the response, to experience it.

Mark Schlichting's Living Books are superb examples of "communities of agents" in the Brenda Laurel sense. Here they are personified, not abstract: you have the characters of the tale, and also the "helper characters" that engage in direct dialog with you – even invite (minor but nice) "complicity."

Christopher Hales's interactive movie "Jinxed" works on similar lines (for more on him, see http://www.uwe.ac.uk).

Beverly and Hans Reiser's work, in the Amiga system called "Mandala" (Chapter 1.7), physically placed you, as user, into the community they'd created for you on the screen.

The "community of agents" idea obviously ties in very nicely with the idea of object-oriented programming – and Peter Small's latest book *Magical A-Life Avatars* (Chapter 2.1) seems the perfect conceptual toolkit for anyone who wants to pursue this approach.

From theater to carnival – Mikhail Bakhtin's "Dialogic Imagination"

It is also an idea that can help us think more clearly about many other things – not just computers – and it has deep roots. As so often, they're found in the Russia of the 1920s, where a remarkable literary scholar called Mikhail Bakhtin formulated his now-influential theory of "carnival" and "multi-voiced texts" (called "heteroglossia" in English, by his translators).

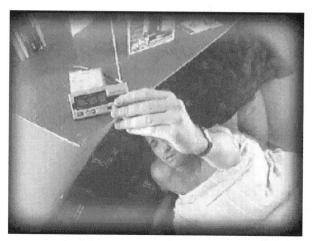

Explicit complicity in Christopher Hales's "Jinxed." In this interactive movie, various objects invite the user to click on them (they swell discreetly, as if to say "psst! – over here!"). If you accept the invitation the object will play a trick on the "hero" (who is trying to get to a job interview), e.g., click on the alarm-radio and it turns off so that he oversleeps; click on the soap in the bathroom and it falls on the floor – and he slips on it. This was inspired by slapstick comedy and British pantomime – where characters regularly invite mischievous help from the audience.

Bakhtin's ideas can sound almost mystical but in fact he is no more a mystic than Joseph LeDoux is, which is to say he looks for hard, verifiable evidence – in his case, in novels.

In a book of essays called *The Dialogic Imagination* Bakhtin shows that a novel is not just one person's voice, but a riot of different voices, drawn from the entire culture in which the author lived – from its remotest past to the living present. Authorship is more what we would now call a "collage" activity than a solitary, painful process of invention. The pleasure and power of authorship come from:

The possibility of employing on the plane of a single work discourses of various types, with all their expressive capacities intact, without reducing them to a single denominator. (Problems of Dostoyevsky's Poetics)

and:

For the prose artist the world is full of other people's words . . . He works with a very rich verbal palette. (ibid.)

Bakhtin then argues that our whole culture is created by this "accumulation" and "recycling" process where, with each generation, new voices, commenting on each other, referring to each other, mocking each other, are added to the "rich palette" available to the next. In this way "mind" evolves, we free ourselves from the past, and are able to think new thoughts. Interesting, how near this is to Richard Gregory's ideas!

The "rich palette" is not just a textual one. We can see our whole environment this way. It is all "heritage," and it is meant to be used. Life is a carnival – and the dead are just as much a part of it as the living.

Bakhtin didn't know anything about computers (he spent much of his life in exile in Kazakstan and Southern Russia) but his way of looking at things is a gift to workers in the computer-medium.

This is the ultimate "multi-voiced" or "collage" medium, and it puts vast realms of "heritage" at our fingertips. This is like what Vannevar Bush had in mind – and then some. It's also like what Ted Nelson has in mind at Xanadu – and adds great depth to Brenda Laurel's idea of the "computer as community."

What you create is a carnival, and being here is often participation enough.

Notes

1 In *Descartes' Error*, 1995.

2 Guy Claxton (author of *Hare Brain, Tortoise Mind*) presented these figures in a talk at the University of the West of England in early 1998.

3 LeDoux's book is *The Emotional Brain* (1998). He is an ex-pupil and co-worker of Michael Gazzaniga (Dartmouth College, MD) whose work on "split-brain" patients revealed that the two halves of the brain have different specialities – and launched a spate of sometimes simplistic books and courses on "right-brain" thinking.

4 In *Emotion: A Psychoevolutionary Synthesis*, 1980. I presume Plutchik's system is an approximation and therefore almost certainly wrong to some extent – but LeDoux has no fundamental problem with it, and uses it in *The Emotional Brain*.

5 The full text is at http://www.ubiq.com/hypertext/weiser/ACMInteractions2.html.

6 Dennett proposed this is in his 1996 book *Kinds of Minds*.

7 Source: *The Guardian* 28 May 1998 (Colin Campbell's Videowatch column). Media Metrix "fixed a special device to 28,000 PCs in the US to see what was taking up game-playng time." "21 per cent of users are likely to play parlor games, while only 0.8 per cent will play something like Civilization II."

8 The ones on the website are mostly made in Macromedia Director, and delivered to the Web via Macromedia's ShockWave "player," or plug-in. Stringer's young protégé Danny Thomas makes most of the toys you'll find on the site. Roy gives him free rein, and a 32k "budget" (he can make anything he likes, but it has to be under 32k in size).

3.5

"Cognitive dynamite": Multi-sensory effects that blow you away

HOW MANY "LANGUAGES" do people use – and what do they do to each other? Computers have made this question an important one.

A few years ago a friend came back from Moscow, very excited by a paper by a distinguished academician called Gennady Uzilevsky.[1] He had listed 12 kinds of language that, he said, humans have developed over the last few hundred thousand years. His diagram (approximation below) may not entirely match Western scientific orthodoxy, but it does dramatize the state of affairs rather well:

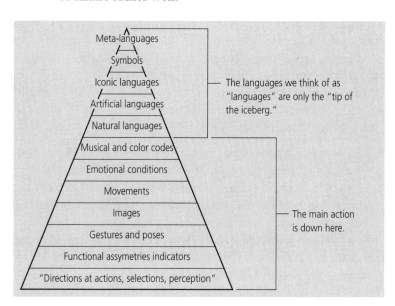

Meta-languages
Symbols
Iconic languages
Artificial languages
Natural languages
Musical and color codes
Emotional conditions
Movements
Images
Gestures and poses
Functional assymetries indicators
"Directions at actions, selections, perception"

— The languages we think of as "languages" are only the "tip of the iceberg."

— The main action is down here.

Approximation of Uzilevsky's diagram of "An empirical set of different languages and codes that are inherent in humans"

Only the top five languages are what we think of as "languages": these are the least powerful of the 12, but they are what most "conventional" media focus on. Most human communication is done by the lower seven, of which the most easily named (in decreasing order of power) are gesture,[2] images, movements, emotional conditions, music and color – things few "traditional" media designers have ever had to deal with, but all of which are suddenly activated by interactive multimedia computers. As soon as work become interactive, it gets judged by the whole, primeval arsenal of human cognition.

Uzilevsky's "triangle of languages" illustrates a generally accepted fact: most of the "languages" we use are unconscious ones – and they influence us more easily than the consciously recognized ones. As Richard Gregory, Guy Claxton, Antonio Damasio, Joseph LeDoux, and many others are proving, it's these unconscious modes of perception that make us "smarter than we think."

Perception seems to be a team effort: each sense helps the others. People who work in older media invest great effort and skill, assisted by techniques developed over centuries, coaxing one sense to evoke all the others. Now we can use several sense-channels at once – and we've barely begun to explore the ways they affect each other. However, some things are known.

Mixing media is "sensory dynamite"

Media change whatever you put into them. A joke can die the death on the page. So will a novel if you try transferring it to the TV-screen lock, stock, and barrel. And as soon as you add one medium to another, remarkable things happen. The art critic John Berger (in a famous book called *Ways of Seeing*) draws our attention to the way that a gilded frame turns a picture into "a work of art"; add a text caption to it (e.g., "the artist killed himself the day after he painted this") and you transform its meaning; change the caption and you change its meaning again.

Movie-makers have made many important discoveries of this kind. Add music to a scene of someone taking a shower, and you have either a shower-gel commercial or the stabbing sequence from *Psycho*. Musicians have been playing this kind of "mix-and-match" for centuries: songs can have quite banal words that, when added to a particular tune, become dynamite. This is "sensory chemistry" – cheap ingredients that become explosive when combined. The art is to get a "free ride" from the explosive force, and avoid getting blown up: that happens too.

Sound improves graphics and animations

Back in 1991, Brenda Laurel (then at Telepresence Research) reported an interesting experiment that they'd carried out. They showed test-subjects two identical video-clips with *almost* identical sound tracks – one sound track was of lower quality than the other. Then they asked the subjects "which clip looks better?." Everyone replied that the one with the higher-quality sound track had the better graphics.

Mark Schlichting (in his experiments while making his "Living Books") also found, independently, that *"Good audio makes poor graphics look better, (but the reverse is not true)."*

What's more: *"Good audio also lets you imply a lot – animation that actually takes place in the viewers head. (Character slips and crashes off screen with sound fx.)"* (email to author, Summer 1998)

Going further back, Joe Henderson (Chapter 1.6) discovered that a "sound bridge" (sound that continued in the background while the user made a decision) intensified the user's experience – *even though what was happening on the screen had exactly the opposite effect.*

What happens here? Going back to mind science, it *appears* **sound gets priority** in mental processing. This makes evolutionary sense: our eyes can't be everywhere but danger can come from anywhere; sound is our "early-warning" system. By the time you consciously "see" something, aural processing has already worked out what class of thing it is in general terms (something nice, something threatful, something amusing) and you interpret what you see in those terms.

The economics of sound; Psygnosis's "Wipeout 2097"

Combining media can be like combining physical materials to make "composites" that are many times stronger than the sum of their parts.

Games designers started using sound as soon as it was possible to do so – even though the quality was crude (think of the original "Space Invaders," "Pong," and "PacMan"). Even a crude "system beep" gave the on-screen interaction (ball hitting paddle) an almost a physical quality. Today there is a rich synergy between games designers and the dance music scene.

For a fine example of this, see Psygnosis' "Wipeout 2097" (1997, for the Sony PlayStation), which features music by various stars of the UK dance and drum-and-bass scene (Future Sound of London, Chemical Brothers, The Prodigy, and others), and fascinating ambient sound – by (I presume)

Wipeout 2097® (©Psygnosis, 1997 – for Sony PlayStation®). Ambient sound is close-coupled with the action, creating an intensely immersive experience.

Tim Wright (of Psygnosis's own studio: CoLD SToRAGE). The ambient sound is scarcely anything more than white noise – yet it's not a mere accompaniment: it's a big part of the experience. It has a hint of echo that changes as you fly past objects and through tunnels. Then, the *quality* of the echo changes depending on the type of terrain you're flying through: rock and concrete give a harsher echo than snow. Collisions produce echoey "thumps" that you can almost feel – again the amount of echo you get depends on whether the collision happens "out in the open" or in one of the tunnels.

The voice in "Wipeout" is interesting too. (It counts you down at the start, and warns you of hazards.) It cuts from "echo" to "no-echo" in mid-word as you fly past objects. Most other games use real actors' voices. I imagine Psygnosis could have afforded Bruce Willis or even Marlon Brando if they'd wanted – but here they used a synthesized voice, heavily processed on an old Amiga 1200. It does not sound like a robot voice, but it is much more calm than a human voice would ever be: a little bit like the voice of HAL9000 in Kubrick's *2001*. Somehow the voice seems to be inside your own head. It's very different from the cheery, hyped-up, commentator-voices used in other games (where the sound files occupy acres of disk space). As with the sound effects, I find calculated subtlety here that easily goes unnoticed by the conscious mind, and could be a major reason for its classic status.

This use of sound is supremely elegant, achieving enormous effect very "cheaply" in computing terms: the sound files must be tiny; it is very easy for the program to pick the right one for the context (tunnel, rock, snow, etc.) and switch rapidly between them as the context changes.

Tim Wright was also responsible for the award-winning music in DMA's[3] 1991 hit, "Lemmings" (later published by Psygnosis). There, a wonderful variety of rib-ticklingly witty pastiche tunes were created, at run-time, from a fairly small assortment of sound clips, morphing from tune to unlikely tune without missing a beat. The "lemmings" marched in perfect step to these tunes wherever they led: from the *Turkish March*, to *O Little Town of Bethlehem*, to the theme from *The Good, the Bad and the Ugly*.

Wright has been close-coupling music and sound to on-screen action in this wickedly clever and economical way for years, helping Psygnosis to become a world leader in games design from one of the least advantageous starting points in computerdom: down-at-heel Liverpool. Despite Psygnosis's success, relatively few other games houses (and even fewer software houses) have latched on to this way of doing things. Sound is usually more an accompaniment to the action than a part of it.

Wright has recently created a mix-your-own music application for the PlayStation called "Music!" – see http://jesterinteractive.com.

If sound and graphics together produce such interesting results, what other combinations are there, that we need to be aware of? What other senses get priority?

Richard Gregory: interactions speak louder than anything else

Physical interaction is a new(ish: see "tools and toys," Chapter 3.4) medium for an artist, but a very ancient one for living beings. As Joseph LeDoux has shown, emotion is our first-line mechanism for handling it.

In fact, physical interaction makes us what we are – as Richard Gregory has pointed out over the past 20-odd years in a series of important books and experiments. His view is now rapidly becoming scientific orthodoxy, supported by brain scientists like LeDoux and Damasio, and by certain artificial intelligence researchers mentioned in a moment.

Gregory is particularly interesting for anyone who works in this new "heavy-on-the-visuals" medium, because vision is his "home turf." He wrote the classic work on the subject, *Eye and Brain* (five editions since it was first published in 1986).

How the body makes vision possible

In this book he explains that vision is as much a hands-on, physical business as an optical one. The eye is like a ridiculously badly designed video camera where all the wiring and circuitry has been dumped right on top of the "film-plane." It's amazing that we see anything at all with it. Yet somehow, we imagine ourselves surrounded by vivid, "lifelike" images. In a recent talk, he says: "*The ghostly images in eyes are almost absurdly inadequate representations of objects, yet we see amazing richness in the world around us. This is the miracle of perception.*"[4] How does this miracle work? Much of what we *think* we see is conjured up by the brain from other cues – in particular, from information supplied by our hands and bodies.

Objects have and are seen to have solidity, and complex interactive causal properties that are entirely lacking for images. Young children learn to read their eyes' images in terms of objects by experimenting, essentially by disturbing things – which is why children are destructive and are given toys to play with – for active touch is necessary for the innumerable discoveries that make sense of signals from the eyes. *(My emphasis)*

It is *our own actions* that help to produce the "miracle of perception." This is why Richard Gregory has spent a good part of his life championing the cause of "hands-on science": the kind of science education where people are not just *told* things, or even just *shown* things, but allowed to *discover* things with their own two hands. He helped Frank Oppenheimer (Robert Oppenheimer's brother) to set up the famous "Exploratorium" in San Francisco. His "Exploratory" at Bristol has since carried the agenda forward in Europe.

The whole mind-science community has coalesced around Gregory in recent years. Evidence accumulates each year of the way our hands and bodies help us make sense of the world. In robotics, this has led to the fascinating field of "embodied intelligence" (whose leading light is MIT's Rodney Brooks). One of Brooks's colleagues, an English worker called Andy Clark, describes the field in his book *Being There*; "*perception*," he says, "*is itself tangled up with possibilities for action – so tangled up in fact that the job of central control often ceases to exist.*"

If interactive, physical engagement is so fundamental to perception, it's no wonder that a medium that allows interactive engagement should be a runaway success. Interaction is our natural *milieu*. (Hence there is something quite remarkable about the apparently "non-interactive" media – how on earth do things like novels and paintings and films capture our attention so well?[5] I've already touched on this in the previous chapter and I'll return to it – briefly alas – at the end.)

Unconsciously perceived movement helps vision

Richard Gregory also explains in *Eye and Brain* that although the eye is a very bad camera, it is an excellent motion-detector. Our peripheral vision does nothing *but* detect motion. In fact, all kinds of eyes started their evolutions as motion-detectors. The computer community has always liked the idea of "languages of movement" – while producing computer interfaces that look stone-dead most of the time.

Frank Thomas: one of the cadre of great Disney animators who found a second career explaining their economical art to computer interface designers at Apple, MIT, and elsewhere during the 1980s – to the benefit of computer users everywhere. Frank worked on *Snow White and the Seven Dwarves* and was lead-animator on *Jungle Book*. (Author's photo)

Animation has made some headway – for explaining things, and to help navigation (the "zoom" effects in the original Macintosh interface[6]). Animation was one of the features that made Macromedia Director a runaway success in spite of its apparent disadvantages – see Chapter 1.7. Cartoon-film animators have made important contributions to the art of interface design – and could probably contribute much more. But maybe we are only scratching the surface so far.

The real world is full of movement-information – and so could computer displays be. Much of this kind of information is so subtle, and absorbed so easily, we do not notice it – but we get a lot of pleasure and subliminal information from it, and we can interpret this consciously as we learn to read the signs.

A birdwatcher can identify tiny birds that are fields away, just by the way they bounce through the air. Many anglers can sense the presence of a particular fish in a certain pool from the merest of clues. It's improbable that they use magic or telepathy – they do it through unconsciously registered cues which they would not get from a photograph of the same scene: again, it is probably to do with movement. Birdwatchers and anglers become highly attuned to these effects – as other connoisseurs do – but there is no reason to think they have no effect at all on other people: most of us prefer "being there" to being in front of a picture, and this could be why.

Yet when we design computer interfaces, static pictures are usually all we provide.

Two neglected explorations, and one challenge

Whatever happened to micons?

Around 1991 there was a lot of interest in micons (or animated icons). A researcher called Hans Peter Brondno at MIT demonstrated the idea in 1989: there are many things where a still picture simply doesn't help. His demonstration included a photo of the splash made by a drop of milk falling into a glass: you can't identify it unless someone explains what it is. But once you see the animated sequence you realize immediately what you're seeing. This principle obviously had the power to explain many things that still pictures couldn't. Like anything hailing from MIT, the micons were considered miraculous – but they were not too difficult to do, even with the modest computer power available at that time. Colin Holgate (later of Voyager, but then working at Apple UK as resident multi-media expert) built a few very nice micons on his MacII over a weekend.

The idea got prime-time airing in Douglas Adams and Max Whitby's excellent BBC documentary *Hyperland* in 1990.

In 1991, Ronald Baecker[7] and colleagues applied the technique to HyperCard's interface. Little animations replaced the usual static pictures in the tool-palette (paint-tin, spraycan, line tool, etc.). They proved that people understood the animations much more easily than the standard, static pictures.

The idea seemed to have been forgotten – until suddenly, thanks to animated GIFs and the Web, we have whole websites populated by animated "buttons and banners." Mostly, these serve trivial purposes and add nothing much more than "visual noise" but occasionally you find ones that are quite helpful. Out of the noise a new element of visual grammar may yet emerge.

Bill Gaver's "Auditory Icons"

Going back again to 1989, a researcher at Xerox's EuroPARC, at Cambridge UK, developed an add-on for the Macintosh's "Finder," which he called "SonicFinder." It attached sounds to common actions: when you clicked on an folder, the sound you got was deeper if the folder contained a lot of items than if it only contained a few. As you dragged items around, again, the sound reflected the "weight" of the object.

This seemed a neat way of giving valuable extra information: to this day you cannot tell how many files a folder contains just by looking at it. However, you still had to do something to the folder (click on it) to get the sound effect – and having clicked you might as well go on and open it. I also found the sounds surprisingly intrusive, even though they weren't loud. A high degree of subtlety seems to be needed for this to work well: our auditory system works on a hair-trigger.

Later on, Gaver developed the idea of "Soundholders"[8]: these provide what he calls "auditory landmarks" and are a bit like "sound rollovers." As your mouse-pointer approaches an object the sound associated with it swells in volume, and diminishes again as the mouse moves away.

Alex Mayhew's team at Real World (mentioned at the beginning of Section 2) created lots of nice examples of what can be achieved by coupling sounds to actions in the interface, in "Ceremony of Innocence."

A screen from "Ceremony of Innocence" (©Real World Multimedia 1998), which provides a very rich "sound world" and lots of aural feedback. Here, the user's mouse-pointer has been eaten, and emits plaintive noises from the belly of the beast on the right.

The "stuffed dog" challenge: information from subliminally perceived movement

If a computer program is supposed to be someone's "ever-helpful servant," why shouldn't it signal its eagerness the way a good dog does? A really good dog barely moves – but could never be confused with a stuffed dog. Tiny movements, bristlings of the hair, breathing, and glances signal her instant readiness to "go fetch!" whatever you desire.

Most computer interfaces are "stuffed dogs" – and don't need to be. The monitor's electron-guns are going hell-for-leather across the screen, 75, 85, 100 times a second, and the computer processor is churning away at 200 MHz, but on the screen nothing happens. It's quite unlike the natural world, which is alive with subtle movement – although it takes a certain modest "connoisseurship" to notice it consciously.

While the user sits in front of the screen, a veritable Niagara Falls of computing power is going to waste, meticulously handling the "idle" message 200,000+ times a second, which could easily be driving a wealth of subtle and unconsciously informative movement. This kind of information could be exactly what's needed to reduce what some HCI people call the "cognitive overhead" of interpreting the system's affordances.

You've got to be subtle, and quick!

All these "non-verbal" languages seem to require a lot of subtlety – and they must be highly responsive. This is what one would expect from the findings of mind-science: humans are supremely sensitive to them, and respond to them fast: even tiny delays between the action and the associated sound or movement destroy any illusion of naturalness and turn it instead into a source of irritation.

The medium's constraints are a surprisingly good guide

In all media, simply following the medium's own constraints can lead you, as if by magic, to the right answers. (We can't do anything the constraints won't allow anyway, so we may as well explore them.) Think of carving wood, or oil-painting: the best work seems to allow the material's natural tendencies to be "part of the action." Wood-carvers let the wood's grain do some of the job for them; many great painters (since Rembrandt) have allowed thick oil paint to "do its own thing" instead of wasting effort, making it look like a photograph.

Bandwidth will always be a constraint with computers – and the need to coax the maximum out of scarce processor-cycles seems to be an excellent discipline. It produces effects that are far richer than ones produced as if computer-power were limitless – as Tim Wright's work (above) demonstrates. His methods seem to produce a tremendous sense of involvement – in some essential way *precisely* because he "works with the machine": giving it tasks that it can perform easily and quickly.

Notes

1 The paper was called "View on the information technologies, from the position of information environment evolution," by Gennady Uzilevsky and Vladimir Andreev, Techn&com, Moscow. Presented at the Moscow HCI meeting in August 1992.

2 Gesture recognition is being explored at various places. The most famous is Patti Maes' "Alive Project" at MIT Media Lab: see: http://www.mediaport.net/CyberScience/.

3 DMA is in Dundee, Scotland – founded by Dave Jones. DMA = "Doesn't Mean Anything." See http://www.dma.co.uk for the whole story. Their most (in)famous recent hit is "Grand Theft Auto."

4 Richard Gregory – from a talk given at the Exploratory in 1997.

5 Marie-Laure Ryan, of Boulder, Colorado, is tackling this subject in a fascinating book called *Immersion versus Interactivity*: *Literature as Virtual Reality*, which should be out in 2000. Some of it is available at her website: http://lamar.colostate.edu/~pwryan.

6 The "zoom" effects happen so fast on modern machines you barely notice them – but on the original Macs (e.g., the Mac Plus) they took an appreciable fraction of a second, and seem (to me) to create a much better sense of working in a 3-D "information space" than you get with the latest machines.

7 "Bringing Icons to Life" – Ronald Baecker, Ian Small and Richard Mander. In *Readings in Human-Computer Interaction*: *Toward the Year 2000*, edited and written by Ronald Baecker, Jonathan Grudin, William Buxton and Saul Greenberg, Morgan Kaufmann, 1995.

8 Written up in "Auditory Icons in Large-Scale Collaborative Environments," in *Readings in Human–Computer Interaction: Toward the Year 2000*, edited and written by Ronald Baecker, Jonathan Grudin, William Buxton and Saul Greenberg, Morgan Kaufmann, 1995.

3.6

"Cognitive train wrecks" and "user expectations"

❝What can we do about the little cognitive train wrecks that occur at the interstices between modes in a drawing program, a word-processor, or a virtual-reality system? The hand wavers between the keyboard and mouse button, and the mind, even though it is working thousands of times faster and more elegantly than the computer itself, cannot predict the bahavior of the interface❞

Brenda Laurel, preface to *Computers as Theater*

"USER EXPECTATIONS" SPRING to center-stage in an interactive medium – making you realize how important they are in every other medium as well. The great art historian and theorist Ernst Gombrich said that "art itself is a game the artist plays with the beholder's expectations." Modern cognitive science has shown that expectations are fundamental both to perception and to mind itself. The neuroscientist William Calvin observes that the human mind has a fundamental "what-happens-next orientation."[1]

There has never been a medium where you can play so many, or such elaborate, games with other people's expectations as the computer. All manner of "playing with expectations" is, at times, appropriate. But when expectations are mishandled we get what Brenda Laurel has called "cognitive train wrecks." Nobody gets killed but they destroy users' confidence in the system – which is just as bad if you hope to make a living in this medium.

Differences: the beauty of "wallpaper"

In the real, real-time world, differences are what we notice most. For example, if you hear a sound of constant pitch and volume, your conscious mind rapidly ceases to notice it; you only notice it again if it changes. A beautiful landscape makes you go "wow" the first time you see it, but then becomes "wallpaper" – until you change your viewpoint and notice things about it you hadn't noticed before. (And if you've got beautiful wallpaper in your home, you don't spend a lot of time admiring it.)

Sometimes, it's appropriate to create things that become "wallpaper." A reliable kitchen faucet may be a thing of beauty in its own right – but it never gets noticed because it never does anything different: that's its real beauty. It's nice to have light switches that always behave the same way: you can use them without conscious thought: they require little "cognitive overhead."

The nicely designed "back" and "forward" buttons in your Web browser are examples of well-behaved "cognitive wallpaper." Their behavior and appearance are completely predictable so you don't even think about them – and your mind's free to concentrate on the work in hand.

"Affordances" tell users what to expect

Donald Norman adopted this term from the American psychologist J.J. Gibson. Norman was a cognitive scientist before becoming a professional critic of computer interfaces (and also of "psychotic artifacts" in general, including automatic doors, modern phones, and video recorders).

Norman explains that certain objects have "knowledge built into them," as it were. For example, when you see an old-fashioned doorknob, you don't need to be told what it does. It "affords" turning, pulling, and pushing – but not lifting or sliding. An old-fashioned bellpush affords pushing and nothing else. These are just two out of thousands of things in our everyday environment that "make us smart."

It makes a lot of sense to use objects like these in interfaces because the user won't have to learn what they do and you won't have to waste effort and valuable "screen real-estate" explaining them. But beware: some things have "natural affordances" that lie: we've all encountered door handles that look as if they can be pulled, which in fact can only be pushed. And what's more, putting a sign that says "PUSH" beside the handle does not stop people trying to pull it: the written information may be in 6-inch-high letters, but it does not speak as loudly, or as directly to us, as the object's natural affordances do.

(This is thanks to the superior speed and power of "unconscious" brain processes, compared to the much slower ones that handle consciousness and language.)

Once you start looking at things through Norman's eyes you don't stop at the computer interface. You find yourself reinterpreting your whole environment – as in fact Norman does in his books. As you do so, you discover that many confusions you've suffered for years are not actually your fault (for being stupid) but the designer's fault (for creating stupid objects).[2]

Before interactive media came along, stupid objects could only be made, with some difficulty, by architects and product designers. With the computer you can make them very easily – and you may never know what you've done. As Norman says, people usually blame themselves for their confusion – not the designer. It can take careful testing to unearth these design bugs – people are too ashamed to admit to them voluntarily. They just steer clear of the product – it's a flop and nobody knows why.

"Slavish adherence to a metaphor"

Norman's work on "natural affordances" has led some thoughtless people to take interface design up a blind alley by assuming that we have to use "real world" objects, with well-known "affordances," in computer interfaces.

The Apple "Desktop Metaphor" has unintentionally provided ammunition for this view. Its success led many people to believe that "real-world metaphors" are the be-all and end-all of computer interface design. It's assumed that people will not be able to understand what's going on on the screen, unless it's represented by some familiar, friendly item from the "real world."

They ignore two things: (a) the Apple Desktop is not necessarily a literal metaphor: it is perhaps better seen as a playful parody – see below – and (b) they forget that the "real-world originals" were themselves novel once, and gained public acceptance perfectly well even though they were not metaphors for anything. Doorknobs are not metaphors for anything – they just do the job, and as soon as we've successfully used them once, they're part of our "internal toolkit." People (being "Gregorian") "internalize" new tools very quickly. We have assimilated such non-real-world tools as menu- and scroll-bars so quickly that they now seem natural.

Metaphors can help the user's expectations – insofar as their "natural affordances" truly reflect what's on offer. Otherwise they mislead, conceal, and complicate. If we're using the computer to do new things (and why else would we use them?) we soon run out of real-world objects to represent them. But if real-world objects could do the job they'd be doing it already; we wouldn't need the computer.

Interface metaphors (to use a metaphor) are perhaps best used as booster-rockets: to be handled carefully, and jettisoned immediately the user is "airborne." (End of metaphor.)

As usual, Ted Nelson put it really well ages ago. He wrote this back in 1989 (the italics are his):

the metaphor becomes a dead weight. Once the metaphor is instituted, *every related function has to become a part of it.*

... It becomes like a lie or a large government project: more and more things have to be added to it, and they have to be in some ... possibly obscure way, consistent. ...

The alternative to metaphorics *is the construction of well-thought-out unifying ideas ...*

... slavish adherence to a metaphor prevents the emergence of things that are genuinely new.[3]

He calls these "unifying ideas" "virtualities." These are built from the "conceptual structure" outwards – rather as TV sets, bicycles, lathes, potato-peelers, and other functional artifacts are, I suppose. His example of a good, computer-interface virtuality is the "Replicate" feature of the first spreadsheet, VisiCalc, which:

corresponds to nothing that was on earth previously; and when metaphoric thinking was dismissed, it could be designed cleanly with no reference to anything that had come before.

Brenda Laurel offers an even earlier authority in *Computers as Theater*: Aristotle – who said (in the Poetics – fourth century BC) that the proper function of art is not to represent what exists, but *what might be.*

However, this does not mean that "real-world metaphors" are uninteresting. You can play with metaphors in ways you can't play with the originals.

Ted Nelson (in the article quoted above) scorns the Apple Desktop because it's not really like a desktop: "I do not believe such desks exist and I would not want one if they did." But in a sense, the Apple Desktop succeeds precisely because of the humorous and playful ways it diverges from its real-world origins. Its original trashcan, which bulged when full, was one of the things that caught the public imagination when the Mac was launched. Being "inconsistent with the real-world model" was a plus, not a minus. It was fun, and functional. The trashcan's replacement in System 8.XX with a more realistic, non-bulging one suggests Apple has lost its original light, and winning, touch.

Talking heads you want to punch: Getting a sermon when you expected interactivity

Many early "interactive" systems were designed by people who mistook them for TVs. There were the "information kiosks" that could tell you all kinds of useful things – like where the nearest bathroom was – but wouldn't let you find anything until they'd given you a long, and probably quite lovingly produced, title sequence, during which you had to stand there grinding your teeth. ("Long" is relative. A good rule seems to be: *The user's awareness of time varies in inverse proportion to their distance from the screen –* and perhaps *as the square of the distance* if other people are watching.)

A lot of these early applications featured TV-style presenters, or "talking heads," which, again, took over and stopped you interacting with the system till they'd finished – and they did this every time you "went" to a new screen. These could turn users into homicidal maniacs. We tested one during our Interact project (Chapter 2.5) and even very gentle, unassertive users declared they would like to strangle or punch her. As they moved to the next part of the program they'd go, "no! not her again!" They found her "condescending," "arrogant," and "stupid." After a very brief exposure to the system they'd become reluctant to touch anything for fear of triggering another talking-head session.

Providing a "shut up" button didn't quite provide the answer: people seem to feel bad about shutting another human being up, even an annoying, digitized one.

Mark Schlichting provided the answer in his "Living Books" where, if you click to explore the book before your cartoon presenter has finished talking, he doesn't just stop dead and disappear. The animation branches to a half-second sequence where he shrugs self-deprecatingly, says "OK" and *then* shuts up. His tone of voice and facial expression are just right: a little wistful, but with no trace of resentment. That one little bit of animation turns an irritant into an asset.

Talking heads with unexpectedly shallow personalities

Talking heads set up expectations that could wreck everything – for example, when you came back to a place in the program that you visited only seconds before, and the "presenter" didn't remember you. You got the same "clip" all over again. You expect a lot from human beings – even digitized ones – and the very least you expect is that they'll recognize you next time they see you. Robert Carr's MacJesus – Chapter 2.1 – at least remembers your name. And of course you expect him to be a bit odd.

On the other hand, a few words from the programmer can make the system unexpectedly delightful Error messages and "system beeps" are also messages from another human (the programmer). The famous message that goes: "The Application 'Unknown' has unexpectedly quit because an error of Type 1 occurred" tells us that the programmer doesn't really want to talk to us. That's fair enough in a way – the programmer had his work cut out just getting the program to run. All the same, error messages alienate.

But error messages can be a system's most delightful and useful features (after all, trial-and-error is the typical human's preferred learning method). With Interact we knew our users would make mistakes because we were explaining complicated investment products. We spent some time developing a routine that used variables and conditionals to create messages like:

"Sorry – you can't put £8,000 into a Personal Equity Plan: the legal maximum is £6,000. Shall we try that instead?

"If you like, we can put the other £2,000 into our Special SuperDuper Interest Bond – which pays 9.5% (gross) at the moment."

Users were surprised and delighted when their errors were handled this way.

The interface as initiation rite

Among first-time multimedia designers, there is general agreement that the interface "has to be fun." Problems happen when this gets confused with making the application itself fun to use. What is the user expecting? If they're expecting puzzles, fine; but if they're expecting to get some information, don't frustrate them. If you want to give them a nice surprise, give them better information than they expected.

Many tests on website design have found that people are every bit as irritated when they get big, slow information-free graphics in response to their enquiring click, as they are to non-shut-uppable talking heads.

Gestapo interfaces: systems that unexpectedly change the rules

In the interactive puzzles in Alex Mayhew's "Ceremony of Innocence" the "rules of engagement" change constantly – which is fine: we're in a puzzle-world and expect that kind of thing. If we're not expecting it, it's profoundly disturbing.

I once tried a system called "Silver to Silicon," put together by students and teachers at a number of British colleges, which attempted to present the multifarious ways media affect our perceptions. It seemed a very good use of interactive media and the content itself was excellent. But each section was created by a different team, and the whole thing was only assembled at the last minute. Predictably, interaction worked differently depending on where you were in the application.

Sometimes mouse clicks did nothing because you were in a section that presented images or stories in a strictly linear way – but you didn't necessarily realize it: you thought that maybe this was a "hypermovie" and your clicks were making it branch into an alternative plot. In other, interactive sections the screen would just sit there doing nothing unless you clicked on something. What's more, in these interactive bits, the "rules of engagement" varied enormously: in some places, the same thing would happen wherever you clicked on the screen, in others you had to click on precise objects; other places used "rollovers": the mouse-pointer would change into a hand when it went over a "hot area," showing that that area was "clickable"; in others, there was nothing to show which areas were hot; in yet others, simply moving the pointer over a hot area triggered a transition to another screen.

It was acutely disorienting: like a conversation with a paranoid schizophrenic, where the rules are liable to sudden change at any moment, or one where confusing rules are set, and changed, by a small inner circle of initiates, or being interrogated: you never know whether your answer will get a you a sympathetic word, or a slap. You feel foolish at best. Do I look stupid when I click/don't click? The feeling was compounded by the fact that this was happening in a "fine art" environment, which is notoriously a shifting minefield of initiatory rites and subtle but crucial behavioral taboos.

Confusing the "spatial modeling" mind

The concept of "information space" is absolutely fundamental. The human mind seems to have evolved for finding our way around places. We can never see these places in their entirety so we make internal models of them, which we then refer to, adjust, etc. – largely unconsciously. Our "spatial modeling software" is so fundamental that it gets applied to just about everything we encounter – including multimedia applications. Good applications turn this powerful "software" to advantage, carelessly designed ones make it crash.

For example, current "help" systems (like Microsoft Help) give you a clear sense of the "space you're in": the help window comes "to the front" and your work remains "behind it." But in earlier systems you might click the "help" button and you'd "go" from the screen you were "in" to a different screen entirely. It felt as if you'd been whisked away into a distant part of the building: the basement where the help system lived: straight out of Kafka's castle or Orwell's 1984 (the actual 1984 was in fact the heyday of that kind of help system!).

This happens all over again on the Web – unless the site's designer has specified that the new information appears in a new browser window.

Cinematic tricks that help spatial expectations

The cinema learned how help the mind's "spatial modeling software" very early on with wipes, fades, and dissolves. Bill Atkinson built these into the Macintosh operating system at the very beginning. Transitions needn't take a lot of time but they really help: close or open a folder on the Macintosh desktop and observe the "zoom" effect. Atkinson's HyperCard authoring package included a wide range of transition effects, which made it easy to create a sense of "information space," and your current position in it. A "zoom open" took you "deeper," "zoom closed" took you out again, "wipe left" took you to adjacent information on the same conceptual level, etc. The Miller brothers' early works ("The Manhole," "Cosmic Osmo") relied heavily on this kind of visual clue. Of course, it was also easy to use transitions gratuitously so that users lost their bearings completely! Most of HyperCard's early imitators didn't provide transitions, perhaps considering them a superfluous gimmick.

In Interact we were working in Visual Basic, which didn't provide transitions at the time, so my colleague Chris McEvoy wrote some from scratch in C++. We were able to prove, in user tests, that they really did help users to find their way around the system.

I think Microsoft's "Musical Instruments" CD-ROM (1991) suffered from having no visual transitions. This was the first fruit of the short-lived collaboration with the original content-owners, Dorling Kindersley: based on their "Eyewitness" guide of that name. Transitions were abrupt. You clicked on the little picture of the instrument you were interested in, then bam: you found yourself in the screen that tells you all about it. OK, you got there and you got there with no messing about, but it felt uncomfortable – and it happened every time you moved from screen to screen, making it difficult to build up a mental model of the "information space." If the transitions didn't work quickly (because the next batch of graphics was being hauled into RAM from the CD-ROM), there was a very conscious hiccup: "delay … bam!": the pulling-a-brick-across-your-desk-with-a-piece-of-elastic effect: nothing happens, then it knocks your teeth out. "Musical Instruments" earned praise for its excellent graphics and information content – but it wasn't a big seller. Later DK titles have been much more successful – and pay great regard to visual transitions.

One of the limitations of the World Wide Web, as a medium, is that it is quite difficult for designers to "choreograph" visual transitions there. Transition from one "page" to another may be instantaneous, or take many seconds – depending on the speed of the user's modem, or even on the time of day.

Making the application seem smarter than it is, by pre-conditioning people's expectations

An application does not have to be deep to be good. People just need to know what to expect – and you can "flag" this subliminally.

As Harold Thimbleby puts it (*User Interface Design*, p. 172) people explore interactive applications like scientists exploring a new world:

the designer strives to build a system with … "natural laws" for the user to understand and exploit.

As soon as an application opens we start constructing theories to explain what's going on – and we do it unconsciously. If a graphic, when clicked, turns into an animation, we expect all other graphics to do that too – unless "non-clickable" graphics are made to look different. Two general techniques are worth mentioning.

"Heading the user off at the pass" – arranging things so that people don't expect what they can't have

Lisa Anderson's "Critical Mass" (Chapter 2.3) is a good demonstration of how to prevent the "hidden shallows" feeling. Here, you're never in any doubt as to "what's hot and what's not." There are plenty of "non-hot" graphics but you don't click them because you don't expect them to lead anywhere. Why? Because you learned in your first seconds that "hot" graphics always change state when the mouse is over them – and *you learned this without even noticing what you'd done.* How is that achieved?

As soon as you arrive at the "main menu" screen you move the mouse around *without even thinking about it* – and discover the "rollovers": graphics that change state and sprout a label when the mouse-pointer is over them. Thereafter it never occurs to you to click on anything that doesn't produce a rollover – hence you're never disappointed.

You've learned the system's limitations and basic rules *instantaneously and unconsciously*.

Note that this wouldn't work nearly as well if that menu screen wasn't absolutely packed with hot, "rollover" graphics: if it were more sparsely populated your random mouse-movements might not find a rollover, you'd click on a "dead" graphic, get no response, and decide that CD-ROMs are rubbish. After that menu screen, there are fewer rollovers but that doesn't matter by now: you've learned to look for them and don't bother clicking unless you find one.

Constraining the context: the "Eliza Effect"

Another way to "constrain expectations," which involves no work at the computer at all, is to "constrain the context."

This is why Joseph Weizenbaum's famous "Eliza" (the computerized psychoanalyst – Chapter 1.5) is so convincing, even though she isn't actually very "intelligent." You know she's supposed to be an analyst – so you automatically expect to have a certain kind of conversation with her: a rather formulaic one where your remarks are fed back to you in mildly modified form, and the (presumably very wise and perceptive) analyst sometimes changes tack abruptly, and asks you about something completely different. "Eliza" is programmed to hold that type of conversation and no other – she feeds key words back to you within a ready-made sentence. If she hasn't got a ready-made sentence, she just changes the subject. It simply doesn't occur to you to expect any other kind of response from her, so you assume she's intelligent. Her ruse ceases to work if we try to engage her in an ordinary, free-ranging conversation.

Games depend entirely on "constraint of context." Games like Simon Pick's "Die Hard Trilogy" offer realistic-looking worlds that *could* be hugely disappointing: we can't have conversations with people, we can't browse in the shops; all we can do is shoot people and run them over – but that's OK because that's all we expect.

Having narrowed our expectations, Pick and his team are then able to give us plenty of variety within its narrow confines.

Notes

1   William H. Calvin – "The Emergence of Intelligence," *Scientific American*, October, 1994. "Language, foresight, musical skills and other hallmarks of intelligence are connected through an underlying facility that enhances rapid movements." The ideas are developed in his latest book, *How brains think* (Basic Books, 1996).

2 For example, a friend's cottage contains a rather handsome kitchen stove that rejoices in the name of "Smeg" (it's from Sweden, not Red Dwarf). It reeks of "Scandinavian Design" with its discreet, enigmatic, label-free controls, and I have to consult the manual every time I go there. Harold Thimbleby (professor of Computer Science at Middlesex University in the UK) has described an occasion when he and another professor of computer science were reduced to a supper of corn-flakes because they could not operate the microwave oven in their vacation cottage.

3 "The right way to think about software design," in *The Art of Human–Computer Interface Design*, ed. Brenda Laurel, Addison-Wesley, 1990.

3.7

Storyspace: From the path to the landscape itself

> ❝I say I say I say – my dog's got no nose!
> Your dog's got no nose? How does he smell?
> Terrible!❞

> Bud Flanagan and Chesney Allen (I think), 1940s

STORIES ARE THE ULTIMATE GAME that people play with each others' expectations. The computer has stimulated tremendous interest in them – and this begins to yield important new understanding, as I hope to show.

First, what do we mean by "a story"? All stories – from movies, operas and novels, right down to jokes – are *generally*[1] agreed to have beginnings, middles, and ends.

- In the beginning: we (the audience) have something presented to us that's unresolved, or promises something: we're intrigued. ("I say I say," etc.)

- In the middle: the "story" gets going and we try to predict what may happen next – watching attentively to see if it really will turn out like that. ("Your dog ...?", etc.)

- In the end: whatever happens, happens: but not quite as we expected. ("Terrible!" – tumultuous laughter, or other emotional response.)

A story is (let's say) any "chunk" of experience that's organized in that particular beginning/middle/end way. Lots of things fit that description: from theories of the universe, to making a phone call, to switching on a light: not just the things you experience at your grandmother's knee. Many things we experience in life are like this. Maybe, *that's how we experience them*. Many real, physical phenomena – like gravity, and light – were simply not noticed by people, until acutely perceptive individuals came up with satisfactory stories about them.

Brief but recognizable events have "story" shape: raindrops falling on water for example.

A story "wraps up" some part of life's uncertainty. Where no suitable story exists, we always seem to try to invent one (the mind's "what happens next orientation" is always at work – Michael Gazzaniga has identified the brain region that does this: mentioned shortly). Storification is what drives science. It's also behind paranoia, superstitions, and religions that provide a satisfactory solution to the problems of life, after death. If we can neither find nor invent a suitable story to fit events, we're confused; we may even suffer psychological trauma and simply cannot function.

Is trauma the opposite of a story?   Here's a conjecture: If we can't perceive events as "stories," we can't perceive them at all. Events that have no discernible beginning, middle, or end are just meaningless "cognitive noise," and we just live with them the way we do with the weather or bad wallpaper. Too-abrupt events can be impossible to assimilate, even causing trauma. A real-life bombing or road accident is like that: one moment everything is perfectly normal, the next you are in the road and absolutely everything has changed. There's none of the gracefully managed buildup and letdown that makes movie violence so appealing.

"Stories" can be very quick – but not as sudden as an explosion, heist, or a car crash. They have a sequence – even if it's a very short one.

The all-important "sub-three-second domain"

How short is the shortest possible narrative? Apparently, somewhere between 50 milliseconds and about 3 seconds.[2] Under 50 ms, events simply don't make it into consciousness (although they do get to us unconsciously, with very powerful effects – see final chapter). The Czech poet and scientist Miroslav Holub calls this timespan "the duration of the present."

Why is this important? Because in interactive media the most obvious action is *precisely* in the sub-three-second domain: the way things respond to the user's actions, screen transitions are made, and information is fed back to the user.

Writers, film-makers, and stand-up comedians are virtuosos with these brief events: timing is everything (it's not what you do, it's the way that you do it). But they are able to do it simply through practice, without thinking. But when you work with the computer you *have* to think: an event that lasts 1 second has to be built up deliberately and logically, often in code, and can take hours to build and fine-tune. If we want to make our work as riveting as some writers and comedians make theirs, we need to know precisely what we're doing. We can't rely on unconscious intuition: we need to become conscious connoisseurs of the "sub-three-second domain."

Most computer-events can be looked at as little stories: You start off seeing clearly what kind of action you can take (a button you can "click" on maybe), confirmation that something is about to happen when you make the mouse click (the button highlights), then something does indeed happen (you go to a different screen, something is deleted, etc.).

If you just "clicked and went" (without the button highlighting) it wouldn't be as nice. It is perhaps like the difference between splitting stone neatly with a cold-chisel (a complete, satisfying action: preparation, commitment, and result), and having it suddenly fall apart in your hands (a confusing surprise: a real downer).

To some extent this is simply what HCI experts say already: clear choices are presented to you, you get feedback as you make the choice (so that you know you are indeed doing something and can back out of it if you need to), and you then get the result you thought you'd get. But that description is quite bland; it misses the element of delight, emotional engagement that we get from really good and useful things.

In "story" terms, something extra is happening: anticipation (mouse over the button), a moment of commitment (the mouse is down – now what will happen?), and release (we get a result – and ideally one that's *better* in some way than we expected): there is emotional involvement all the way, and emotional reward at the end.

It could be worth spending time and imaginative effort to give things a brief, even as menu choices, "story shape." These are the "small change" of computer interaction, but they are used again and again and again. They are its "everyday things."

On the larger scale, the whole interaction can have "dramatic shape": from the moment you open the application, to the moment you exit from it.

This sounds a tough challenge. A multimedia application is a bit like life: there is lots of it. You may be able to explore the information it contains by thousands of routes, of unpredictable lengths. Is it possible to design systems in such a way that whatever route the user takes, and whatever its duration, it will have the characteristics of a good story: a beginning, a middle, and an end, with some delight provided? Is this an impossible goal? As we'll see in a moment this is perhaps *exactly* what happens in successful software, like spreadsheets.

But first, I want to show that this really does tie in with accepted, road-tested psychology and Human–Computer Interaction (HCI) theory – as well as adding some useful extra "top-spin" to it.

Stories provide "closure"

The term "closure" originated in mathematics and migrated to psychology, where it connects to the idea of "chunking" (developed by the psychologist George Miller in 1956).[3] Miller noted that while our short-term memory (which lasts for about 20 seconds) can hold only seven items – plus or minus two – we can remember very large numbers of things if we arrange them into "chunks." For example, you can remember seven individual letters (±2) – but you can also remember seven dozen letters – if those letters make up seven 12-letter words. And so on.

It seems we have a structure in our brains (left lobe, where 98 percent of people's language centers live) that strives to put sense-impressions into meaningful units, or chunks: it can turn a stream of sounds into words, or a bunch of colors and shapes into "a flower" or "a car." It gives us a certain pleasure when it succeeds in doing so. The short-term memory, as it were, "breathes a sigh of relief." Richard Gregory has dubbed this the "ahah!" effect. His co-worker Priscilla Heard likens it to having your arms full of shopping, and being given a bag.

The British HCI guru Harold Thimbleby notes that: "*The sense of closure may be sufficient to eclipse other goals the person still has outstanding*" – for example, you buy your ticket but forget your change; or get your money from the ATM (automated teller machine), and leave your card behind: which is why nearly all ATMs now eject your card before they give you your money: the "money-getting experience" is turned into a complete "chunk."

"Chunking" and the "7±2" rule for short-term memory have long been very important for computer interface designers. It explains why interfaces with dozens of buttons can be such a bad idea, and why you should not leave users in situations where necessary tasks aren't completed. (That's why software designers assist chunking with "forcing functions" – like the "no-cash-before-you've-removed-your-card" rule in ATMs, and the "modal" dialog boxes in applications, that prevent you doing anything until you've finished "saving" a document.)

Also, you need to help the user "chunk" things *correctly*. The distinguished American neuroscientist Michael Gazzaniga[4] has done experiments that show the left-brain "chunking mechanism" is so keen to do its work that it will chunk things incorrectly, rather than forgo the pleasure of closure.

This, he says, could be how false memories are created. It also fits perfectly with computer users' now-famous tendency to create quite elaborate (and totally wrong) explanations of what the computer is doing when things go wrong.

You can follow this fascinating subject up for yourself in Thimbleby's and Donald Norman's books (Norman doesn't mention "closure" specifically – but his writing relates to it strongly. His work in cognitive science was largely in the area of attention and short-term memory). What I want to do now is put these concepts into the context of "stories." It may be that "chunks" and "stories" are in fact the same thing – but whether they are or are not, what follows fits the neuroscience quite well – while putting it into a context that dramatizes its relevance to the task in hand: creating good experiences for other people.

"Chunking" and "closure," then, deliver an "emotional payoff." What stories seem to do is strive to maximize the "emotional payoff." If you like, the payoff was originally a byproduct of the brain's need to organize sensory data – and has now become an end in itself. We are addicted to it; stories feed our addiction. Presumably it's an addiction that carries an evolutionary benefit.

Stories (in the grandmother's knee sense) play constantly with the "user's" expectations: from the initial "promise" or "fascinating problem," though the "what-happens-next?" midsection, to the "so *that's* what happens" of the finale (or *dénouement*, to use the literary term).

I think it is worth considering whether other successful artifacts do this too – and if they don't whether they should. If our websites, VR worlds and other applications can engage people's interest as well as jokes and fairy tales do, we'll be well ahead of the game.

Stories have shapes – and so does good interaction

In *Computers as Theater*, Brenda Laurel proposes that, when interaction goes well, it has many of the characteristics of a good play. This was described very simply in a famous diagram by a nineteenth-century German novelist and playwright called Gustav Freytag (in 1863, in a book called *Technique of Drama*).

A stage play (or a good tale) has a period of "rising action" where the uncertainties of the action build up (like Priscilla Heard's groceries), a climax (where they're almost falling all over the floor), and a period of "falling action" where the uncertainties fall into place until you get to

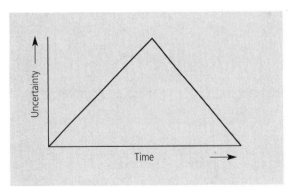

The basic "Freytag Triangle"

the dénouement – and carry the whole experience home, happily, in its "cognitive carry-bag." Laurel shows that good human-computer interaction proceeds in a very similar way.

She points out that plays, novels, and computer tasks are all, in fact, a little bit more complicated than Freytag's diagram shows. You have subsidiary "peaks and troughs" – see second diagram – but the basic shape is still there. This is like a graph of a "dance with user expectations."

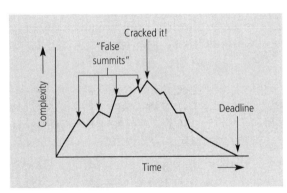

With a little modification, the "Freytag graph" fits all manner of other activities – including work projects, as here.

Interest is constantly stimulated and rewarded both on the way "up" and on the way "down." She suggests this could explain why spreadsheets are such a success. Dan Bricklin's "Visicalc" (the first spreadsheet program – for the Apple II) turned the personal computer from a hacker's toy into a mainstream product because it turned the messy business of juggling numbers into a satisfying, complete, and engrossing activity that has just this kind of structure: there are problems to overcome all the way but they are enticing challenges, not daunting obstacles (most of the time).

You could do sums on the computer before – but the spreadsheet gives the job a dramatic shape and wholeness it never had before. It is actually fun to use (OK – for quite a lot of us)! You proceed from puzzlement, through uncertainty as you try to marshal figures on the "virtual page" in a meaningful way, through frustration – where the calculation comes out wrong – to anticipation – where you begin to see daylight – to delight and pride as the neatly formatted results emerge from your printer.

Cash-machines as theater A speculation: Could this be the real reason why ATMs became such a hit with the public? The interaction with the machine was brief, but it was definitely dramatic: there was always the dreadful possibility that the machine would swallow your card, huge relief when it didn't, and a superb dénouement: cash in your hand.

At every stage there's a lot of "what happens next?" going on in your mind, followed by an "emotional payoff." This suggests to me that maybe we should look at other successful artifacts and see if they do that too.

Fun and function in artifacts of all kinds: is "storification" manufacturing's real agenda?

When we make things, we focus consciously on getting the job done. Getting it done *interestingly* is every bit as important to human beings: makers and users alike.

If we look at the world of "serious" artifacts (cars, microwave ovens, ATMs, houses, etc.) very few of them merely "do the job" – they all strive to do it delightfully. As I said right back in Chapter 1, people have been striving to cause delight with the media they use almost from the beginning. This is not just a matter of "prettification." Making things fun to use also makes them more functional: a good sharp knife is a pleasure to use, and you carve better with it too. It also makes them more desirable: in a world where there are plenty of cars to choose from, a car that's no fun to drive goes nowhere faster than anything else on wheels. Ditto, personal stereos, computers, software packages, dishwashers, packaged holidays, retail operations ... everything.

A lot of attention is paid to the visual detail of artifacts – but relatively little seems to be paid (by HCI writers at any rate) to the fine detail of their *behavior*. There may be a major gap in my knowledge here, but I have not found any analysis of the effect of "well or badly shaped behavior" in, for example, car gear-shifts – although people do seem to prefer ones that have a "nice feel," and motor manufacturers invest a lot of effort in making car doors that shut with a satisfying "Ker-Lunk": it seems a brief event, but I think it lasts quite a bit longer than the 50 ms required for conscious awareness; it seems to have a definite, and apparently very important, "shape" to it.

"Storytelling" maybe gives us a way of analyzing effects like these, and enhancing the user's experience.

Fractals: The story is (maybe) the same at every level of magnification

Brenda Laurel offers another very interesting insight: the individual segments of the "story graph" are *perhaps* "fractally self-similar" (just as the "wiggliness" of a twig is similar to the "wiggliness" of the tree as a whole).

For example, it could be (if we could measure it) that each of Tolstoy's sentences in *War and Peace* has a similar dramatic shape to *War and Peace* as a whole. That *seems* plausible – I think I can identify a Tolstoy sentence in isolation, and maybe even tell that it is a sentence from *War and Peace*, rather than *Anna Karenina*. We certainly do this kind of thing with music (identify the composer, or the band, from just a few bars – even though we don't know the particular tune). Many people can do it with films as well: there is plenty to go on: the "pace" of cutting, the way the camera moves, the ways speech, ambient sound, and music are paced, fade in and out.

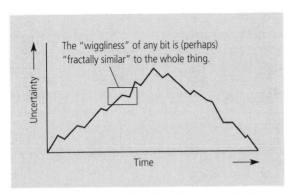

The "wiggliness" of any bit is (perhaps) "fractally similar" to the whole thing.

Uncertainty

Time

A more realistic version of Freytag's Triangle – with its intriguing fractual implication!

It would be very nice if we could make each little piece of interaction in an interactive title a microcosm of the interaction as a whole: the way a menu highlights, or a recalculation appears, and so on. Looking back at my examples, I think many of them do this. In "Lulu" I certainly get a sense of languid, dreamy movement that's consistent on all timescales: from the turning of a page and the way an animation appears, to the development of the story itself. Every event has a distinct beginning, middle, and end and proceeds through that sequence in a similar, graceful way. There are no sudden events. Rushed ones would stick out like sore thumbs. The same comment applies to Alex Mayhew's "Ceremony of Innocence." It also applies to Robert Carr's "MacJesus" – abruptness is the rule there, rather than grace.

One question this raises is: how can we achieve this kind of consistency on the Web – where we have no control over the pace at which things load into the user's browser? To what extent does that restrict its usefulness as a medium?

It seems to help if we consider even very small events (like clicking "close" boxes) as stories. They may be quick, but they seem to work best if they have a definite beginning, a middle and an end – and proceed through these stages with a certain grace.

In stories, only one thing can happen at a time

There are lots of situations in new-media design where lots of things can happen at once. But if you have ever made a movie or a video, you have probably discovered how carefully each step of the action has to be spelled out – and if you rush things, or try to introduce even two new things at once, you completely lose the audience.

For example, Interact (Chapter 2.5) had lots of situations where the user would change one figure (e.g, the price of the house they wanted to buy) and that would cause several other figures to change (the monthly repayment, insurance cost, total interest paid, etc.). The computer can calculate all of these things before you can blink. Just dumping them on the screen is very confusing for the user: they may not notice some of the changes; if they were looking at the one figure that *didn't* change, they were apt not notice that the others *did* change. We found it was vital to "choreograph" the way figures appeared, so that the changes rippled through the screen from top to bottom. The sequence can tell a story, and save you from having to provide text explanations (and the user from having to read them). Without that careful pacing, one thing at a time, it's like an explosion: everything changes and the mind is thrown.

Narrative flow (why people watch rivers and bad TV)   Why shouldn't new media have "narrative flow"? It could be the perfect answer to the "stuffed dog effect" (see Chapter 3.5).

Leaning over a bridge and watching the river is an age-old pastime that's very satisfying. There is no grand narrative but hundreds of little, similar-shaped events are developing and decaying, of different durations, mostly of three seconds or less: there is a constant, low-key "what-happens-next" game going on that sustains interest. Perhaps TV and film benefit from this effect where CD-ROM usually doesn't. In London's Museum of the Moving Image you can see a short film-sequence, made in the very early 1900s, of people simply disembarking from a cross-channel ferry: nothing more to it than that. It was quite a hit in the music-halls where it was first shown – and is still absolutely fascinating. Again, there is that busy sequence of short, similar-shaped events – a species of "narrative flow." Pathé called it *actualité* and made many such sequences for his new movie theaters, so they are pretty much what got cinema started.

Almost any film or video has a narrative flow that makes it watchable, even if the flow isn't particularly strong. Most "multimedia" has no narrative flow unless the user instigates it. It is "user-driven." The Norwegian new-media scholar Espen Aarseth calls it "ergodic" (it requires some work-input from the user). Finding out what happens next carries a slight but significant cost; but with a film, it carries no cost at all; you just sit there and let it happen – and you will still sit there even if it does not happen to be very good. Few movie-makers are as good as Alfred Hitchcock but perhaps the movie medium is successful *precisely because* it does not need authors as good as Alfred Hitchcock to make it work.

There is no reason why multimedia shouldn't be like this. Multimedia titles could give themselves a "free ride" by making the interface come alive. As I said in the last chapter ("stuffed-dog syndrome"), we have millions of spare processor-cycles to play with and could use these to make interfaces that are as watchable as rivers or the wind on trees.

Narrative as landscape

I'll now bring another dimension to this business of narrative: the third dimension.

I'm suggesting that we think of narratives not as a linear things, paths, but as three-dimensional spaces, or landscapes, through which we happen to *take* paths.

Brenda Laurel's "modified Freytag triangle" looks like a cross-section through a mountain range:

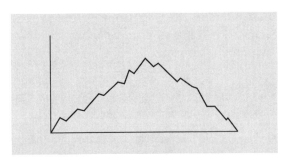 

Graph of the action in a farce like *Charley's Aunt*, and the Auguille du Midi, in the French Alps. Are they by any chance related? (Author's images)

Recall (when I spoke about advertising) that a series of ads and commercials (and all the brochures and leaflets that go with it) tell the same story – but in different ways. It's as if they are offering the audience a wide choice of different "routes through the territory": long ones, short ones, easy ones, technical ones, ones with different starting and end-points, but always giving you at least a glimpse of the main "features of the landscape" on the way.

Campaigning through Volvo-land   An advertising campaign for a car may have ads that
start off telling you how fast it is: "You can only tell it's a Volvo from behind" (front-view of the
Volvo 850 in someone's rear-view mirror; rear view as it overtakes), how safe it is: "If the door-
handle breaks, the copywriter dies" (shot of a Volvo suspended by its door-handle above the
recumbent writer, David Abbott), how convenient it is for large families, etc. Each ad "covers the
same ground" – but by different "routes."

Good salesmen work in exactly this way: their "terrain" is the product, and
they take every single customer through it by a different route, tailored
exclusively for them, on the fly, in real time. A bad salesman, by definition,
is one who only knows one route – his "sales script" – and gets "lost"
when distracted from it.

Good teachers excel at finding "multiple paths through the same territory": they work very hard to "find a way in" for each pupil. Indeed, we all
know that we all have different "ways in" to subjects of all kinds: one
person may "get into" Roman history via Robert Graves's "Claudius"
novels; another will get into it by discovering pottery fragments on the
edge of a ploughed field. I got into computing by a completely different
route from the one you took. Both of us will eventually cover a lot of the
same ground, but by different routes, and have a lot of pleasure comparing
experiences when we meet. Much as real-world travelers do.

Writers seem to do it. It's often said that novelists have one novel in them,
and keep retelling it in different ways. Maybe this really is the case.
Perhaps Tolstoy's *War and Peace* really is a "conceptual landscape" in
Tolstoy's head, and the text he published is simply a route he found
through it; his other works perhaps traverse different parts of the same
landscape, by different routes, of different lengths. I certainly get a similar
experience from all Tolstoy novels. It seems rather like when I go walking
though a familiar bit of countryside: I may take a different route each
time, but I always feel I've visited the same landscape.

Good stories have digressions

Tolstoy *behaves* as if he is in a landscape. He is famous for his "digressions," where he "leaves the main path" of the tale to explore some
philosophical or historical issue at length – just like a good mountain
guide who takes you off the track for a while to show you some ruins, or
an interesting geological structure, or a fantastic view, or to sit in the
shade and eat lunch. (And he shares this tendency with just about every
other story teller, from Homer to William Shakespeare – who take their

audiences off on spectactular detours into extended metaphor – to stand-up comics, to you or me.)

Of course, digressions are the whole point of hypermedia. It aims to let people find their own best routes through the "information space." They're not forced to follow some predefined route. Freedom to digress, at our own pace, is one of the computer's most general attractions: popping up definitions in "Encarta," following links on the World Wide Web – and trying different fonts and formats when word-processing, and exploring "what-if" calculations in Excel. We digress under our own steam – but within a world created by the software designer. These may be virtual worlds, but their natural laws are every bit as real as those of the natural world: you can't defy computer logic any more than you can gravity.

Does the landscape idea shed any new light on the design of CD-ROMs, websites, or whatever?

Here are some thoughts – and their implications for design:

Good landscapes needn't have many paths ...

Some of the best ones have hardly any. Just as Everest has only two main approach routes, so a new-media product can be highly attractive with only one or two. "Go everywhere from everywhere" isn't aways what people want. Alex Mayhew's "Ceremony of Innocence" has only one main path; so does Romain Victor-Pujebet's "Lulu."

... but you can go "off piste" if you want to

A good landscape may only have a few major routes, but there's also plenty of scope for the Reinhold Messner types, who want to tackle the North Face without oxygen.

Bill Atkinson's HyperCard did this very well with its five "user levels," from "browsing" (where you simply "click around" in a ready-made HyperCard application, without changing it) to "authoring" (where you program in HyperTalk). Atkinson also considered a sixth "hacking" level, where you'd be able to get at the Pascal source code as well. Considered as a landscape, HyperCard has a "terraced" topography – like the Grand Canyon, or Ordesa in Spain.

Microsoft's Excel spreadsheet seems a bit like the English Lake District, which has something for everyone. There's a seamless progression from "easy routes" (for example where, like most users, you only use the "sum" function) to "moderate" routes (where you use more advanced functions, use the output of one calculation as the input for another, and use "named" cells to simplify function-writing) to "very hard severe" routes (where you can write "macros" that automatically create entire new suites of interconnected custom-worksheets, complete with built-in functions and formatting).

My main wordprocessor (Nisus, for the Macintosh) has a more ravine-like landscape: it lets most people do all the basic stuff pretty easily, but it also has a programming language that lets you turn your documents into Web pages, generate haikus, and reinvent Excel (badly) – but it's a stiff, near-vertical climb from the "low-level" stuff to the "high ground" and falling off is normal (there again, it's never fatal – which is nice).

People like to know challenges are there – even if they don't attempt them themselves

Whether the landscape is accommodating (like Excel) or scary (like Nisus), the very fact that it offers high-level challenge is a very real part of its attraction to novices and hard cases alike. This seems to apply to everything: for example, the millions of rugged, off-road vehicles that people buy, never to tackle anything more terrifying than a trip to the supermarket.

The paths don't have to be easy – just satisfying

This links back to Doug Engelbart's observations about not making things easy for the user, if that limits what the user can do. Gratuitous obstacles aren't a good idea – but people love challenges if they feel they're "getting somewhere" (as they say).

All good landscapes have distinctive "fractal dimensions"

A good landscape has a distinctive "overall shape." There is no single "right shape" – but its shape tends to recur in tiny features as well as large ones. Hence, even a brief, easy stroll gives you a sense of "having been there." (This echoes what I said earlier, about stories being "similar on every scale" – Romain Victor-Pujebet's "Lulu" being my chosen example.) Any route, to some extent, gives you the feeling of knowing the whole thing.

The best landscapes have landmarks – but few road signs

Road signs are an intrusion in real life, but computer "desktops" and websites offer little else.

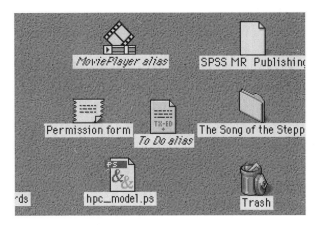

A bit of my Mac's desktop: nothing but "road signs"

It might be nice if these things had landmarks that, like mountains, give us a *general* sense of where we are and what's "out there."

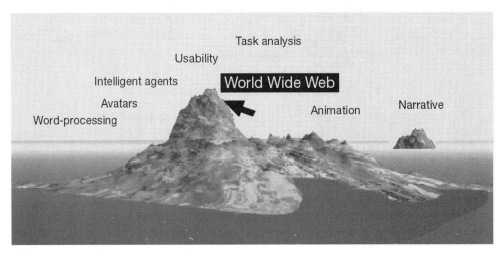

A world of information at a glance. Matthew Chalmers, then at Xerox Europarc, built a system called "Bead" that built "landscapes" out of data in 1993. It looked a bit like this. The most-mentioned subjects became the most prominent features; you could "zoom in" to find out more. Chalmers is now at the Union Bank of Switzerland's UBILAB. This kind of thing is called a Geographical Information System – and it has made little impression on the world of personal computing. (Author's image)

Note that in a real-life landscape, landmarks do not entirely guarantee you won't get lost – but nobody seems to object to that arrangement. That's partly because the landmarks tell "landscape users" what they're in for when they start out.

"Souvenirs" are an important part of the experience

Rocks and pebbles that you bring home are continuing reminders of what it was like. Their computer equivalent might be printouts: on the Interact project (Chapter 2.5) we wanted everything that the system printed for users (mortgage quotations, etc.) to be attractive "mementos" of their Interact session – not just "system excreta."

Good landscapes are full of surprises – but they are always in character

You don't expect to find a supermarket halfway up Everest, or rhododendrons in the Sahara.

Landscapes are usually discovered and explored, not manufactured

In the popular imagination, creative work seems like a matter of inventing things – but for creative workers (and people who study them) it seems more often to be a process of *finding* things. Remember what James Webb Young says (Chapter 3.3) about "feeling the subject with the tentacles of your mind." Creative work seems to be about exploration. What you're exploring may be a "possibility space" (like the "world of Money," or probability, or Middle Earth) or a world that's taking shape in your own mind. Either way, it has its own "physics," flora and fauna, and "overall shape."

The "landscape metaphor" seems to shed useful light on the way we do creative work – as I'll explain in the next chapter.

Notes

1 Some people point out that soap operas just go on and on with no apparent beginning or end. But in fact every soap opera is a very skilful interweaving of lots of stories, with three or so very carefully crafted ones going on at any time – and these *do* have clear beginnings, middles, and ends. I'd say soap operas are a very good use of the "narrative flow" principle, discussed later in this chapter.

   I believe there are also some postmodernists who believe "story structure" is passé. If so, I'd argue that (1) there's no evidence and (2) if it is passé the human brain is passé too.

2 These figures come from various sources: The physicist Paul Davis's "About Time," the philosopher Daniel Dennett's *Consciousness Explained*, Guy Claxton's *Hare Brain Tortoise Mind*, Steven Pinker's superb *The Language Instinct*, and Miroslav Holub's *The Duration of the Present Moment*. Three seconds is the maximum duration of a line of poetry in all cultures, apparently.

3 Miller's famous paper is "The magical number seven, plus or minus two: some limits on our capacity for processing information," *Psychological Review*, 63.

4 Gazzaniga, Michael S., "The split brain revisited," *Scientific American*, July, 1998. See also his book *The Mind's Past* – University of California Press, 1998. Gazzaniga, who works at Dartmouth College, Maryland, has studied "split-brain" patients since the 1960s – work that has proved that the two halves of the brain work in different ways. Joseph LeDoux (mentioned elsewhere in this book) has worked closely with Gazzaniga.

3.8

Working in Cyberia: From storyspace to the real world

❝Enjoyment ... is the cutting edge of sociocultural evolution❞

Mihalyi Csikszentmihalyi: Optimal Experience

WHAT IS THE BEST WAY TO WORK in Cyberia? The most successful examples mentioned in this book have these common features:

▨ They are by small teams: ten people or fewer. Some are by lone workers.

▨ Most of them have deep roots (they grew, often over many years, from important personal experiences that had little, originally, to do with computing).

▨ The work itself was usually done in a single, fairly short, intense burst of work: nearly always well under a year.

▨ Every project was led by the person who had the original vision, and kept "ownership" of the project all the way through to completion.

▨ At the same time, there's a strong sense of "shared ownership" within the team.

There are other common features – but I'm singling these ones out particularly because they are so at odds with the way work is done in conventionally organized businesses – and because they happen to match very closely the characteristics of successful teams, described by two acknowledged "heavyweights" of computer project management, Frederick P. Brooks (in his classic *The Mythical Man-Month*) and Tom Love (*Object Lessons*).

Brooks's *The Mythical Man-Month* was first published in 1975, has never been out of print, and is now available in a revised, expanded twentieth anniversary edition.

Brooks challenged the whole military/hierarchical approach to computer work. His observations rang bells in many other areas of work: he was surprised to find that "lawyers, doctors, psychologists, sociologists" were as inspired by his message as software people. He argued for "surgical teams" of no more than ten very able persons – as opposed to the "brute force" or "hog butchering"[1] approach favored by traditional businesses.

His *bête noire* is macho management, and its tendency to throw people at a problem in a great, glittering phalanx. The reasoning seems to go: "It took Tolstoy (an old amateur with no proper qualifications) five years to write *War and Peace*: that's 60 man-months. We'll hire 60 top professionals and have it cracked in one month." Creative workers have rarely felt happy with this approach, but Brooks supports the intuition with hard figures.

He found that while "*cost does indeed vary as the product of the number of men and the number of months, progress does not. Hence the man-month as a unit for measuring the size of a job is a dangerous and deceptive myth.*"

His recommended regime is strikingly similar to the one we find in successful new-media work: "small, sharp teams" (ten or fewer) that feel a sense of ownership of the work they're doing – and do it within a human time-frame. Above all, there is a guiding sense of "audience": the user for whom the work is intended. He found that:

the most important action is the commissioning of some one mind to be the product's architect, who is responsible for the conceptual integrity of all aspects of the product perceivable to the user. This includes the detailed specification of all of its function and the means for invoking and controlling it.

The "architect" role is very similar to that of Romain Victor-Pujebet (Chapter 2.4) or any of the leader-authors in this book. Curtis Wong's description of his "producer/author" role (Chapter 2.3) echoes Brooks strikingly clearly.

The architect is "the user's agent" on the system and, says Brooks, it is a full-time job. "Only on the smallest teams" can it be combined with the role, say, of manager – and maybe not even then. In his afterword to the 1995 edition, he reports applying this role, successfully, to teams as small as four people. It seems new-media workers have intuitively adopted something like the "approved" approach. Which isn't to say that they have nothing to learn from Brooks: his "architect" is solely the "user's agent" – not necessarily the project's instigator – although it's probably best if the instigator can play the "architect" role. But where the instigator is the client, or some other remote figure or committee in the company you're working for, a specialist architect becomes vital. Victor-Pujebet was also project manager – a notoriously stressful role. Production can be terribly intense – 12- and 20-hour days with no letup for weeks – and a good, specialist manager can be an absolute godsend (see my remarks about our own manager, Julie Cutts, on the Interact project – Chapter 2.5. There, we had one manager for just two of us).

Brooks is particularly good on management: something that commercial organizations seldom seem to get right (the fortunes they spend on management training are probably more a symptom of the problem than evidence that they've got it under control). Inexorably, managers seem to turn into policemen or minor feudal lords. You'll be pleased to know that kick-ass techniques are not approved by Brooks. He recommends another book that is really worth owning: Tom DeMarco and Timothy Lister's *Peopleware* (mentioned again below).

DeMarco and Lister have studied the effects of different styles of management under almost laboratory conditions, and found that the dictatorial, "military" style, so detested by creative workers, is hugely (and measurably) unproductive. They say: *"The manager's function is not to make people work, but to make it possible for people to work."*

Since these books were written, even stronger evidence has come in. I specially recommend Guy Claxton's *Hare Brain, Tortoise Mind* for its wealth of scientific experimental evidence, which supports DeMarco and Lister's findings. Claxton's examples demonstrate the extent to which fear, insecurity, and criticism drastically reduce people's creative abilities.

In one of several well-designed experiments, two groups of non-golfers were taught putting. Both were instructed in exactly the same way, but one group was told that they'd be inspected at the end of the course by a famous professional. This group's performance (measured in balls successfully "sunk") was far lower than the other group. The small anxiety of knowing a professional would be watching them devastated their ability to learn (for reasons that are now well understood: see "Good managers are guardians, not guards," later in this chapter).

Claxton mentions an illuminating, rather disillusioned, comment from George Prince (who had co-founded "Synectics" – a system for "enhancing creativity" that is widely sold to companies). He:

came to realize that speculation, *the process of expressing and exploring tentative ideas in public, made people, especially in the work setting, intensely vulnerable, and that … people came to experience their workplace meetings as unsafe.*

People's willingness to engage in delicate explorations on the edge of their thinking could be easily suppressed by an atmosphere of even minimal competition and judgement. "Seemingly acceptable actions such as close questioning of the offerer of an idea, or ignoring the idea … tend to reduce not only his speculation but that of others in the group." (Hare Brain …, pp. 77–8*)*

> Joseph LeDoux has now explained the brain-processes that are responsible in great detail, in his book *The Emotional Brain*. I shall mention him again below.
>
> All of these books provide "smoking gun" evidence of the almost-criminal inefficiency of old, fear-ridden, hierarchical, military-style work regimes – and authoritative support for the regimes used by my "eminent Cyberians."
>
> My other "computer-heavyweight" source is Tom Love's *Object Lessons*. Love's book is mainly about the object-oriented approach to computer programming – which he places firmly in the context of working life, and all the so-called "soft" human factors that go with it.
>
> Like Brooks, Love is essentially a "small teams," "human timescale" man. His preferred way of working fits precisely the idea of work-as-exploration I developed earlier.

The software business, like mountain climbing, requires macrodecisions and split-second tactical decision making. We must decide which system to build, estimate how long it will take, and determine the amount of energy it will consume. Then, as the ascent progresses, hundreds of tactical decisions must be made without undue deliberation or dispute. Literally, the careers of a development team hang on every decision.

Software team leaders should think of themselves as leaders of a rope team ascending a rock- and glacier-strewn mountain with all available supplies on their backs. The rope team is tied together; a fall by one person can cause everyone to fall." (Object Lessons, p. 170)

> The climbing team is not the only good analogy. Other people use other ones: Brooks talks about surgical teams; many new-media workers are musicians, and find rock bands a good analogy; for others it is deep-water sailing; still others may prefer the analogy of working in a theater company. All of these types of team, and many more, provide models of work organization that are vastly more effective, more efficient, and more fun than the "glittering phalanx" approach.

A very important researcher into creativity, Mihalyi Csikszentmihalyi[2] (and his circle) has in fact studied all of these types of group in great depth over the years – and found that they share a strong common core of characteristics: especially, there's that clear sense of knowing *what* you have to do and *that* you can do it; a loss of self-consciousness; and a tendency of time itself to become different: it can fly, stand still, and everything in between! He calls this state of mind "flow" (or "happiness").

A working model: Mountaineering vs. civil engineering

In the last chapter, I showed how communicative work can be described as a journey in "information space": a landscape no less; often a demanding, complicated, but interesting landscape such as a mountain range.

Depending on your mind-set, a mountain range can be either a wonderful, inspiring sight, or a huge civil-engineering problem. To climb mountains is cheap, exciting, and good for you physically and spiritually. The engineering approach is horrendously expensive, and "boring": making tunnels can be quite well paid but it is not much fun; using them is quick, but dull.

When a landscape is geologically young and unstable, major investment in road tunnels can quickly become money down the drain. Cyberia is *highly* unstable – a major reason why brute-force, "civil-engineering" style software development has such a low success rate.

Of course, more people will get through the boring tunnel – if it can be completed – but given the choice (and with computers we can, perhaps, offer this kind of choice) many people would probably rather traverse the mountains as mountaineers than as "spam in a can" – if the route could be made acceptably safe, easy, and quick.

Also, when the landscape is complex and rich, it can be far better to give people a route that allows them to learn something about it, than one that hides the reality from them. The terrain may contain other things of interest that they may want to explore – things they had not realized were important to them.

A practical example based on that analogy   A "civil-engineering" mortgage-quotation system might just ask you your salary and age, then tell you what maximum loan you can get (based on standard assumptions about your future earning prospects, disposable income, how much capital you can contribute yourself, etc. – none of which the user can see). A "mountaineering" system would allow you to see all the assumptions (the "main features" of the model), explore them, understand them – and modify your approach. It may turn out that you can actually afford a bigger mortgage – or need to get a grip on your household budget.

I believe that creative work in any medium involves finding a "realm of possibility," exploring it, and building a path or paths through it, so that some (but not necessarily all) other people can traverse and explore it too – but without all the dead-ends and difficulties you had to go through yourself. To this extent, whether we work with words, paint, machinery, or computing machinery, we are all Vannevar Bush's "trailblazers."

The way trailblazing is done in the real world, by actual climbers and explorers, seems to provide a very good, and simple, model for enjoyable, successful, new-media work.

Mountaineering as a model for work

The terrain is the main attraction

Teams have a strong, *shared vision* of the goal, which they feed generously in all manner of ways, long before they start out: with maps, books, conversation, reconnoitering.

This "shared vision" is the obvious, and main, point at which new-media work differs: the "mountains" are invisible. On a commercial project, they may not be your mountains of choice. The vision offered to workers can be very sparse – and workers are usually not automatically inclined to "feed" it themselves – let alone in the enthusiastic way mountaineers do.

Yet it is very noticeable that a team's productivity and morale shoot up through the roof once the job starts to take physical shape: as soon as people can *see* what's to be done, they do it. The problem is establishing this "shared vision" early on in the project. It's the single biggest challenge, according to Microsoft's Jim McCarthy (in *Dynamics of Software Development*). "The vision" cannot be handed down to the workers on tablets of stone or kept in the managing director's filing cabinet; it needs to be something very much richer, which everyone contributes to.

To a great extent, the terrain forms the team for you

Headhunters, big salaries, and relocation bonuses aren't required: the mere rumor of unclimbed mountains brings people across continents at their own expense. Choosing a team is still a critical matter, but it is also true that otherwise-incompatible individuals often find they can work together just fine, once they're in the field.

In new media, team-building can be a headache – but perhaps if we can make the "vision" clear enough, it will draw the right people, draw out the best from the people we've got, and unify the team the way a mountain does. More on this below – as Jim McCarthy says, it is the main issue.

The terrain largely sets the agenda

Nobody attempts to reach goals that self-evidently aren't there, or routes that self-evidently aren't viable. The parameters of choice are very clear.

In new-media work it's easy to set ambitious agendas, and then find that the "landscape" thwarts them. Again – if we could get a better sense of the "terrain" before we start, our work would be simpler and more effective.

There's a definite timescale

This "comes with the terrain." You know you have to be down by nightfall, or back home by the end of two weeks. Even big expeditions seldom last longer than six months. The obvious reason is cost – but another, very big, reason is that people just don't seem to be designed to cope well with longer timescales. Beyond a few months it all gets a bit theoretical and vague.

In new media, timescales are a massive problem. They slip! Tom Love recommends breaking all work down into three-month "expeditions." But what if three months aren't enough?

There's always a "fallback" plan

Well-planned expeditions have "subsidiary goals." If they can't achieve the main peak, they may at least succeed in reconnoitering an untried route. Something is always gained and there's a sense of achievement whatever happens. Organizations that sponsor expeditions always look for ones with good, but achievable subsidiary goals: they know 100 percent success is unlikely

As Tom Love says: "*Large software projects … have a higher risk of failure than do assaults on the world's 10 highest peaks*" (*Object Lessons*, p. 170) – yet failure is seldom contemplated. On the Interact project (Chapter 2.5), our "deliverable minimum" gave us precisely that kind of subsidiary goal.

Lightweight reconnoitering is essential

The team is always free to act on its own initiative because the situation is never quite the way it looks from base camp, or from the map. Exploration is an ongoing activity, not usually done by the whole party but by one or two going fast and light – the rest following only if the route is good. Every expedition schedule allows for this. No expedition sponsor expects the team to follow the planned itinerary to the letter and minute.

New-media tasks can be every bit as demanding and convoluted as real landscapes, so reconnoitering is vital here too. As our experience "under the waterfall" (Interact project, Chapter 2.5) showed, it is very difficult to plan the entire route in advance. The people "on the mountain" have to be free to make responsible decisions on the spot – and whoever is sponsoring the "expedition" must be able to trust them to do that. If they don't have that freedom (and trust) they'll most likely end up in an impasse or a crevasse.

Equipment is constantly reviewed, modified – and even invented on the job

Equipment and technique are respected and discussed at great length – and often developed on actual expeditions out of available materials. For example, the "nuts" that are used for fixing rope-slings into rock crevices were originally actual engineering nuts, "borrowed" from work by British climbers in the 1950s. The original climbing harness was made out of spare rope by Don Whillans, for a climb with Joe Brown in North Wales in the 1950s. Climbers replace these "lashup" devices with purpose-made high-tech ones at the first opportunity – but they have great contempt for people who are obsessed only with equipment: the people who have the best gear, and do nothing much with it. Maximum kudos goes to those who know their equipment intimately, and use it in new ways.

New-media workers are often criticized for being obsessed with technology – but the technology is the medium and one needs to know it and enjoy it just as much as painters enjoy paint or sculptors stone. And the same internal discipline applies here, as in climbing, to people who have great kit and use it in boring ways.

Musicians will also recognize this process: it is considered far better to do great stuff with a cheap guitar than rubbish with a superb, top-of-the-range Stratocaster. This kind of "constraint appreciation" is a powerful (but mainly undocumented) influence in musician culture – and every other of work.

When you know your tools, you can go beyond them: like Peter Small, building his "conversation engine" for "How God Makes God" (Chapter 2.1) and Chris McEvoy with McThing. The World Wide Web itself seems to have been very much a product of this kind of task-centered improvisation. So is MacroMedia Director: Marc Canter and his friends seem to have developed it to answer a series of practical problems that they themselves had, on particular projects (I'm thinking specifically of Director's language, Lingo), then released those solutions to the developer community. Canter left Macromedia when the company ceased to be involved in project work.

Constraints and risks are the whole point of the exercise

Climbers don't bother with mountains that offer no challenge; new technology (new kinds of "protection", for example) makes things safer – but people respond by opening up harder routes. At the same time, you never take on bigger challenges than you can deal with. The criteria seem to be: do something that seems impossible, feel certain that it is do-able – and carefully, logically restrict the possible damage if it isn't. It is more a test of intuition than of equipment.

This kind of challenge seems particularly characteristic of new media. Technologies change constantly; they make old things easy – but make new things possible, which nobody has done before, and these become the focus of effort. There always seems to be this need to find the limits of the available technology.

The approach may seem irrational and dangerous – but it is a major motivating factor. People work harder this way. Dispense with it, and you can remove all the "steam from the boiler." It also seems to produce superior work whatever the medium. For an unusually perceptive analysis of this phenomenon, see the late David Pye's *The Nature of Art and Workmanship*: especially his observations about the "workmanship of risk."

all the works of men which have been most admired since the beginning of our history have been made by the workmanship of risk, the last 3 or 4 generations excepted.

The "workmanship of risk" is the kind (like making pots on a wheel, or wood-carving) where your next action could ruin the whole thing. This sounds dangerous – but good workmen make sure the risks are always small ones. A potter who ruins a pot doesn't get sacked or go bankrupt – or even give it another thought. He or she just chucks the clay back in the bin, makes another and does it better. Programmers do this too when building routines. A big element of the "joy of programming" is anticipating the question "will it run?" when you hit "enter." It's what makes good programmers good.

This kind of risk is unknown to textbook twentieth-century management, where "risk" means one person staking an entire community's future on a single throw of the die; risk management involves eliminating the worker's freedom – including the freedom to take the little risks that produce good work.

But craft-workers, like climbers, are very good risk managers. They use "jigs" of various kinds (often improvised for the particular job) to contain the risk within a small area. Programmers have an exact equivalent in "object-oriented programming" (OOP): code is built up in small, self-contained modules that can be tested and "bullet-proofed" before building the next (see Love's book, or Peter Small's books on Lingo).

Pye was a wood-worker who never touched a computer in his life – but his book sheds wonderful light on these issues.

Some observations about the teams themselves

Teams are small

Ten, or thereabouts, is an ideal maximum. Beyond this it becomes hard to develop the necessary rapport and trust.

This seems to be the rule in computer work too (see above). Brooks and Love recommend many small teams – rather than one large army – for tasks that are too big for one team alone.

Trust can be more important than skill. Individual failure is tolerated

On real mountains, trust can develop surprisingly quickly between strangers. The best teams have climbed together for years – but they are not necessarily all great climbers: some all-star teams have been utter disasters. The same thing seems to apply to rock bands. The important thing is: people know, and respect, each other's limitations as well as strengths. Failure is pardonable. It happens to everyone.

In new media, where you are so often attempting new and difficult things, it is essential to feel trusted. When you fear ridicule, or the sack, you cannot think creatively – so failure is more likely. It can be far better to retain apparently weak team members, giving them useful work that's within their abilities, than to fire them – and thereby create insecurity in the rest of the team. Relieved of the task at which they were failing, they may display hitherto unnoticed strengths.

Criticism is merciless, but never fatal

Climbers don't mince words. (Nor do members of a working band, or of a sailing crew.) This does not contradict what I've said about "fear of criticism": if a solid bedrock of trust is there, you can be spontaneous and truthful in your appraisal of their work and behavior – and that goes for blame as well as praise. Another way of putting it is that people are able to use a fuller range of communicative styles than they can in the office – where much time and creativity are soaked up by second-guessing people's reactions and fine-tuning memos.

You compete "co-operatively"

This is completely unlike the dog-eat-dog competition of dysfunctional workplaces. It's not "me against you," but "us against it." Each of you wants to excel for the sake of the others. Others' achievements are applauded, not seen as a threat.

This contradicts the publicly accepted idea of "competition" (there have to be winners and losers) – yet it is manifestly the norm in the innumerable happy, unofficial social situations, such as families and groups of friends, that are society's bedrock.

Idiosyncracy thrives: a team's unity is the inverse of its uniformity

Successful climbing teams seem to be full of "characters" (as do successful rock bands). They are not uniformed stereotypes. In fact, people go out onto mountains so that they can shed the uniformity of office life and be themselves for a change. People turn out to be much richer and more diverse than they seem in the normal world of work.

A new-media project needs more skills than you have people. Very likely, many of the skills you need are there already, in latent form. A well-enough visualized task may bring them out.

The ideal team member is multi-skilled

Obviously, an expedition doctor or photographer needs to be a reasonable climber as well. Less obviously, the ability to tell a good yarn, to listen well, or to defuse a terrifying moment with a witty one-liner can be every bit as important as technical ability. In fact ...

Humor is a prized asset

Expeditions that are no fun are no fun. Anecdotal evidence strongly suggests that they are less likely to reach their goals, and more likely to have accidents.

Leadership becomes like the stove: it gets passed around

An expedition always has a leader, whose example, and belief in the goal, inspires everyone else. But when things are going well, leadership seems to become, as it were, common property: a piece of essential equipment (such as the stove) that's automatically passed to the most appropriate person as the situation requires. As with the stove, it's not so important *who* has it, as that *somebody* has it. Nobody fights over it.

People who have done successful new media work report this too. There is no sense of someone "ordering us around." (If there is, it's a danger sign.) It's different as anything can be from the leaderless hell of the "Sendak" saga, where people battled for leadership, had it wrested from them amid mutual distrust and fear.

From mountaineering to new media: the "vision" problem

A project always seems to gather pace and purpose as it takes physical shape. Once there is something that can be seen, tried and discussed, everyone suddenly knows what they have to do, and they do it. They work longer, harder, better, and faster, accomplishing more and more in less and less time. The emerging reality has the same galvanic effect a real landscape has.

If we can start to give the "problem space" physical form sooner, rather than later, we're likely to get those famous "creative juices" flowing earlier.

As I said above – it is not just a matter of handing this vision to the team. If they are to work as well as a climbing team (or band or sailing crew) does, they need to contribute their own insights to it – and to do that, they must *want* to contribute. Without this, all the project planning and task-analysis in the world will probably fail.

Model the challenge, not the solution

The first physical reality many projects have is a "demo": a linear demon-stration of some particular (ideal) sequence of interaction. This often becomes the model for the development work proper. There is wide agree-ment[3] that "following the demo" doesn't work. From a "mountaineering" standpoint, one can see that it is *bound* not to work: it is prescribing the route before anybody has even set foot in the landscape.

A real demo, and a fake   Doug Engelbart's famous demo of "Augment" (Chapter 1.4) was a demonstration of an actual, working system. Apple's Knowledge Navigator was not – yet it created enormous enthusiasm at the time (1990–1) and was even featured in *Scientific American* (November 1991). Knowledge Navigator featured a personal "software agent" called Phil who knew all your likes and dislikes, interests and needs, reminded you about things, rearranged your diary for you, and searched the Internet for the precise nuggets of information you needed (even before you realized you needed them). A great idea – except that nobody had any precise idea how to implement it – and still don't.

How do we make the "challenge" visible? The steps I described in Chapter 3.4 can all help you do this: the brief, and the five-stage "technique for producing ideas." In addition, we need better visualization techniques than we have (I give a few suggestions below). But the most valuable "aid" is the audience itself – which is to say, the person who will eventually use the thing you're building: not the client (unless he or she is indeed the end-user) or the project manager.

Use your audience as a "magic mirror"

The "sense of audience" is like a searchlight. The landscape may be invisible, but a real human being's reactions to it are physical, detailed, and full of significant nuance. On the Interact project it was the embarrassment and diffidence of actual people, when faced with the complexities of "Money," that told us where the main problems lay. Their body language and tone of voice were as informative as the things they actually said. For people like Mark Schlichting and Romain Victor-Pujebet, it was their children who provided this "sense of audience," and they were guided very surely by the whole gamut of their reactions, from delight to boredom.

It's vital to keep a sense of audience throughout development. Schlichting and Victor-Pujebet had their audiences around them constantly – but most commercial developers don't. There's a tendency to think that there isn't time to get users involved (but then, there isn't time to do so many things). Then there's a fear that the users may not like what you've built! This fear seems to get bigger, the longer you go before allowing other people to try the work. Yet, as Schlichting's and Victor-Pujebet's work shows, users can be your biggest source of inspiration.

Every new-media project should build user-testing into its schedule – and there are lots of ways to do it. On Interact (Chapter 2.5) we used a two-week "test-and-build" cycle, where our usability expert John Cato gave representative members of the public tasks to do, asked them to think aloud as they did them – and videoed the session. In between times we were constantly asking people to try things we'd built, or just to look at things and tell us what they thought they meant. I had to resist the urge to *show* them things and give them a running commentary. If you do that, you learn nothing.

For a very good introduction to the art of user testing, see Bruce Tognazzini's *Tog on Interface* – especially his chapter on "User testing on the cheap." Everybody should also know about the Danish "illuminatus" of usability, Jakob Nielsen: author of *Hypertext and Hypermedia*. He also maintains a very helpful website: www.useit.com.

It's important to seize any opportunity to study real users – and sooner rather than later, before you've become committed to a landscape that isn't theirs.

If you start with a vivid sense of your audience, it will be your guide.

Visualize the landscape in the most physical way possible, as early as possible

In computer work we tend to forget about the possibility of using cheap, no-tech "intermediate media" – but they can be fantastic value for money. It can take far less time to mock up an interface in card and paper than to do it on the computer, and modifying it is even easier. You learn a lot as you do it, and it can be a lot of fun (desirable). Physical models are "full-bandwidth" devices, which engage the full range of human senses and perception.

As Richard Gregory says, we see, and think, as much with our hands as with our brains. Getting your hands involved helps your brain work better.

Architects make models – often of cardboard and balsa-wood, and they do this even when sophisticated 3-D computer-modeling systems are available. Likewise, sculptors make "maquettes" – quick, small versions of the sculpture they're planning, which they study, handle, experiment with, modify, and keep out on display so that others can comment on them. Jeff Hawkins's PalmPilot prototype was a block of wood.

Things like these are permanent features of the working environment, focusing discussion, reminding everyone of where the design's been, and where it's heading. Permanence is important: the thing is its own reminder, in peripheral vision, keeping the thought processes alive. If you only use the computer you don't get that: the images are usually hidden away on the hard disk.

It is perfectly possible (and some people prefer) to use a no-tech interface to test the system you're about to build, on potential users. You can even make a kind of "penny-plain, tuppence colored" theater, with replacement screens inserted like stage-flats, and menus and dialog boxes made of paper. You can do this in an afternoon – or ten minutes! The interaction is crude but you can debug a design very well this way.

"Wizard of Oz" testing.   The style of testing where an unseen human plays the part of the computer is known as the "Wizard of Oz" technique, after Frank Baum's famous wizard, who didn't actually do anything magical – just cheap, effective tricks that kept everybody happy. It's a valid test because the "wizard" responds to the user's actions according to strictly logical rules. This way, you can simulate a system in one week that might take years to build – and discover the major flaws (and unsuspected opportunities) right at the start. The technique is nothing like as well known as it needs to be. John Cato used it to evaluate an expensive voice-recognition system for Nationwide – revealing problems that simply wouldn't have been discovered otherwise till serious money had been spent. Harold Thimbleby discusses the "Oz" technique a little (but very well) in *User Interface Design*.

Route planning vs. project management. Getting an idea of where you're going, and where you are at the moment

There's a shortage of good "route planning" tools: tools that give a graphical overview of the whole "landscape."

There are *plenty* of project management tools. Maybe these are intrinsically excellent tools – but the way they are often used is not. You have a project manager who sits all day peering into his Gantt-charts, and timelines, tweaking them, disappearing into meetings where he discusses them with his fellow project managers, tweaks them some more. Finally he appears at your shoulder with a "schedule" telling you what you have to do, when – and nothing else. This is a fair-enough way to organize an amusing afternoon treasure-hunt but not a serious expedition.

There is nothing to stop creative teams using project management tools themselves – but they seem not to do this: perhaps because it takes time to learn to use them properly. They (I certainly) prefer some way of getting an integrated vision of what's to be done, even if it's not as detailed: one that represents *what* we're trying to build as well as *how and when* we're going to tackle each stage. Far too often, we rely on mental models.

For example, the current Web design scene is dominated by tools that help you build gorgeous pages, but with relatively little emphasis on the site as a whole: you're expected to attend to that in your mind's eye, as if it were a minor detail. NetObjects Fusion is the notable exception.

There are some computer-based tools that help (diagrammers like "Inspiration," "SmartDraw" and "Visio"). Eastgate's hypertext editor "StorySpace" – see www.eastgate.com – is probably a much better tool: you always have a clear view of the "information space" you're building, and you generate the HTML pages from that (the famous "HyperCafe"

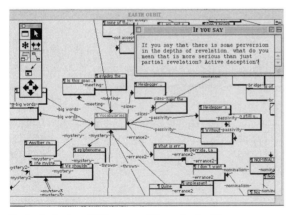

Eastgate Systems' "Storyspace" hypertext editor

project and website – www. hypercafe.com – was built with it). But computer tools (or their designers) have a strong tendency to gravitate towards fine detail – just as we ourselves get sucked into detail the moment we start using the machine. This is another reason for backing off from the computer, and using paper, card, magic markers, and the wall for the "high-level" stuff.

Film-makers' storyboards are a great invention (in fact they are an art form in themselves). Everyone can see the whole film, at a glance. You can show the storyboard to producers, financial backers, cameramen, and set-builders and they'll immediately get a pretty good idea of what you have in mind. As the work proceeds the storyboard is the check-point everyone refers to: you can see what's been done, what's still to be done and what's been changed. Like the architect's model, it's a permanent part of the work environment.

We need as many ways as possible of allowing a lot of information to be taken in at a glance.

Victor Papanek, a veteran product designer who has spent much of his life working in the Third World and in disadvantaged communities, offers some excellent techniques in his book *Design for the Real World*. Papanek was looking for ways of involving communities in the design of public parks and libraries, village irrigation schemes, etc. He wanted to bring children, mothers, elderly people, teachers into the design process – so that what they got was actually what they needed, not what some planner thought they should have.

One method involved a big roll of brown parcel-wrapping paper, a selection of marker pens, scissors, and glue, and someone to wield them. His team would discuss the project with the community and build a kind of "mind-map" of all their needs, with drawings of the proposed solution. This "frieze" became the "design document," up there on the wall throughout the project, and present at all meetings. As time went on it would become a kind of patchwork as changes were made, features added, modified, and removed – so it also became the "design history": everyone could see where changes had been made. Papanek also found it was best to give one member of the team responsibility for the "frieze," and coordinating everyone's requirements.

A good tool I've found, that's only slightly higher-tech than Papanek's, is a big sheet of "poly-board" (the artwork mounting board that has a core of polystyrene, 0.5 cm thick, available from graphic design suppliers), a can of low-tack adhesive, some marker pads, scissors, Post-it pads, and some marker pens. For $50 you have an easy-to-update, highly portable "graphical information system" that shows the whole system at a glance, with the latest screenshots of the system's main sections as they're completed. Following Papanek's (and Brooks's) example, it is probably a good idea if one person takes responsibility for it. But it has to be somebody who's *part* of the team: not merely *attached* to it.

Experiment

A lot of the best work comes precisely from people playing around with new tools to see what they can do, and discovering unexpected possibilities. This, after all, is the "medium," and its charms aren't to be found in any other way.

The work regime: space is vital

Given a strong enough sense of your audience, everything else follows: people can sometimes work in terrible conditions with inferior equipment and still get the job done (just as climbers sometimes extricate themselves from lethal situations, through a keen sense of direction and intimate knowledge of the terrain).

Occasionally, very great art is done in this heroic way – which leads some people to suppose that workers somehow *need* awful conditions. For example, the Voyager Company started in extremely cramped conditions, where bedrooms doubled as offices. An extreme example: Aleksandr Solzhenitsyn wrote his *Day in the Life of Ivan Denisovich* in secret, in a subarctic Gulag labor camp. However, it is usually a recipe for failure (thousands of other excellent writers died in the camps; lots of people work in their bedrooms and never get anywhere). Good conditions never hurt anyone. We all work much better in good conditions, with good backup and good tools. The better the conditions, the better the work.

Pleasant, secure conditions make you more "creative"

The cheapest, easiest way of getting better results is to improve your working conditions. Creative people seem to do *measurably* better work if they have better-quality, physical space in which to to do it. Two factors are important: the amount of space (more is better), and a feeling that the space is your own. Tom DeMarco and Timothy Lister[4] ran "coding war" experiments with software engineers over many years and proved that "*the top performers' space is quieter, more private, better protected against interruption, and there is more of it.*"

This figures: if you feel vulnerable to critical and unsympathetic eyes you tend to take fewer risks – and if you can't take risks you can't be creative. Recall Guy Claxton's "golfing" example, mentioned earlier. Given the important role the body itself plays in thought (see Chapter 3.5), being cramped physically clearly restricts you mentally.

Nearly all my "eminent Cyberians" had either very pleasant working conditions, or ones they'd chosen for themselves and had complete control over. Hardly any of them worked in office blocks with "policemen" watching them. The "Sendak" team (Chapter 3.1) had good *physical* working conditions that were emotionally awful: they were dispersed all over the building, and had no protection from summary criticism and interference.

Disk space is no substitute for physical space

John Perry Barlow's vision of the Electronic Frontier (www.eff.org) can suggest otherwise, but not even he dispenses with physical space: he has a very nice, big ranch in Wyoming – where he *and* his buffalo can roam.

A computer monitor can only show one thing at a time – and it is nothing like as easy to manipulate as paper and pencil.

A decent table where you can lay out visuals, sit and discuss the job, have screenshots and mind-maps permanently on display, can be worth its weight in gold.

The more space you have, the more ways you can visualize the work as it develops, and the more "angles" you can get on it – all of which helps to give the job reality.

Defending your space

Older creative industries (architecture, advertising, the film industry) have learned to keep their most "creative" work separate from everything else. They recognize that, like husbands and wives, clients and workers benefit from spaces of their own. Clients are not allowed to intrude on the creative process, and the creative process (the "concepts" or "idea-getting" stage) is separate from the "production" stage. They've found that without separation, it is almost impossible for creatives to do their stuff.

You also need separation to preserve the client's morale. Creative work can look very messy. When big money is involved (and any money is "big money" as far as a client is concerned: $10,000 is as serious to a small publisher as $10,000,000 is to Disney), any hint of messiness makes people get twitchy. When they get twitchy, they ask for changes, and the creative process gets thrown off track before it can bear fruit. The result is a system where everyone "has an input" but nobody is happy.

Good managers are guardians, not guards

"People tend to imbue their managers with the powers of their parents," says Jim McCarthy. This is not surprising because creative work and childhood play have a lot in common, and both are very serious matters.

Creative work involves a lot of self-absorbed exploration – and indeed self-doubt, when you hit apparently insurmountable problems. At this point a good manager can be priceless.

A good project manager "holds the ring," keeps other people out of your hair, makes sure you've got the things and the information you need to do your job, stays sane, and helps you keep on track and on schedule. Our Interact project manager was just like that. The Sendak team had nobody in that role.

A bad manager, on the other hand, is an added source of stress – and what's worse they're right there in your workspace. Bad managers are rarely bad people; they're usually sick people. Colossal stress is piled onto managers when they are made personally accountable for other people's work: a logical and physical impossibility. Maybe one day soon it will be illegal to inflict that kind of stress on people.

Stressed behavior has a well-understood neurological basis[5]: stress hormones inhibit a person's conscious brain-processes, and stimulate ingrained, unconscious, emotional ones. If that person is in any way fearful (and just about everybody is) they will react fearfully to every novel thing you do. They may constantly challenge, inspect, and try to control you – as inadequate parents do – or retreat into their private nightmare world, fiddle compulsively with their Gantt charts, and be neither use nor ornament. When we accuse them of behaving childishly we are technically correct – these emotional, unconscious behaviors are laid down in childhood. It is vital to suppress the urge to mockery or rebellion, which can only make them desperate. Short-term, their desperation can wreck the project; long-term it makes them physically ill.

People who have already done your kind of work are better able to cope because they understand what you're doing. In Adland, the creative director is nearly always someone with a creative background, often a writer. In film, the best producers are frequently ex-directors – like Martin Scorsese, David Puttnam, and Roger Corman.

"Temporal space": schedules and deadlines based on mutual trust

In work of all kinds, deadlines can become bones of bitter contention. Time pressure is the bane of life. Yet in my favored analogy – the climbing expedition – nobody throws tantrums because they need to get down before dark, and nobody gets angry with an expedition that's overdue; on the contrary, people get concerned about them, and organize search parties. As I've said, the expedition's time-frame is a "given" that everyone understands. It helps to give the expedition its satisfying shape. It helps people decide what's achievable and what's not.

But as soon as people come down off the mountain into the "real" world of work, time becomes the biggest single source of grief – even in the simplest kinds of work (like shoveling coal and laying bricks) where the scope for over- and under-achievement is quite limited. People are under constant pressure to promise more than they are confident of delivering, and work in constant anxiety until they have either delivered, or failed. Either way they cease to be as creative as they were on the mountain; ultimately they get ill. The reason, of course, is that people don't trust each other: the person who commissions the work suspects the worker will waste time unless pushed; the worker suspects the commissioner will go elsewhere, unless he promises the absolute maximum.

But at least, in old media, there *is* a maximum. In new media even this is in doubt. Here, almost everything is possible, and people can easily feel they have to deliver (or have been promised) the Earth.

Hence, we *have* to have a more trust-based way of working.

Notes

1   This is not just a colorful metaphor. Henry Ford got the idea for his famous production-line technique when he saw hogs being disassembled in a Chicago slaughterhouse. The twentieth century's dominant mode of work is hog-butchering in reverse.

2   Csikszentmihalyi works at Chicago University. His key studies are *Beyond Boredom and Anxiety* (1975) and *Optimal Experience* (1988).

3 For example, see Harold Thimbleby's "Internet, discourse and action potential" – keynote speech at the Asia Pacific Conference on HCI: http://www.cs.mdx.ac.uk/harold/singapore/singapore.html.

4 *Peopleware – Productive Projects and Teams*.

5 For example, see *Emotional Intelligence* (Daniel Goleman) and *The Emotional Brain* (Joseph LeDoux) – which explains the neural mechanisms. For evidence of the devastating effect of stress on particular creative tasks, see Guy Claxton's *Hare Brain, Tortoise Mind*.

3.9

Trust, and the paradox of self-absorbed work

IF DESIGN SHOULD BE "USER-CENTERED," why are so many of the things we like best, in every medium, things that people have apparently made for their own self-centered pleasure: from gardens to paintings? Does it mean there are two kinds of creative work: work you do for yourself, and work you do for other people? If so, where do you draw the line?

Many employers live in fear of "creative self-indulgence." This is very often justified. One sees plenty of web-pages where graphic designers have had a whale of a time creating graphics, animations, and strikingly unusual screen layouts that "look good" – but make the site impossible to use.

Yet most, probably all, of the very finest things in every medium are exactly the result of people "playing around" – the designer (or musician, or whatever) intently finding their way through some "problem space" that they've been given, or discovered for themselves, unconcerned whether anyone's watching or not. This is the real joy of creative work!

It seems to drive a coach and horses through the whole idea of careful briefing, precise identification of our audience, recognition of their back-grounds, emotions, and needs. Yet somehow the two approaches often coexist very happily indeed in the real world – and even in the most func-tional things. We have cars (like the British Mini mentioned in my first chapter) that are, simultaneously, supremely well designed for their intended "audience," and one person's obsessive labor of love.

How can we explain this paradox? The first part of the solution is possibly quite simple.

How an audience *permits* you to indulge yourself

In his book *Writing with Power*, Peter Elbow describes the paradox this way (you can substitute the word "writing" for "design"):

- *Writing is usually a communication with others. And yet the essential transaction seems to be with oneself, a speaking to one's best self.*

- *Sometimes you can't figure out what you want to say and how to say it till you get into the presence of your audience (or think intensely about it). Yet sometimes it's only by getting away from your audience that you can figure out your meaning and how to convey it clearly: your real audience can distract or inhibit you.*

- *You can't get an audience to listen and hear you till you have something to say and can say it well. Yet I think the process by which people actually learn to write and speak well is often the other way around: first they get an audience that listens and hears them (parents first, then supportive teachers, then a circle of friends or fellow writers, and finally a larger audience).* Having an audience helps them find what to say *and find better ways to say it.* (*Writing with Power*, p. 179 (*My emphasis*))

> So: an audience "urges you on." If you have ever performed in public, and the performance has gone well, you'll know exactly what that feels like. A good audience doesn't know precisely what it expects, but it has faith in you, that whatever you do will be delightful. Sometimes you will engage them eye to eye. You may even, occasionally, say "help me out here!" – but more as a gesture of reciprocal trust than as an admission of failure. Ultimately, the deal is: you're in control. It's your show, and the audience trusts you to "come up with the goods." As long as you do that now and again, the audience won't mind how self-engrossed you are. In fact, they prefer it that way most of the time. The last thing they want is a performer who's continually asking "what would you like next?" Audiences look for leadership – not followership.
>
> Notice that Peter Elbow mentions the way parents play this "encouraging" role. Child psychologists like the late Donald Winnicott bear him out (see Chapter 3.4). Parents are the original "good audience" that allows, and encourages, you to explore, and become whatever you have the power to be.
>
> This is exactly the same thing that a good creative director does (the "guardian" of your "creative space"). In fact, your audience is your ultimate "guardian." If you are really engaging with them you don't need anyone else.

Creative work as a spectator sport: performance, fine and applied art

Another way of looking at it is: *all* creative work is an expedition through "problem space." When you're negotiating that space successfully, your efforts are intrinsically fascinating to other people.

You may want to negotiate it just for your own private purposes: you take up juggling, hang-gliding or rock climbing – or sketching, wood-turning, fixing old radios, or computer game-playing. Your efforts may be of great interest to anyone who happens to be watching, especially if the challenge you've set yourself really stretches you to your limit: *people are universally fascinated by the sight of other people taking risks*. This is "performance art," whether you get paid to do it or not.

You may also want to leave some record of the route you took – mainly for yourself at first, but if you do it really well then other people may also find the record fascinating. This is perhaps a good definition of "fine art": painting, music composition, sculpture, creative writing, conceptual art.

Thirdly, you may see (or be given) a problem that other people have: they need to get from Situation A to Situation B but haven't the skills to get there. *You make their problem your problem.* First, you "go in there," you "play around" (try different routes – many of which are no fun at all), then somehow, by hook or by crook, you find a way through. Then you go back over your route, improve it in all kinds of ways, and when it's capable of bearing traffic, and safe enough for your clients' level of endurance, you open it up for business. We can call this "applied art": textbooks, consumer appliances, tools, computer programs, etc.

Two ways of "getting the bird": too much audience involvement and too little

In all three cases, intense, personal "engagement with the terrain" comes first – but only because the audience trusts you to do something interesting and/or useful. They will trust you a long way, but woe betide you if you let them down! Here's an analogy.

How to take somebody for a walk   Suppose you are a famous mountaineer, organizing a Sunday-afternoon hike for a bunch of non-hikers. They love the idea of getting up there in the hills with you; they are sure you'll get them there without mishap and give them a memorable experience; they want an adventure – but one they can cope with: nothing nasty.

If you just follow your own inclinations and blast off up the toughest ridge in sight they won't thank you at all (too little audience involvement). Nor will they thank you if you completely subordinate your own inclinations to theirs: asking them how they're enjoying things the moment they get out of their cars, modifying the route according to their responses ("this bit is too steep," "this bit is too muddy"). At that rate you'll never get out of the parking lot and everyone will be sorely disappointed.

A "middle course" is the right one to take – yet it should definitely not be a mere compromise. It is perfectly possible to organize things so that everyone feels they've been stretched, "had an adventure," and discovered new things.

> It's a contract. The audience wants *you* to give a lead – not to ask *them* for a lead all the time. They want you to enjoy yourself *and* to feel safe and appreciated themselves. This seems to fit the way "performance art" works – but what about "fine art" and "applied art," where you're creating a *record* of the "intense, personal engagement," which the audience will encounter in your absence? Can a user of something really get a sense of dialog with the person who made it?

Unconscious awareness and the "connoisseur effect"

It certainly seems to be the case that Picasso's paintings, Gothic carvings, and innumerable other well-loved things are very largely the results of "self-absorbed exploration." We could argue (subjectively) that Alec Issigonis's Mini is a record of his intensely skilful engagement with the problem of creating a small, reliable car that's fun to drive, which can be manufactured cheaply – and that this is why people seem to prefer it to the designed-by-committee Metro.

Yet do we recognize it – and if so, how? "Connoisseurs" give us our first clue. Most people look at Picassos and Minis, enjoy them and prefer them without thinking very deeply about them – but connoisseurs apply conscious thought to their unconscious preferences and discover the reasons for them. The connoisseur explains them to the "lay-person" – and very often the lay-person goes "oh yes! that's absolutely right!"

What happens here? The connoisseur has drawn the lay-person's attention to unnoticed features that reveal the object's "secret history." The lay-person realizes that although they had not noticed those features, they had been *influenced* by them. This is a source of great delight. We realize that a subjective feeling in fact has a real basis. This is probably just what happens when people are moved to tears by Robert Winter's "Beethoven" disk.

Part of the delight is relief: we realize that our vague but real dislikes, and feelings of unease, have a real basis too. That's what happens when one reads Donald Norman's books: we realize that it is not we who are stupid when we can't work the clever-looking multi-function phone, but the phone's own stupid design. It is also what happens, extremely powerfully, in counseling: the person realizes they are not mad or silly – there is a big, solid reason why they feel the way they do.

The "connoisseur" shows there are reasons for our likes and dislikes – but that still doesn't entirely explain how we experience the likes and dislikes in the first place.

This is where we come to "the unconscious." (And it may have been through reading about a particularly famous connoisseur, Giovanni Morelli, that Sigmund Freud came to formulate the first theory of the unconscious mind.[1])

Most of our mental processing happens unconsciously – for the simple reason that it has to. It takes anything from half to three-quarters of a second to register something consciously and act upon it.[2] This is far too slow to deal successfully with most of the things we do in life – everything from keeping ourselves upright as we walk and run, to driving cars and hitting tennis-balls. We can even do very complicated calculations unconsciously. Pawel Lewicki's experiments at Tulsa, Oklahoma (below), and Dianne Berry and Donald Broadbent's work at Oxford (with British factory managers), have shown that people often solve problems unconsciously that completely stump the conscious mind, very accurately – without any awareness that they are doing so.[3] It seems that a great deal of what otherwise looks like telepathy can be explained this way.

One of those experiments, briefly   Lewicki showed test subjects a sequence of seven screens, divided into quadrants, with the numbers 0–9 distributed among them – apparently at random. They had to say which quadrant the "6" was in each time, by pressing one of four buttons, as quickly as they could. Lewicki timed their responses; they spotted the "6" very much faster on the fifth and seventh tries. Unknown to the subjects, there was a complicated rule that predicted where the "6" would appear on the third, fifth and seventh screens – which they'd somehow unconsciously solved. They could not believe what they'd done afterwards, and could barely work it out consciously when it was explained to them!

Presumably we do this kind of "unconscious detective work" all the time. Lewicki claims to have found this "algorithmic" kind of unconscious processing in children as young as four and five.

It seems that we are continuously interrogating and responding to the things around us – swiftly, efficiently, in detail, and entirely unconsciously (unless we have trained ourselves to be connoisseurs). The interrogation is merciless, and nothing is immune to it. This makes evolutionary sense: Human beings evolved in environments where life depended on being able to "read" situations quickly and accurately, without thinking. We now apply the same quick, powerful, unconscious abilities we developed during our hundreds of thousands of years on the veldt to the artificial world we've made for ourselves in the past century. Just as hunters "read" an animal's sex, age, condition, speed and direction of travel, and likely behavior from imperceptible evidence, without being able to explain quite how they do it, so maybe we too "pick up" volumes of information about the makers of the objects we use, from the dumb objects themselves.

Made objects carry their makers' "handwriting" – and we are quite capable of reading and analyzing that handwriting very quickly and accurately, and it could well be that we do just that. If so, we are also capable of "reading" the tangled tale of corporate bumbling, bullying, boredom, competing agendas, and fudge that's written into so many of the things we use every day. We don't form a conscious, scholarly critique – we react, as the hunter does.

When these are things we are compelled to use – like roads, houses, and office buildings – we suffer unconsciously. When they are things we don't have to use – like cars and CD-ROMs – we follow our feelings and vote with our feet.

As far as I know, nobody has yet tested this possibility explicitly on the "world of artifacts," but the evidence of powerful unconscious processing is now so strong that it has to be taken seriously.

Notes

1. Morelli definitely inspired another influential nineteenth-century figure: Sherlock Holmes. Morelli was an "art sleuth" who detected fakes by attending to unconsidered details (such as the way the artist had painted the subject's ears). Conan Doyle based Holmes's entire character and career on this novel approach.

2. Established by Benjamin Libet and others – cited in Guy Claxton's *Hare Brain, Tortoise Mind*.

3. Lewicki's, and Berry and Broadbent's work is described in Guy Claxton's *Hare Brain, Tortoise Mind*. Lewicki's Nonconscious Information Processing Laboratory is at http://centum.utulsa.edu/~PSY_PL/www/.

3.10

Conclusion: Rediscovering workmanship

THE COMPUTER, AND CURRENT BRAIN SCIENCE, have given "human factors" a prominence that might have delighted William Morris – and given him renewed hope. In a surprising way, the computer requires the very same approach to work (and to the users of things) that he championed, but which has been progressively marginalized throughout industrial history: an approach that acknowledges people's emotional needs, individuality, and hard-to-articulate subjective values.

The computer (through its celebrated capacity for interactivity and media integration) brings us face to face with these values. It connects with the "unsleeping giant" of unconscious processing in ways no other medium has done. Simultaneously, the computer (as a spur to mind-research) has helped raise our understanding of the unconscious mind – and given this new understanding a whole industry to work upon.

The medium that's "on its own" the way an actor is

A new-media application engages its audience on the same equal and unforgiving terms a stand-up performer does. It lives or dies at the interface – and has no other habitat.

New-media work has no physical existence. In other media – like books and bricks – physicality gives half-baked designs a "get-out." They may not be any good, but at least they are there – and they can survive on that fact alone. A trivial item like an advertising brochure doesn't need to be readable or informative (and often isn't) because its physical form has value: as an *aide-mémoire*. Steven Hawking's *Brief History of Time* is allegedly read by very few of the people who buy it, but it is a hugely desirable object: as a gift (an immensely flattering one), an advertisement of one's intellect, even a magical object: just owning it makes you feel clever. Its "talismanic" value gives it a toehold in the world. A CD-ROM, somehow, has no such secondary appeal. It succeeds at "run-time" or not at all.

Larger items, like buildings, can use their physical presence to present the user with a *fait accompli*. If people do not like your horrible building, so what? They must learn to live with it or live somewhere else. People's adaptability is the undeclared part of the twentieth-century production equation, which makes rubbish look efficient.

Computer companies *do* dump rubbish on captive audiences, and on an outrageous scale. There is no technology that dumps so many of its costs onto its customers (few computer systems are ready to run until you've invested a lot of your own time in them, setting them up), or disowns responsibility for defective workmanship so blatantly (see the disclaimers on any software package).

But when it comes to "discretionary use" – the kinds of computer-based creations that people *don't* have to use – it's a totally different story. Either it works for the user, or the user switches it off, and it vanishes. It has no fall-back position. A website has no coffee-table role, no gift value, no role as a household ornament, and certainly cannot interpose itself between you and the rest of your life the way a highway or a building does (although the advocates of "push technology" would like to do this).

This stuff has no way to insinuate itself into anyone's life other than by being very good at what it's supposed to do. Working under this constraint, the only way forward seems to be via the irreducible complexities of perception, cognition, and human-to-human interaction. And what is *really* new is: all of these complexities have to be *consciously understood*.

Here, things that otherwise are "intuitive" (which a writer would "just write" in the heat of work, or a comic would "just say") have to be built in cold blood, step by step, studied, dismantled, then rebuilt properly. We have never had to understand these things before to anything like this extent – and this is already having some effect: without it, there would be no need for the large, thriving science of "human factors" we now have, and which is already gaining a wider audience beyond the computer community: Donald Norman's books, for example, have a very wide readership, and address many of the same concerns Morris had:

I watch technology, especially the small, common, everyday variety. In particular, I watch the way people interact with technology. I am not happy with what I see. Much of modern technology seems to exist solely for its own sake, oblivious to the needs and concerns of the people around it, people who, after all, are supposed to be the reason for its existence. – Preface to Turn Signals are the Facial Expressions of Automobiles

This kind of awareness is gradually but definitely becoming part of the culture. To work in the computer medium gives you *the chance* to be at the leading edge of this kind of awareness, and contribute to it.

As we've seen, the workplace has to be different – and again this echoes William Morris. A leading-edge Web-design or games studio is much more like an arts-and-crafts movement pottery or furniture-making workshop, than a Henry Ford-style automobile plant. It is not a "soft" way of working: on the contrary it is intensely disciplined and hard – but it nourishes people's unique, intuitive capacities instead of trying to eliminate them, as the Ford regime does.

Not everyone has to work in a Web-design studio for this to have an effect on society. People always carry the language, habits, and insights acquired at work out into the world – and influence it.

I have a strong feeling that the computer's biggest benefits will be "Gregorian" ones. We will not use computers for everything, any more than we use levers or clocks for everything. Instead, the computer and the disciplines that come with it are becoming part of our "mental toolset" – just as, Richard Gregory argues, levers and clocks did, allowing us to think in new ways.

From the cult of perfectionism to a culture of workmanship

The twentieth century has pursued visible "perfection" to its baroque outer limit and way beyond. It started with exquisite mass-produced fountain pens and shirt buttons. Strictly speaking these were "sacred art"[1]: artifacts that bear no consciously perceptible trace of human origin; eternally delightful things in their place. It ends with "exquisiteness" being the only production language we know – alarmed to find that 99 percent of the world cannot afford it, and that 99 percent of its problems do not submit to it.

Visible perfection is an easy goal in products whose boundaries can be well defined. In the material world, tasks seem to be self-contained exercises that have little impact on anything else.

There are practical limits to the amount of material you can cram into a building or a TV program. Marlon Brando's fee sets a known maximum on voice-overs. Buildings can have solid-gold lavatory seats – but they too have a maximum price, and no building can have an infinite number of them. A "perfect" building or TV commercial is just about possible. The price may be high and the timescale may be long but both are finite.

New-media creations are not finite. They have "elastic sides" and can consume material indefinitely. Perfection becomes an elusive target unless you take very firm steps to constrain the information space (see "Combinatorial explosion" – Chapters 2.3 and 3.6) or enforce "site-wide design standards" (which people always seem to break, no matter how carefully you codify them).

Perfection is further subverted because this medium lacks the accustomed conventions for preliminary, intermediate, and finished images that other twentieth-century media have. In the world of print, the "working medium" (layout pad) and the "delivery medium" (printed item) are two distinct things, and everybody can see which is which – but there's no such distinction here. The working medium *is* the delivery medium. People assume that whatever you put on the screen is the final product – and very often they're right!

Workers may intend certain images, code modules, or sounds to be temporary – but they have a way of ending up in the finished product anyway. As the deadline rushes towards them, they realize just how many items they meant to tidy up later. But "later" never comes!

Because working- and delivery-medium are the same, the computer is more like a traditional fine-art medium, such as oil-painting or sculpture, or a traditional craft like furniture-making or pottery, than print or film.

This stile in the Mendip Hills, cobbled together from available materials, is an excellent example of "good-enough" design, or "rough workmanship." A highly finished stile in concrete, steel, and machine-planed teak would look and feel very "wrong."

I suspect that this really does call for a richer esthetic – one that recognizes that "exquisiteness" is not the only good. We may find what we need in older media and other cultures: not just fine art and craft – but also from arts like dry-stone walling, hedge-laying, etc., where there is a respected and well-understood tradition of "rough workman-ship." There, users see the problem and the solution in context. A field gate that is "just good enough" looks precisely right but a highly finished suburban one in the same setting looks utterly wrong.

In physical media we tend to hide problems (the easiest thing to do usu-ally). In new media it becomes important to show problem and solution in context. The "problem spaces" we represent tend to be dynamic, very much more elaborate than the ones older media deal with, and they are often "mission-critical" (people part with money on websites; some graph-ical interfaces affect human safety).

Harold Thimbleby has drawn attention to the mismatch between "con-struction complexity"[2] and "comprehension complexity" in computer devices like video cameras and calculators – which present a deceivingly simple model to the user, and quickly cause problems.

It is a consequence of the way development effort leaks into "visible per-fection" in physical media, and away from the original problem. This is a very general problem for society. We end up with roads, cars, super-markets, and innumerable other artifacts that present simple, complete-looking solutions to situations that are in fact very complex and unresolved. People come to rely on these solutions. They compound the problems not in ignorance, but because they have no choice.

Donald Norman and Harold Thimbleby appeal for better design – but there is far too much to do, to have it all designed "perfectly." I think the answer is more *good-enough* design. Perhaps we already see something like a culture of "rough workmanship" emerging on the Web, in its millions of homespun "home pages."

Will this medium always be "new"?

The best time to be working in any medium is when it's new but, after a while, media have tended to become "old," well understood, and the old feudal ways have reasserted themselves, driving out idiosyncratic human input. Happily, the computer shows no sign whatever of becoming "mature." It keeps acquiring new technologies, and these keep changing the landscape. Also, every attempt at forcing it into some standardized (and thence controllable) shape only seems to complicate matters, rein-force its immaturity – and prolong its youth.

Continuing change means continuing exploration, experimentation, and plenty of scope for the individual.

It would, of course, be bitterly ironic if this William Morris-like world were to be realized only behind the thick glass of a computer monitor. But I suspect that the habits and insights we acquire here will be very infectious. The knowledge we gain from working with the machine could be every bit as subversive as anything we make with it.

Notes

1   I am using the precise definition of "sacred art" (as opposed to "religious art") given by the late Martin Lings in *The Quranic Art of Calligraphy and Illumination*.

2   See his paper "Detection and elimination of spurious complexity" at http://www.cs.mdx. ac.uk/harold/uitp.html.

Bibliography

Aarseth, **E**. (1997) *Cybertext – Perspectives in Ergodic Literature*. John Hopkins, ISBN 0-8018-5579-9

Adams, **A**. (1992) *Bullying at Work*. Virago

Ambron, **S**. and **Hooper**, **K**. eds (1988) *Interactive Multimedia*. Apple Computer and Microsoft Press, ISBN 1-55615-124-1

Andersen, **P**. **B**. and **Holmqvist**, **B**. (1992) "Narrative computer systems: the dialectics of emotion and formalism." In *Computers and Writing – State of the Art* (Holt and Williams, eds). Oxford: Intellect Books, ISBN 1-871516-20-X

Baecker, **R**. et al., eds (1995). *Readings in Human–Computer Interaction: Toward the Year 2000*. Morgan Kaufmann

Bakhtin, **M**. **M**. (1981) *The Dialogic Imagination*, Trans. C. Emerson and M. Holquist. University of Texas, ISBN 0-292-71534-X

Barker, **J**. Inside Multimedia newsletter. http://www.phillips.com/PhillipsUK/im.htm

Berger, **J**. (1977) *Ways of Seeing*. London: Penguin

Blinn, **J**. (1996) *Jim Blinn's Corner: A Trip Down the Graphics Pipeline*. Morgan Kaufmann, ISBN 1-55860-387-5

Blinn, **J**. (1998) *Jim Blinn's Corner: Dirty Pixels*. Morgan Kaufmann, ISBN 1-55860-455-3

Bolter, **J**. **D**. (1991) *Writing Space – The Computer, Hypertext, and the History of Writing*. Erlbaum, ISBN 0-8058-0428-5

Brand, **S**. (1987) *The Media Lab – Inventing the Future at MIT*. Viking, ISBN 0-670-81442-3

Brooks, **F**. **P**. **Jr**. (1995) *The Mythical Man-Month*. Addison-Wesley, ISBN 0-201-83595-9

Bush, **V**. (1945) "As We May Think." In *Literary Machines* (Nelson. T.H.), 1987 Mindful Press

Calvin, **W**. **H**. (1994) "The Emergence of Intelligence," *Scientific American*, October

Calvin, **W**. **H**. (1996) *How Brains Think: Evolving Intelligence.* Basic Books

Carrington, **M**. and **Languuth**, **P**. (1997) *The Banking Revolution: Salvation or Slaughter?* Pitman, ISBN 0-273-63055-5

Clark, **A.** (1997) *Being There – Putting Brain, Body, Mind and World Back Together Again*. MIT Press

Claxton, **G**. (1997) *Hare Brain, Tortoise Mind – Why Intelligence Increases When You Think Less*. 4th Estate, ISBN 1-85702-709-4

Crompton, **A**. (1979) *The Craft of Copywriting*. Business Books, ISBN 0-220-67006-4

Csikszentmihalyi, **M**. (1975) *Beyond Boredom and Anxiety*. Jossey Bass

Csikszentmihalyi, **M**. (1988) *Optimal Experience*. Cambridge University Press

Csikszentmihalyi, **M**. (1996) *Creativity* HarperCollins

Damasio, **A**. (1994) *Descartes' Error*. Picador

Dawkins, **R**. (1998) *Climbing Mount Improbable*. W.W. Norton & Co.

Dawkins, **R**. (1988) *The Blind Watchmaker*. Penguin

Davies, **P**. (1996) *About Time*

DeMarco, **T**. and **Lister**, **T**. (1987) *Peopleware – Productive Projects and Teams*. New York: Dorset House Publishing, ISBN 0-932633-05-6

Dennett, **D**. (1991) *Consciousness Explained*. Penguin

Dennett, **D**. (1996) *Kinds of Minds*. Weidenfeld & Nicholson

Dewdney, **A**.**K**. (1989) *The New Turing Omnibus*. Freeman, ISBN 0-7167-8271-5

Eco, **U**. (1990) *Travels in Hyperreality*. Harcourt Brace and Company

Eisenstein, **E**. **L**. (1983) *The Printing Revolution in Early Modern Europe*. Cambridge University Press, ISBN 0-521-27735-3

Elbow, **P**. (1981) *Writing with Power*. Oxford University Press, ISBN 0-19-502913-5

Engelbart, **D**. (1985) *Workstation History and the Augmented Knowledge Workshop*. Bootstrap Institute. www.bootstrap.org

Freytag, **G**. (1863) *Technique of the Drama*

Gardner, **H**. (1983) *Frames of Mind – the Theory of Multiple Intelligences*. Basic Books

Gardner, **M**. (1998) "A quarter-century of recreational mathematics," *Scientific American*, August

Gazzaniga, **M**. **S**. (1998) *The Mind's Past*. University of California Press

Gazzaniga, **M**. **S**. (1998) "The split brain revisited," *Scientific American*, July

Gelernter, **D**. (1994) *The Muse in the Machine*: *Computerizing the Poetry of Human Thought*. Free Press

Gelernter, **D**. (1998) *Machine Beauty*: *Elegance and the Heart of Technology*. Basic Books

Gibson, **W**. (1984) *Neuromancer*. Voyager Expanded Book version (1991 – Apple Macintosh only) includes the two subsequent "Cyberspace" novels, *Count Zero* and *Mona Lisa Overdrive*, and additional notes by the author

Goldstine, **H**.**H**. (1973) *The Computer: from Pascal to von Neumann*. Princeton

Goleman, **D**. (1995) *Emotional Intelligence*. Bantam

Gregory, **R**. **L**. (1966, 1972, 1977, 1990, 1997) *Eye and Brain – the Psychology of Seeing*. Oxford, ISBN 0-19-852340-8

Gregory, **R**. **L**. (1981) *Mind in Science*

Henderson, **J**. (1981) "Designing Realities." In *Virtual Reality – Theory, Practice and Promise*. Meckler

Hill, **C**. (1972) *The World Turned Upside Down*. Maurice Temple Smith; Penguin, 1991, ISBN 0-14-013732-7 (the English Revolution of 1641)

Hodges, **A**. (1983) *Alan Turing: the Enigma*. See also Hodges' website: http://www.wadham.ac. uk/~ahodges/main.html

Holub, **M**. (1990) "The Dimension of the Present Moment." Faber

Jackson, **D**.**S**. (1988) "Palm-to-Palm combat," *Time*, 16 March, **150** (10)

Johnson-Laird, **P**. (1989) *The Computer and the Mind*. Havard University Press

Kidder, **T**. (1981) *The Soul of a New Machine*. Little, Brown and Company, ISBN 0-7139-1482-3

Krueger, **M**. (1983) *Artificial Reality*. Addison-Wesley

Landauer, **T**. **K**. (1995) *The Trouble with Computers – Usefulness, Usability and Productivity*. MIT Press, ISBN 0-262-62108

Landow, **G**. (1994) *Hypertext*

Lane, **M**. (1975) *The Tale of Beatrix Potter*. Allen & Unwin

Laurel, **B**. (1990) *The Art of Human–Computer Interface Design*. Addison-Wesley

Laurel, **B**. (1991) *Computers as Theater*. Addison-Wesley

LeDoux, **J**. (1998) *The Emotional Brain*. Simon and Schuster, ISBN 0-297-84108-4

Levitt, **T**. (1986) *The Marketing Imagination*. Free Press

Lings, **M**. (1976) *The Quranic Art of Calligraphy and Illumination*. World of Islam Festival Trust, ISBN 0-905035-01-1

Love, **T**. (1993) *Object Lessons*. New York: SIGS Books, ISBN 0-9627477-3-4

MacCarthy, **F**. (1994) *William Morris, A Life for our Time*. Faber & Faber

McCarthy, **J**. (1995) *The Dynamics of Software Development*. Microsoft Press, ISBN 1-555615-823-8

McKnight, **C**. **Dillon**, **A**. and **Richardson, J**. (1991) *Hypertext in Context*. Cambridge University Press

McLuhan, **M**. (1964) *Understanding Media*. MIT Press

Miller, **G**. **A**. "The magical number seven, plus or minus two: Some limits on our capacity for processing information," *Psychological Review*, **63**

Mithen, **S**. (1996) *The Prehistory of Mind*. Thames and Hudson

Moody, **F**. (1995) *I Sing The Body Electronic – A Year With Microsoft On The Multimedia Frontier*. Viking Penguin

Moravec, **H**. (1990) *Mind Children: The Future of Robot and Human Intelligence*. Harvard University Press

Murray, **J**. **H**. (1997) *Hamlet on the Holodeck – the Future of Narrative in Cyberspace*. Free Press, ISBN 0-684-82723-9

Nelson, **T**. **H**. (Ted) (1980, 1981, etc.) *Literary Machines*. Mindful Press, 3020 Bridgeway Suite 295, Sausalito CA 94965. Also available from Eastgate Systems: www.eastgate.com. The version cited here is 87.1 (1987)

Nelson, **T**. **H**. (Ted) (1997) *Computer Lib* and *Dream Machines*. Microsoft Press, ISBN 0-914845- 49-7

Nielsen, **J**. (1997) *Multimedia and Hypertext*

Norman, **D**. **A**. (1988) *The Psychology of Everyday Things*. HarperCollins

Norman, **D**. **A**. (1992) *Turn Signals are the Facial Expressions of Automobiles*. Addison-Wesley, ISBN 0-201-62236-X

Norman, **D**. **A**. (1993) *Things that Make us Smart*

Norman, **D**. **A**. (1994) *Defending Human Attributes in the Age of the Machine*. Voyager Company, CD-ROM

Ogilvie, **D**. "Ogilvie on Advertising."

Ong, **W**. **J**. (1982) *Orality and Literacy – The Technologizing of the Word*. Methuen

Pangaro, **P**. (1993) "Pask as Dramaturg." *Systems Research*, **10** (3), ed. Ranulph Glanville

Papanek, **V**. (1971, 1984 (2nd edn)) *Design for the Real World*: *Human Ecology and Social Change*, Thames and Hudson, ISBN 0-500-27358-8

Pask, **G**. (1961) *An Approach to Cybernetics*. Hutchinson

Pask, **G**. (1976) *Conversation Theory*. Elsevier

Pask, **G**. (1978) "A comment, a case history and a plan." In *Cybernetics*, *Art and Ideas* (J. Reichart, ed.) Studio Vista

Pask, **G**. (with Susan Curran) (1982) *Microman*. Century

Pilcher, **D**. (1987) *Winning Ways*. Harper & Row

Pinker, **S**. (1994) *The Language Instinct*. Penguin

Plutchik, **R**. (1980) *Emotion*: *A Psychoevolutionary Synthesis*

Propp, **V**. **Y**. (1927) *Morphology of the Folktale*. English translation, Bloomington, 1958

Pye, **D**. (1971) *The Nature and Art of Workmanship*. Herbert Press (first published 1968)

Reeves, **C**. and **Nass**, **B**. (1996) *The Media Equation*. Cambridge University Press

Rheingold, **H**. (1989) *Tools for Thought*

Rheingold, **H**. (1991) *Virtual Reality*. Martin Secker & Warburg

Rhodes, **R**. (1986) *The Making of the Atomic Bomb*. Simon & Schuster, ISBN 0-671-65719-4

Schor, **J**. (1992) *The Overworked American*. Basic Books

Sculley, **J**. (1988) *Oddyssey – Pepsi to Apple*. Fontana, ISBN 0-00-637284-8

Shah, **V**. and **Musser**, **J**. (1996) *Director Lingo and Shockwave*. Wiley

Small, **P**. (1993) "How God Makes God." CD-ROM – Genome Publishing

Small, **P**. (1994) *Lingo Sorcery*. Wiley

Small, **P**. (1998) *Magical A-life Avatars*: *A New Paradigm for the Internet*. Manning Publications Co.

Spence, **J**. (1984) *The Memory Palace of Matteo Ricci*. Viking

Stewart, **I**. and **Cohen**, **J**. (1997) *Figments of Reality – The Evolution of the Curious Mind*. Cambridge University Press, ISBN 0-521-57155-3

Thimbleby, **H**. (1991) *User Interface Design*. Addison-Wesley ACM series

Thimbleby, **H**. (1998) "Detection and elimination of spurious complexity" at http://www.cs. mdx.ac. uk/harold/uitp.html

Tognazzini, **B**. (1992) *Tog on Interface*. Addison-Wesley, ISBN 0-201-60842-1

Weisberg, **R.W**. (1986) *Creativity: Genius and Other Myths*. Freeman and Company, ISBN 0-7167-1769-7

Weisberg, **R.W**. (1993) *Creativity: Beyond the Myth of Genius*. W.H. Freeman & Co., ISBN 0-7 167-2365-4, 0-7167-2367-0

Wiener, **N**. (1948, 1961) *Cybernetics – or Control and Communication in the Animal and the Machine*. MIT Press

Wiener, **N**. (1950, 1989) *The Human Use of Human Beings*. Houghton Mifflin (1950) and Free Association Books (1989)

Winnicott, **D.W**. (1982) *Playing and Reality*. Routledge, ISBN 0-415-03689-5

Yates, **F.M**. (1969) *The Art of Memory*. Penguin

Young, **J.W**. (1975, 1994) *A Technique for Producing Ideas*. Crain Books (1975), NTC Business Books (1994), ISBN 0-8442-3000-6

Zachary, **P.G**. (1997) *Endless Frontier – Vannevar Bush, Engineer of the American Century*. Free Press, ISBN 0-684-82821-9

Index